C03CDH-570

DISCARDED
University of Winnipeg, 515 Portage Ave., Winnipeg, MB. R3B 2E9 Canada

Building
for Women

Books from
The Lincoln Institute of Land Policy

The Lincoln Institute of Land Policy is a school that offers intensive courses of instruction in the field of land economics and property taxation. The Institute provides a stimulating learning environment for students, policy-makers, and administrators with challenging opportunities for research and publication. The goal of the Institute is to improve theory and practice in those fundamental areas of land policy that have significant impact on the lives and livelihood of all people.

Constitutions, Taxation, and Land Policy
Michael M. Bernard

Constitutions, Taxation, and Land Policy—Volume II
Michael M. Bernard

Federal Tax Aspects of Open-Space Preservation
Kingsbury Browne

Taxation of Nonrenewable Resources
Albert M. Church

Taxation of Mineral Resources
Robert F. Conrad and R. Bryce Hool

World Congress on Land policy, 1980
Edited by Matthew Cullen and Sharon Woolery

Incentive Zoning
Jerold S. Kayden

Building for Women
Edited by Suzanne Keller

State Land-Use Planning and Regulation
Thomas G. Pelham

Land-Office Business
Gary Sands

The Art of Valuation
Edited by Arlo Woolery

HD
108.6
B84
1981

Building
for Women

Edited by
Suzanne Keller
Princeton University

LexingtonBooks
D.C. Heath and Company
Lexington, Massachusetts
Toronto

Library of Congress Cataloging in Publication Data

Main entry under title:

Building for women.

    Includes bibliographical references.
    1.   Women and land use planning—Addresses, essays, lectures. I. Keller, Suzanne Infeld, 1927–

HD108.6.B84	363.5'9	80–8783
ISBN 0–669–04368–0		AACR2

Copyright © 1981 by D.C. Heath and Company

All rights reserved. No part of this publication may be reproduced or transmitted in any form or by any means, electronic or mechanical, including photocopy, recording, or any information storage or retrieval system, without permission in writing from the publisher.

Published simultaneously in Canada

Printed in the United States of America

International Standard Book Number: 0–669–04368–0

Library of Congress Catalog Card Number: 80–8783

Contents

Foreword

The 1980s will see many changes in the ways Americans live and work. The suburban dream is expected to erode further as areas on the urban fringe confront their own problems of crowding, pollution, delinquency, and strained resources. The changing American family, increasingly dependent on two paychecks and vulnerable to stresses, is creating new realities for men and women, hence new demands for housing, services, and space.

Ours is an era of entitlement in which demands for equal rights and equal shares in public goods multiply. This includes access to transportation, safety, shelter, and services. As we attempt to learn more about the ingredients necessary for a satisfying quality of life, the neglected needs of our citizens for fellowship and community and for jobs and housing must receive increasing attention. This raises complex questions of priorities and finances, of identity and participation.

Land-use planning necessarily addresses diverse and competing interests. This book is particularly enlightening as it alerts us to the importance of interests neglected in the land-use arena—specific needs of the individual. The unmet needs of women, highlighted in this book, reflect the special needs of other groups deserving and demanding attention in planning policy.

The drastic societal evolution of the current era continues to redefine roles. Just as women have parted from traditional life patterns, adjustments also have been made in the roles of men, children, marriage, and the entire family structure. As the authors suggest, each in her fashion, these changes seek an outlet in planning for housing, communities, and open space. The large number of women on the job market and the expanded participation of men and children in house care necessitate new kitchen placement. The increase in single-parent mothers stimulates a new demand for a particular form of tenure or type of housing. More women are seeking housing, requiring adequate dissemination of information regarding mortgage financing. The appropriate land-use response must avoid stereotypes in order to be sensitive to the demands of the relevant groups involved. The voices of individuals need to be heard. Children's preferences, for example, have long been neglected in the planning of communities. Community planners must be willing to depart from standard middle-class-neighborhood arrangements. Public-building arrangements can be enhanced by the input of personal preference from exhibition space to public gardens.

Although differing in specific recommendations, there is agreement that the special needs of the "new woman" have not been taken into account adequately by contemporary planners. This poses challenging questions for everyone concerned with creating safe, serviceable, and humane environments for our citizens.

The Lincoln Institute of Land Policy is pleased to have sponsored the Round Table at which several of these chapters were first presented and discussed. In its promotion of research and organization of forums for the exchange of ideas and recommendations among scholars, specialists, and students, the Lincoln Institute puts questions of land use and land policy at the center of its agenda. This book alerts us to the neglected needs of contemporary American women as they expand their traditional maternal and domestic roles. The chapters represent a variety of perspectives on novel legal, economic, and sociological considerations and their impact on urban planning and design.

This symposium exemplifies the Institute's concern for exploring new needs and emergent problems in the development of sound land-use policies. As such, it hopefully contributes to the creation of a national agenda on the role of land use, shelter, and space in our time.

Charles M. Haar
Lincoln Institute of
Land Policy

Introduction

For the past few decades, the new roles and needs of women have aroused considerable public and private attention. We have witnessed the passage of new legislation and new policies on a broad range of issues from jobs and credit to housing and birth control.

One of the areas relatively neglected in this pursuit of a new bill of rights for women has been that of land use and the provision of services and facilities needed by jobholding mothers, self-supporting unmarried women, widows, and the divorced. This neglect creates serious hardships for many categories of the female population.

Manuel Castels in *The Urban Question* makes much of site, space, and place as social constructs that embody the differential resources with which various groups struggle for their place in the sun. Space is always "historically defined space-time" organized around political, economic, and social relationships and ideologies.[1] Access to space and facilities is thus crucial for opportunities to improve one's life chances.

The history of land use is a history of social change, as site and design are inextricably interwoven with political and economic policies.

All political revolutions, as indeed all cultural and technological ones, have their spatial aspects as they rename, reshape, and reform spatial traditions along with social and political ones.

The contemporary feminist revolution constitutes a current example of new demands being made on the environment as lifeways and identities change.

The environments that women's new obligations and identities require are in the process of being created by the social transformations of gender currently taking place.

Among these is the dramatic increase in female employment, especially that of wives and mothers of very young children; the emergence of the two-breadwinner family as a national norm; the increase in the number of women solely responsible for economic and child support; new needs of single mothers; and the change in self-image and ideology as to what it is appropriate for men and women to aspire to and undertake, which reflects the sexual and gender revolutions of the sixties and seventies.

These dramatic developments are not unique to the United States. They are prevalent in all contemporary industrial societies and reflect the pervasive changes in the demographics of our planet and in the concomitant patterns of work and family life.

The history of modern suburbia is a prime example of the interconnections between house, site, design, and spatial access in the search for the good life. Territorial resources, housing, transportation, and geographic mobility have been shown to affect not only economic well-being but opportunities to get ahead, to pursue the American Dream.[2]

The suburbs began when the rich moved beyond nineteenth-century city boundaries in their search for space, beauty, and, some have suggested, to preserve their status superiority from immigrant onslaught. Only in this century did suburbs become a mass symbol of middle-class respectability.

But just as the feudal castle could function only with an extensive support system of services, laws, and labor so the suburbs had to learn about their dependence on urban centers and facilities. Among these supports was a family system based on a strict division of labor by gender and oriented to consumption, togetherness, privacy, and space.

After World War II, the good life spelled suburbia replete with the single-family house, two-car garage, and backyard barbecue. This suited a war-weary generation trying to fulfill postponed dreams of home ownership and children, and while there were sporadic rumblings about suburban problems, it was not until OPEC that Americans had to reconsider and redefine their patterns of getting and spending, growth and limits, and male and female. Long before that reappraisal became widespread, many had warned of suburban escapism, insularity, and their undesirable, as well as illusory separation from the problems of the wider society. Thus Paul and Percival Goodman pointed out decades ago that community planning and physical design is all too often "carried out with eyes shut to the whole pattern."[3]

Charles M. Haar, who anticipated many of the problems of contemporary suburbs, has recently commented that suburbs now have "become heirs to their cities' problems. They have pollution, high taxes, crime." More importantly, they are "predicated on a way of life that is endangered in an era of two-paycheck families, childless couples, and frequent divorce," not to ignore the energy crunch which poses special problems for the car culture in modern suburbia.[4]

The erosion of the American Dream is in part due to the changing roles and identities of American women who are increasingly breaking out of their nuclear nests. Better educated than ever before, with more time on their hands as family size shrinks, and pressed by rising costs, these women seek access to employment, shopping, learning, and diversions near to their homes, to be sure, but away from home nonetheless. If this is the case for the traditional wives and mothers, it is even more so for the women who become divorced or single parents in communities designed for intact, conventional families.

Indeed, it has been estimated that 85 percent of currently married women will live alone at some point in their lives. In 1977 single women were the "fastest growing segment of the home-buying market" especially for condominiums and town houses, and builders have a new acronym to describe their category of buyers: SSWDS, that is, single, separated, widowed, or divorced. One-fourth of all heads of households are women, many of them poor women.

An increase in single households alters aggregate buying and spending habits. Singles use restaurants more and certain household appliances less. They are interested in a whole range of services and products geared to their special needs.[5]

Divorced women, who comprise a special subgroup of singles, are increasing by one-half million each year, as are widows who account for one-third of all one-person households. As is well known, older women dramatically outnumber older men and most of them choose to be independent, preferring their own housing accommodations to moving in with their children or other relatives.

Thus changing social realities compel women to make new demands on their communities for jobs, education, childcare, and other services. The new realities include employed mothers, two-breadwinner families, long journeys to work in search of employment, and children needing care when parents are at work. As the following list indicates, these needs are mirrored in the demands women are making increasingly in their efforts to cope with contemporary change. Women are calling for:

1. Jobs, particularly those close to home and part-time;
2. Job-training opportunities, again close to home;
3. Transportation within the community and outside it;
4. Day-care facilities in a variety of forms: full and part-time; daytime and evenings; with special facilities for handicapped or sick children;
5. Opportunities for higher education to upgrade skills and obtain needed credentials for desired jobs, again part-time and close to home;
6. Counseling services including job counseling, marital counseling, and a whole range of information services;
7. Household help for emergencies.

These are not exotic or unusual demands by this or that woman nor are they particularly extravagant, but the truth is that they are not met in most communities partly because of established traditions and partly because of ideas out of step with current developments.

There is every reason to suppose that the trends we have noted will persist into the future and, therefore, will require that a major aspect of planning in the coming decades will involve the changing needs of women.

When planning with women in mind, planners will increasingly need to pay attention to the design of dwellings and neighborhoods geared to part-time or full-time employment of women and their specialized needs for safety, comfort, accessibilty, and space.

To improve the quality of life in the 1980s requires not only decent housing, safe streets, and unpolluted air and streams but also an awareness of the changes that have taken place in the social fabric of the family, work patterns, and the roles of women and men.

The chapters in this book try to spell out the implications of changing patterns of family life, work roles, and ideologies of gender for land use and the provision of desired facilities and services. Although each chapter has a unique focus that stems from the perspective of a particular discipline, there is nonetheless a common thread of concern for the current and future needs of an increasingly visible majority.

Notes

1. Manuel Castells, *The Urban Question: A Marxist Approach* (Cambridge, Mass.: The MIT Press, 1977).

2. S.I. Fainstein and Norman I. Fainstein, "National Policy and Urban Development," *Social Problems* vol. 26, no. 2, (1978):126.

3. Paul and Percival Goodman, *Communitas: Means of Livelihood and Ways of Life* (New York: Vintage Books, 1960), p. 223.

4. William Lenerini Kowinski, "Suburbia: End of the Golden Age," *The New York Times Magazine,* 16 March 1980, pp. 16–19, 106–109.

5. June Kronholz, "On Their Own," *Wall Street Journal,* 16 November 1977, pp. 1, 2.

Part I
Housing

In these four chapters, housing and its accessibility, design, and symbolic significance for women are the key concerns.

Dolores Hayden describes the efforts of two turn-of-the-century visionaries to reorganize women's lives and work through design in "Two Utopian Feminists and Their Campaigns for Kitchenless Houses." Marie Stevens Howland and Alice Constance Austin each developed proposals to alter private household arrangements in favor of a collective provision of food and services. Kitchenless houses were their answer to domestic drudgery and women's social isolation. Their ideas, influential in their own time, still seem innovative today.

Susan Anderson-Khleif, in "Housing Needs of Single-Parent Mothers," analyzes the housing needs, preferences, and frustrations of divorced women with children. She notes the crucial role played by housing in women's post-divorce adjustments. Noting in particular the impact of inequalities of social class on the magnitude of housing need, she proposes "transional housing security" as a policy concern for the future.

Donna E. Shalala and Jo Ann McGeorge explore the reasons why women do not enter the mortgage market in proportion to their financial resources in "The Women and Mortgage Credit Project: A Government Response to the Housing Problems of Women." The authors review the efforts of HUD to extend information and organizational know-how to diverse groups of women across the nation via workshops, media campaigns, and education in the ABCs of credit and housing markets.

Sheila Levrant de Bretteville, in "The Woman's Building: Physical Forms and Social Implications," describes the experience of creating the Woman's Building in Los Angeles as an environment for self-awareness, feminine consciousness, and personal growth. The struggle to find a place in which to create that environment provides important insights into the "painful and productive tension" between architectural ideals and human realities.

1

1

Two Utopian Feminists and Their Campaigns for Kitchenless Houses

Dolores Hayden

American women have designed many utopias, usually to insist that utopian socialist communities be constructed as socialist, feminist ones. Writing in 1848, Jane Sophia Appleton described the domestic arrangements of Bangor, Maine, in the year 1978:

> . . . you have noticed the various houses for eating which accommodate the city. . . . You would hardly recognize the process of cooking in one of our large establishments. Quiet, order, prudence, certainty of success, govern the process of turning out a ton of bread, or roasting an ox!—as much as the weaving of a yard of cloth in one of our factories. No fuming, no fretting over the cooking stove, as of old! No "roasted lady" at the head of the dinner table! Steam machinery, division of labor, economy of material, make the whole as agreeable as any other toil, while the expense to pocket is as much less to man as the wear of patience, time, bone and muscle to woman. . . .[1]

Despite the frequency with which such visions of efficient collective domestic work occur in nineteenth-century utopian literature, their creators do not always elaborate on the consequences of domestic reform for architecture and urban design. This chapter will deal with the careers of two utopian feminists, Marie Stevens Howland and Alice Constance Austin, who did promote innovative architectural concepts linked to proposals for domestic reform in their plans for the utopian socialist cities of Topolobampo, Mexico, and Llano del Rio, California. Between 1874 and 1917 both women worked with cooperative colonies whose underfinanced rural settlements dissolved before extensive construction could take place. Their plans, however, dealt with some of the major issues of twentieth-century urban and suburban life and provide important evidence of the contacts between communitarian socialists and feminist activists creating cooperative housekeeping projects in cities and suburbs in the United States and England.

Howland's and Austin's work emerges from the ideological controversy about feminism and housing design that animated reform circles dedicated to communitarian socialism. Communitarians who believed that the

Reprinted from *Signs: Journal of Women* in Culture and Society 4 (no. 2) by permission of the University of Chicago Press. Copyright 1978 by the University of Chicago.

construction of a single ideal community would transform the world through the power of its example often described the model community as a world in miniature, a concept which at once domesticated political economy and politicized domestic economy. Therefore, many utopian socialists of the nineteenth century hold special appeal for feminists because of their strategies to change traditional concepts of power and property in the private household. Foremost among male utopian socialists who criticized the private home was Charles Fourier, who argued that the development of a society can best be judged by examining the position of women within it.[2] Fourier identified the isolated single-family dwelling as one of the greatest obstacles to improving the position of women; for his followers, the socialization of domestic work was essential to improving women's status.

Believing (however misguidedly) that architectural design could shape the workings of an experimental community, many early nineteenth-century American utopian socialists, including Fourier's followers, sought to create ideal dwellings to house their idealistic societies.[3] Some made a cult of the perfect single-family home but tended to abandon socialist principles in favor of private property. Others favored elaborate communal mansions but often became involved in sexual and religious practices which isolated the members from society at large. A few groups did build family dwelling units supported by communal services, allowing some privacy while eliminating the wasteful duplication of domestic labor. Unfortunately, the more rigid utopian groups of this persuasion were the ones that tended to be rich. Thus, by 1860, some communities, like the Amana Inspirationists, had developed the kitchenless apartments, but not the ideological commitment, to improve women's situation, while others, like the Fourierists, had developed the ideological commitment to feminism without the resources to build much new housing.

It remained for the next generation of communitarian socialist architects to design and build housing which would encourage women to become full participants in utopian socialist experiments. By the late 1860s they had allies in American women who may have heartily disapproved of socialism and communal life but were anxious to lighten domestic labor in their own lives. Foremost among these women was Melusina Fay Peirce, founder of the Cambridge (Massachusetts) Cooperative Housekeeping Society which organized a cooperative store, laundry, and bakery near Harvard Square beginning in 1869. Peirce argued for the inclusion of such cooperative facilities in the apartment houses then being designed for middle-class Bostonians, but her practical experiment lasted less than two years. Although her experiment was incomplete because the centralized housekeeping facility required the complement of kitchenless apartments or houses, between 1868 and 1884 she did succeed in interesting many social reformers in cooperative housekeeping and in her feminist critique of conventional dwellings.[4]

While Peirce's followers attempted to establish small cooperative kitchens, dining clubs, and laundries in middle-class neighborhoods, Marie Stevens Howland, Alice Constance Austin, and other communitarian socialists developed plans for housing to complement centralized housekeeping facilities, designing entire cities to eliminate private domestic work. They attempted to synthesize the utopian socialists' strategy of building egalitarian communities in isolated locations with the cooperative housekeepers' designs for collective facilities for urban and surburban women. The inherent weakness of social movements based on building isolated model communities rather than on organizing existing communities did not halt these reformers' inventiveness, as examination of their careers will show.

Marie Stevens Howland, born in New Hampshire in 1836, a Lowell millworker in her teens, attended normal school and became a school principal before she met the radical Fourierists of the New York City "Unitary Home" in the late 1850s. Already a successful career woman, she became a campaigner for free love and the "Combined Household" advocated by the American disciples of Charles Fourier.[5] In the 1860s she lived for one year at the Familistere or Social Palace established by Fourierists in Guise, France, an elaborate complex of buildings offering centrally heated apartments, extensive day-care facilities, and cooked-food service for some 350 iron-foundry workers and their families (figure 1–1). After Howland's return to the United States she published a novel, *Papa's Own Girl,* describing the establishment of a Social Palace in the United States.[6] In 1874 Albert Kimsey Owen contacted her about the cooperative colony which he proposed to establish at Topolobampo, Mexico. Owen was a supporter of the single-family home, but Howland persuaded him to consider the merits of the cooperative housekeeping arrangements she had observed at Guise.[7] She became involved in the colony as a strategist who worked with Owen and John J. Deery, the rather conventional Philadelphia architect who provided the detailed plans for the dwellings.

Organized on a grid plan overlaid with diagonal streets, Topolobampo included three types of dwellings: residential hotels, row houses, and picturesque freestanding cottages with adjoining cooperative housekeeping facilities (figure 1–2). The city plan, consisting of dozens of residential hotels and row houses and hundreds of private houses, makes the transition from early nineteenth-century concepts of a single Fourierist phalanstery housing an entire community to late-nineteenth-century notions of mass housing consisting of complementary urban and suburban building types. The city plan also boasted extensive child-care facilities, lakes and flower gardens, cooperative stores, and factories, homes for the sick, libraries, and concert halls, all suggestive of endless supply of communal and private resources and leisure to enjoy them.

Figure 1-1. Childcare Facilities, the Familistère, Guise, France, from
        J.A.B. Godin, *Social Sollutions,* translated by Marie Howland,
        1873.

Like the provision for public facilities, the space allotted to both private
dwellings and collective housekeeping facilities was inflated. The residential
hotel recalled phalansteries built in the United States at different Fourierist
communities before 1860, as well as the Familistère at Guise. It provided
huge suites as well as single rooms, since Topolobampo's planners, in the
Fourierist tradition, did not insist upon the immediate abolition of economic classes. All inhabitants of the hotel could make use of the public
rooms, which were only slightly more grand than those allotted to the row-
house blocks (figure 1-3) where twelve two-story patio houses with enormous rooms overlooked a central garden, and shared parlor, library, kitchen, dining room, and laundry. For those who might prefer freestanding
homes, in the suburban blocks four large picturesque cottages, each slightly
different from its neighbors, shared access to a cooperative kitchen, laundry, bakery, and dormitories for men and women who staffed the facility
(figure 1-4). Although financial speculation and administrative chaos prevented any of this ideal housing from being constructed, the plans were
published in 1885 in a treatise, *Integral Co-operation,* and discussed in various colony publications.[8]

Unfortunately, Howland's feminism was not shared by many of the
other members of the community—her views on free love were enough to
have her labeled as a "loose woman." She lived in Topolobampo for sev-

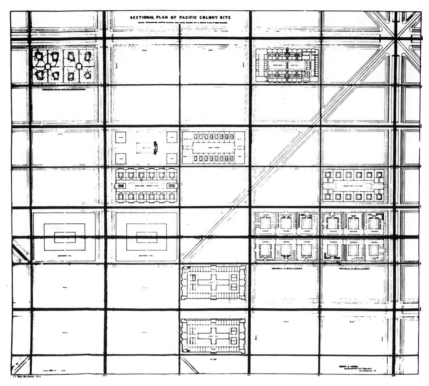

Figure 1-2. Marie Howland, Albert Kimsey Owen, and John Deery, Partial Site Plan, Pacific Colony, Topolobampo, Mexico, 1885, with Residential Hotels, Row Houses, Free-Standing Houses, and Various Cooperative Facilities.

eral years but ultimately sensed the failure of "Integral Co-operation," and moved to a single-tax community in Fairhope, Alabama, where she worked as the community librarian until 1921. Although her plans were unrealized, they were influential in both the United States and England. Two years after the designs for Topolobampo were published, Edward Bellamy wrote *Looking Backward: 2000–1887.*[9] This best-selling novel popularized the ideal of a city of kitchenless apartment houses and collectively run kitchens in the year 2000. Some commentators have cited Marie Howland's fictional account of a Familistère located in New England and the Topolobampo publications as architectural precedents for Bellamy's work.[10]

Whatever his sources, Bellamy proved a powerful advocate of collectively organized domestic work. He inspired a number of minor novelists, inventors, and architects who gave cooperative housekeeping more concrete

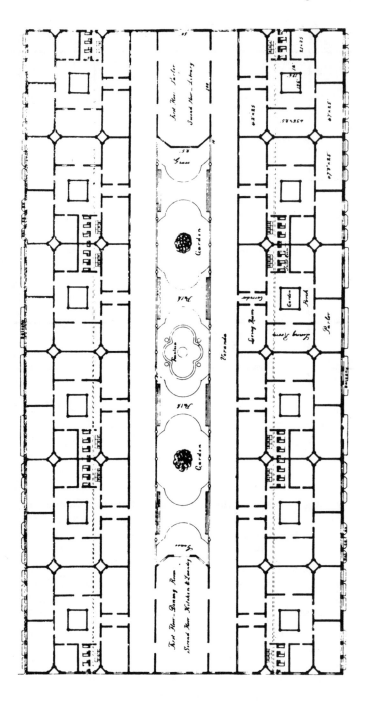

Figure 1-3. Howland, Owen, and Deery, Plan for Block of Pacific Colony with Twelve Row Houses Sharing Dining Room, Kitchen, Laundry, Parlor, and Library.

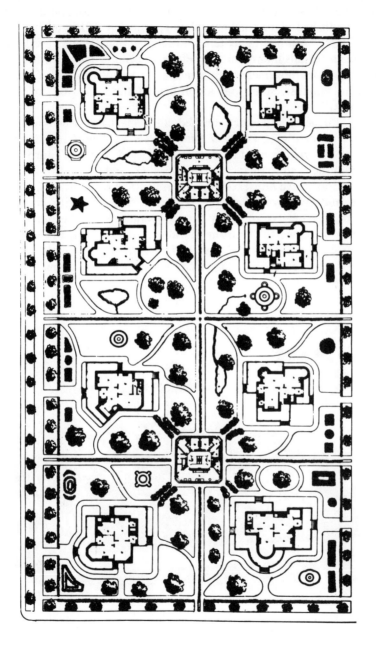

Figure 1-4. Howland, Owen, and Deery, Plan for Block of Pacific Colony. Four Houses with Private Dining Rooms Share One Service Building with Kitchen, Laundry, and Servants' Quarters.

architectural expression, including Leonard E. Ladd, who patented a plan
for an urban block with a central kitchen in 1890 (figure 1–5), and Bradford
Peck, who published plans for kitchenless apartments and municipal restaurants in 1900.[11] Among the writers who claimed that Bellamy awakened
their interest in socialism and housing reform, Ebenezer Howard, founder
of the Garden Cities movement in England, and Charlotte Perkins Gilman,
the American feminist, stand out as influential supporters of collective
domestic work.[12]

In 1898 Ebenezer Howard launched his remarkable town-planning
career with *To-Morrow: A Peaceful Path to Real Reform*.[13] Howard had
read *Integral Co-operation* and *Looking Backward*. He was thoroughly
impressed with the need to socialize domestic work, and within two decades
he launched cooperative housekeeping experiments at the Garden Cities of
Letchworth and Welwyn, England. Howard and his wife lived in
"Homesgarth," a project of thirty-two cooperative housekeeping units
built in 1909 in Letchworth. Thus, he was able to realize some of the housing plans which Howland and Owen had published for Topolobampo,
though only in the context of a larger city building project dominated by
traditional homes.

Figure 1–5. Leonard E. Ladd, Patented Design for Urban Block with
Twenty-four Kitchenless Row Houses and Central Kitchen and
Laundry Building, 1890. A Covered Passageway from the
Kitchen Connects with Private Dining Pavilions.

In the same year that Howard published *To-Morrow,* Charlotte Perkins Gilman finished her best-selling *Women and Economics,* which advocated kitchenless houses in suburban blocks and kitchenless apartments with dining rooms and day-care centers in cities. She deplored mistress-servant relations as much as husband-wife exploitation and suggested that female entrepreneurs organize cooked-food delivery, child care, and cleaning services on a "business basis."[14] In her serial novel, *What Diantha Did* (1909–1910) Gilman created an efficient entrepreneur who develops a cooked-food service and revolutionizes women's situation in a California town.[15] The heroine Diantha's friend, Isobel Porne, an architect who provides her with a residential hotel and kitchenless houses, the perfect environment for running her business, is a prototype, if not an inspiration, for Alice Constance Austin. By 1915 some form of collective housekeeping was the favored solution for the problem of domestic drudgery, and some American feminists were running cooked-food services while others, such as the members of New York's radical Feminist Alliance, were attempting to organize a feminist apartment house in Greenwich Village.[16]

It remained for Alice Constance Austin, a disciple of Ebenezer Howard and Charlotte Perkins Gilman, to integrate programs for collective housekeeping back into an American utopian socialist context, designing an entire city in California in which every house was an expression of the citizens' social and economic equality. Austin, an upper-class radical from Santa Barbara, California, read George Pullman's propaganda on model company towns in 1893 and then educated herself to become the designer of a model community which would be owned and run by workers themselves.[17] In her plans for the cooperative colony of Llano del Rio, near Palmdale, and in her book, *The Next Step,* Austin articulated an imaginative vision of life in a city of kitchenless houses.[18] She maintained that the traditional home functioned as a Procrustean bed to which "each feminine personality must be made to conform by whatever maiming or fatal spiritual or intellectual oppression." In her Socialist City, labor-saving devices in the home and a central laundry and kitchens would relieve woman "of the thankless and unending drudgery of an inconceivably stupid and inefficient system, by which her labors are confiscated. . . ."[19] The substantial economies achieved in residential construction without kitchens, she believed, would permit the construction of the centralized facilities.

Austin first developed her kitchenless house, with living room, patio, two bedrooms, and bath on the first floor and sleeping porches above, about 1915. Her client, Job Harriman, the organizer of Llano, a lawyer and a leader in the Socialist party, called upon his supporters in 1914 to build a cooperative colony in the Antelope Valley. He presented Austin, as the community's architect, with 900 people who wanted a plan for something better than the subdivisions that land speculators were creating in Los

Angeles. Criticizing the "suburban residence street where a Moorish palace elbows a pseudo French castle, which frowns upon a Swiss chalet," Austin proposed a city composed of courtyard houses of concrete construction.[20] Built in rows, they would express "the solidarity of the community" and emphasize the equal access to housing supported by the socialist municipal government (figure 1-6). Austin allowed for personal preferences in the decoration of her houses by providing renderings of alternative facades. She also thoughtfully set aside land in her city plan for future architects' experiments as well as for conventional single-family dwellings.

Austin's housing designs emphasized economy of labor, materials, and space (figure 1-7). She criticized the waste of time, strength, and money which traditional houses with kitchens required and the "hatefully monotonous" drudgery of preparing 1,095 meals in the year and cleaning up after each one.[21] In her plans, hot meals in special containers would arrive from the central kitchens to be eaten in the dining patio; dishes were then returned to the central kitchen. She provided built-in furniture and roll-away beds to eliminate dusting and sweeping in difficult spots, heated tile floors to replace dusty carpets, and windows with decorated frames to do away with what she called that "household scourge," the curtain. Her affinity with the Arts and Crafts movement is apparent in her hope that the production of these window frames would become the basis of a craft industry at Llano, along with simple furniture.[22]

Each kitchenless house was connected to the central kitchen through a complex underground network of tunnels. Railway cars from the center of the city would bring cooked food, laundry, and other deliveries to connection points, or "hubs," from which small electric cars could be dispatched to the basement of each house (figure 1-8). Although this infrastructure was obviously going to be expensive, Austin argued the economic and aesthetic advantages to a socialist government of placing all gas, water, electric, and telephone lines underground in the same tunnels as the residential delivery system. Eliminating all business traffic at the center would produce a more restful city—residents had access to the center on foot, public delivery systems handled all their shopping, and goods coming to the city could arrive at a centrally located air-freight landing pad. Private automobiles would be used chiefly for trips outside this utopia of 10,000 people, perhaps to neighboring towns built on the same plan.

Austin's diagram for Llano shows Ebenezer Howard's undeniable influence on her basic design, but while his kitchenless dwellings were built as small enclaves within larger cities of conventional homes Austin added the urban infrastructure necessary to build all of her dwellings without kitchens. At the time Austin designed Llano one could find articles advocating kitchenless houses in various liberal and radical journals published in California as well as in architectural periodicals, but no one else besides Marie

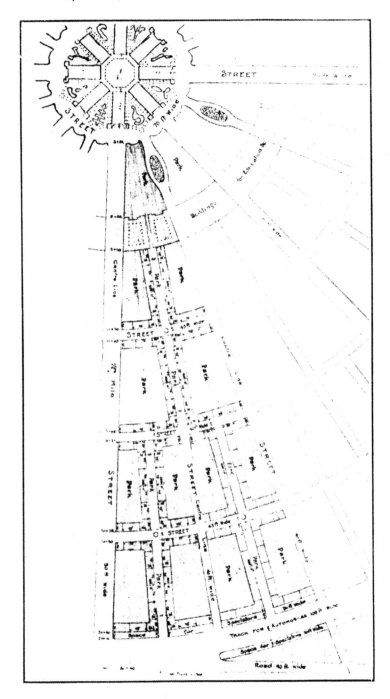

Figure 1-6. Austin, Partial Site Plan, Llano del Rio, Showing One Sector of a Circular City.

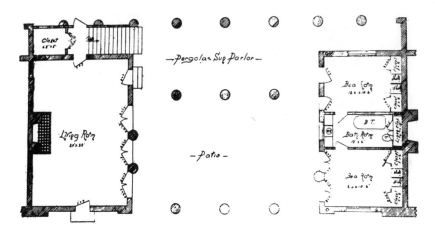

Figure 1–7. Austin, Plan of Kitchenless House, First Floor.

Howland, Owen, and Deery had attempted to design an entire city of this kind. Marie Howland and her colleagues had planned Topolobampo as if it were a city of infinite resources; Austin made some of the same utopian gestures at Llano del Rio. She planned large parks and gardens knowing the community did not have an adequate water supply, and she designed extensive communal infrastructure knowing Llano lacked capital. She was very practical, however, when she designed thick-walled courtyard houses for the desert climate, and her kitchenless houses were taut and efficient compared with those proposed for Topolobampo. Unfortunately, the community's financial condition worsened, and by the fall of 1917 it was clear that Llano's California land would not be fully developed.

After the colony's move from Llano del Rio, California, to New Llano, Louisiana, Austin set up an architectural office in Los Angeles and reworked her Llano designs to appeal to other potential clients. She stressed her design's adaptability to many sites, climates, and economic systems, arguing that the uniformly sized socialist patio houses could expand or contract, even to the point of allowing a palace to be built side by side with a cottage.[23] In *The Next Step: How to Plan for Beauty, Comfort, and Peace with Great Savings Effected by the Reduction of Waste,* she abandoned socialism so far as to write about the problems of the real estate developer and the difficulties of accommodating domestic servants, but she died with her plans unfinanced by either utopian socialist or capitalist developers.

Like Marie Stevens Howland, Austin has been viewed as a minor figure in American communitarian history, a marginal participant whose theoretical contribution has been largely forgotten. Yet because both women advocated housing designed to reorganize "women's" work, they represent a level of innovation which has still not been achieved in American residential

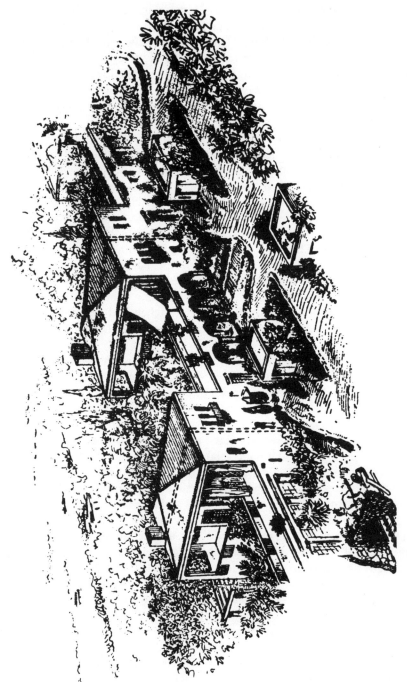

Figure 1–8. Austin, View of Housing, with Underground Service Tunnel at Lower Left.

construction today. Since their proposals, many other attempts to socialize domestic work have been launched and abandoned, such as collective apartment complexes built in the Soviet Union in the 1920s and 1930s and collective dining halls built in China in the 1950s. In all these cases, difficulties in providing family privacy and in integrating such facilities into industrial cities were not completely resolved. The burden of isolated domestic work in the private household remains an economic and architectural problem for women in all societies.

As contemporary feminist groups begin to investigate housing reform, evaluating the work of earlier activists becomes a political as well as historical task.[24] Both Howland and Austin are difficult cases. Howland manifested little concern about economic inequality; Austin was somewhat more egalitarian but more conservative about women's ability to combine careers outside the home with motherhood, when freed of domestic responsibilities. Perhaps because they worked between two movements they were never able to galvanize either. The utopian socialists at Topolobampo and Llano del Rio were somewhat skeptical of feminism and concentrated their scanty resources elsewhere. The feminist cooperative housekeepers, with the exception of Ebenezer Howard, avoided major planning ventures and centered their efforts on establishing small collective kitchen and day-care facilities rather than working out broader plans for cities of kitchenless houses and apartments.

Unfortunately, the problems of isolated domestic work which these plans address (and the related waste of space, time, food, and fuel) still exist. The Topolobampo drawings can be seen as a guide to suburban renovation. One can also imagine Llano del Rio realized as a new condominium development, with some changes in transportation technology. The central kitchens and day-care centers Howland and Austin proposed could replace the tennis courts, swimming pools, elaborate saunas, and recreation rooms some developers now provide. Surely there exists a clientele which would prefer them, especially among single parents, two-career families, and the elderly. Yet Howland and Austin were seeking something more than enclaves of feminist housing within capitalist society. Both of these reformers attempted to sketch the outlines of life in a society based on equality for women, and it is in this context that their work must ultimately be judged. Cooperative colonies have the same relation to a socialist revolution asserting the economic power of the working class as cooperative housekeeping experiments have to a feminist revolution asserting the economic power of women: they are isolated and utopian efforts. Yet Howland's and Austin's attempts to link these premature movements provide surprising glimpses of a socialist, feminist world we have not yet seen. In spite of all their ideological shortcomings, the city plans advocated by Howland and Austin transmit important prophecies about housing, women, and the future.

Notes

1. Jane Sophia Appleton, "Sequel to the Vision of Bangor," in *Shorter American Utopian Fiction,* ed. Arthur Orcutt Lewis (New York: Arno Press, 1974).

2. Charles Fourier, *Design for Utopia, Selected Writings of Charles Fourier,* trans. Julia Franklin (New York: Schocken Books, 1971), p. 77.

3. For an extended discussion of some of these projects, see Dolores Hayden, *Seven American Utopias: The Architecture of Communitarian Socialism, 1790-1975* (Cambridge, Mass.: The MIT Press, 1976) and "Challenging the American Domestic Ideal," in *Women in American Architecture,* ed. S. Torre (New York: Whitney Library of Design, 1977).

4. Melusina Fay Peirce, "Cooperative Housekeeping I-V," *Atlantic Monthly* 22-23, (November 1868 through March 1869): 513-24, 682-97, 29-39, 161-71, 286-99; and *Cooperative Housekeeping: How Not to Do It and How to Do It: A Study in Sociology* (Boston: James R. Osgood & Co., 1884). Also see Nathan C. Meeker, "Cooperation: Model Tenement Houses and Cooperative Housekeeping," *New York Tribune* (August 31, 1869). I have discussed Peirce's career in, "Kitchenless Houses: The Cooperative Housekeepers' Next Step for Women," a paper prepared for the 1977 American Studies Association meeting. All of these proposals for feminist housing reform are the subject of my book in progress, *"A Grand Domestic Revolution": American Visions of Household Liberation* (MIT Press, 1979).

5. Biographical information is drawn from Ray Reynold's history of the Pacific Colony, *Cat's Paw Utopia* (El Cajon, Calif.: published by the author, 1972); Madeleine Stern's biography of Steven Pearl Andrews, *The Pantarch* (Austin: University of Texas Press, 1968); and Robert Fogarty's introduction to Howland's novel, *The Familistere* (formerly *Papa's Own Girl*) 3d ed. (Philadelphia: Porcupine Press, 1975). Klaus Roesch has been helpful in putting this information together.

6. Marie Howland, *Papa's Own Girl* (New York: J.P. Jewett, 1874).

7. Reynolds, p. 39, states that Howland suggested versions of the Social Palace at Guise to Owen. I conclude that she was the major ideologist of the housing while Owen was more involved in the overall city plan and railroad promotions. Reynolds is now editing Howland's letters and publication of them should provide much new material to evaluate her role.

8. Albert Kimsey Owen, *Integral Co-operation: Its Practical Application* (New York: John W. Lovell, 1885). Robert Fogarty, in his "Introduction" to a 1975 edition by Porcupine Press, Philadelphia, states that Howland authored part of this book.

9. Edward Bellamy, *Looking Backward: 2000-1887* (Cambridge, Mass.: Harvard University Press, 1967), pp. 168-69.

10. Reynolds, p. 85, cites Arthur E. Morgan's evaluation of her influence and discusses Bellamy's familiarity with Topolobampo materials. Peirce suggests that her *Cooperative Housekeeping,* which elaborates on the advantages of collective domestic work, was also a source for Bellamy. I can support this assertion only by the circumstantial evidence that it was issued by James R. Osgood and Co. in 1884, the same year that Bellamy published a minor novel with that firm (*Miss Ludington's Sister*), but Peirce's book was very widely reviewed in 1884 (see M.F. Peirce, *New York: A Symphonic Study,* pt. 3, "What's Wrong with the World" [New York: Neale Publishing Co., 1918], p. 14).

11. "Ladd's Improvement in Dwelling Houses," *Scientific American* 63 (3 August 1890): 66; Bradford Peck, *The World a Department Store* (New York: Arno Press, 1974).

12. Dugald MacFayden, *Sir Ebenezer Howard and the Town Planning Movement* (Cambridge, Mass., The MIT Press, 1970), p. 20; Charlotte Perkins Gilman, *The Living of Charlotte Perkins Gilman, an Autobiography,* ed. Zona Gale (New York: Harper Colophon Books, 1975), p. 131.

13. Ebenezer Howard, *To-Morrow: A Peaceful Path to Real Reform* (London: n.p., 1898, republished in 1902 as *Garden Cities of To-Morrow*). For bibliography and further details of Howard's projects, see Dolores Hayden, "Redesigning the Domestic Workplace," *Chrysalis* 1 (Winter 1977): 19–29.

14. Charlotte Perkins Gilman, *Women and Economics,* ed. Carl N. Degler (New York: Harper Torchbooks, 1966), pp. 242–243.

15. Charlotte Perkins Gilman, "What Diantha Did," *Forerunner* (November 1909 through December 1970).

16. Henrietta Rodman was the leader of this movement (see George MacAdam, "Feminist Apartment House to Solve Baby Problem," *New York Times* [24 January 1915], p. 9).

17. Walter Millsap, transcript, UCLA Oral History Project, 15 July 1962, UCLA Library, Los Angeles, p. 66.

18. Alice Constance Austin, "Building a Socialist City," and "The Socialist City" (series of seven articles), *Western Comrade,* vols. 4–5 (October and November 1916; January, February, March, April, and June 1917), and *The Next Step: How to Plan for Beauty, Comfort, and Peace with Great Savings Effected by the Reduction of Waste* (Los Angeles: Institute Press, 1935).

19. Austin, *The Next Step,* p. 63.

20. Austin, "Building a Socialist City" (October 1916), p. 17.

21. Austin, "The Socialist City" (June 1917), p. 14.

22. Ibid.

23. Austin, *The Next Step,* p. 23.

24. See, for example, Jean H. Quataert's discussion of the debate between Lily Braun, who favored cooperative housekeeping, and Clara Zetkin, an orthodox Marxist, in "Unequal Partners in an Uneasy Alliance: Women and the Working Class in Imperial Germany," in *Socialist Women: European Socialist Feminism in the Nineteenth and Early Twentieth Centuries,* ed. Marilyn J. Boxer and Jean H. Quataert (New York: Elsevier, 1978), pp. 129–131. I see cooperative housekeeping projects aimed at economic equality for women, such as those proposed by Melusina Peirce, Alice Constance Austin, and Lily Braun, as having a much greater importance than projects aimed at more efficient domestic life, such as those proposed by Marie Howland or Charlotte Perkins Gilman. The distinction for me depends on a desire to abolish economic classes as well as women's economic dependence on men.

2

Housing Needs of Single-Parent Mothers

Susan Anderson-Khleif

This chapter addresses the problem of unmet housing needs of divorced women with children. I analyzed data from my interviews with divorced mothers about their housing experiences, problems, and preferences. That analysis was part of the Joint Center for Urban Studies project on changing lifestyles and housing needs of single heads of households.[1] A preliminary report of the findings was presented to members of the Department of Housing and Urban Development in Washington, D.C., in January 1979. This chapter outlines certain patterns in housing strategies or choices after divorce; and discusses the unmet resource, design, and spatial needs which are related to these patterns.

Factors Influencing Housing Choices

A change in a family's personal situation often means a change in the family's living arrangements. This is true of recently separated or divorced women who are suddenly faced with the challenge of heading single-parent families. Analysis of interviews with divorced mothers suggests that they face severe difficulties in making decisions about where to live and that they often encounter real hardships as a result of their housing arrangements. The starting point for their decision process is usually a reduction of income, with the severity of this reduction depending on the specific arrangements between husband and wife in each case. Within the limits set by their reduced or low income, the women decide where to live on the basis of several considerations:

1. Maintaining social contacts and established school settings for the children;
2. Maintaining their own social status and sense of community;
3. Finding help with childcare and other supportive arrangements;

This research was funded by the Joint Center for Urban Studies of MIT and Harvard University on the Department of Housing and Urban Development grant number 4.

21

4. Making new social contacts for themselves;
5. Being within reasonable commuting range of jobs or job training.

These different needs usually conflict with one another; no housing choice seems able to satisfy all of them. For instance, women who remain in their suburban homes find that they succeed in keeping up social and school contacts for their children but that they themselves have a hard time making new friends and keeping up a social life. Women who move in with their parents in order to find help and support discover that this move threatens their independence, privacy, and their authority over the children. Moving to a cheaper neighborhood in order to save money results in a loss of social status and raises fears about the friendships and sometimes the safety of the children. Moving to a cheaper home puts the women in with families in a different stage of their life cycle (usually young marrieds) and results in a loss of social contacts and feelings of downward mobility. These conflicts and tensions help explain why some women make a series of moves in rapid succession during the early stages of separation or divorce. They discover that each move produces new problems and try to find reasonable solutions through additional moves. It is possible to start identifying major problems and areas where new policy initiatives are greatly needed.

Method

I completed in-depth interviews with a sample of fifty divorced mothers drawn at random from the divorce-court records in a large Eastern Massachusetts county. All had been divorced from one to five years and all had custody of their children. The interviews, conducted during 1975, covered several areas of single-parent family life and averaged over five hours each. One section of the interviews centered on taking a residential history and exploring attitudes to housing and neighborhoods. This was part of my larger study of divorce and single-parent families, but since the study was focused mainly on other issues, not all the housing data had been analyzed.[2] The data were primarily qualitative. In my reanalysis of this material, for the new Joint Center study, I constructed a housing profile for each single-parent famiily and then completed a content analysis of the profiles.

A wide spectrum of working-class, middle-class, and upper-middle-class families were represented in the sample in terms of age of the interviewees, length of marriage, time since the separation and divorce; and number, sex, and ages of the children. For instance, ages of the mothers ranged from twenty-two to fifty-four years; the median age was thirty-three years old. There was a wide range in length of the former marriages; they ranged from thirteen months to twenty-eight years and ten months before divorce. The median length of marriage was ten years and seven months. The former marital incomes ranged from $4,800 to over $50,000 per year. Single-parent incomes at the time of the interviews ranged from $2,800 to $25,000 per year (from all sources). Support settlements ranged from "zero" to over $20,000 per year. Extensive data on the social-class background of interviewees was gathered. Using Coleman's Index of Urban Status to identify class level, 40 percent were from working-class marriages, 30 percent from middle-class, and 30 percent from upper-middle-class marriages.[3] Family stages ranged from very young families with preschoolers to families in the middle years to families with teens and young adults. Eighty-eight percent of the mothers were working full or part-time at the time of the interviews.

Divorce and Housing Patterns

The divorce rate and the proportion of families headed by women have risen sharply since the 1960s. About 40 percent of women in their late twenties who are now marrying will eventually divorce.[4] An increasing proportion of children are experiencing the disruption of their parents' marriage.[5] At least 15 percent of all families with children are now headed by a woman. The heads of these female-headed households are increasingly divorced and separated women rather than widowed or single.[6] These trends highlight the importance of looking more closely at the impact of divorce on family living and the difficulties women encounter in establishing and supporting their new single-parent families.

   Deciding where to live and how to pay for their housing are among the first problems single-parent mothers must face. There are three main patterns in housing after divorce and these vary by social class.[7] The first pattern is characteristic of professional or business families of the upper–middle class. Most live in their own single-family houses during marriage. When a separation occurs, the woman and children usually get the house and furniture; the husband moves out. After divorce, these upper-middle-class women remain in their former marital residences and are sustained, in part, by regular and fairly substantial child-support or alimony payments. So most of these women avoid any housing move whatsoever and live in their own single-family houses.

   The second pattern is characteristic of middle-class families—the families of average white-collar workers with median incomes. They have a more difficult time. Most of the women in this group live in single-family houses during the marriage but are forced to relinquish their homes after the separation and divorce. Many move into inadequate apartments, usually in what they consider undesirable neighborhoods.

Third, women leaving working-class marriages have an even more difficult time finding a suitable place to live. Compared to the other two groups, they are the most likely to move after the separation. They are also most likely to live in apartments as single parents. Many move from a former apartment to another apartment. Some older women who have a house in marriage are able to keep it. Younger working-class women usually do not have a home of their own when the divorce occurs. After divorce, many of them end up living in cramped, run-down, poor apartments. For instance, a mother and two small children may be living in three little rooms—no living room, the small kitchen used for both cooking and family living, with a shared bedroom for the children, and the "living room" converted into a bedroom for the mother. (Tables 2A–1 and 2A–2 in appendix 2A demonstrate this relationship between social class and housing patterns.)

Money is the first consideration in the decision about whether to move or not after separation and divorce. For most women it is the most important factor. Typically, women either say, "I moved because I had to . . . ," or they say, "I couldn't afford to move." After that, there are other important considerations.

There is what I would call a *hovering phenomenon* in the housing choices of single parents. This manifests itself as a pattern of *regional loyalty* to a particular part of the city or neighborhood. They usually hover around a particular target area for their housing and may move to a series of accommodations all within the same general area. This hovering may be targeted on the former neighborhoods or areas of the city where relatives live. Divorced mothers often try to stay in familiar territory.

The assistance, advice, and attraction of relatives has a strong impact on housing moves for women after divorce. Younger women who do not own a house and, especially those from the working class, tend to move back to the neighborhood of their own parents.

The sense of community and desire to live among friends is also a major consideration. This is especially true for women from middle income and professional marriages who often live far from relatives. Many women in these groups want to stay in their former marital residences for this reason. Women from the working class also hover around or stay in their old neighborhoods because of their sense of community there. For the working class this is closely tied to their tendency to stay near their relatives.

The behavior of the divorced father has a very strong impact on the housing circumstances and choices of the single-parent mother. If he signed over the house in the divorce settlement and/or if he is paying support regularly so that the woman knows her rent is "insured," a divorced woman can start planning her housing strategy from a solid base. Furthermore, if the father is visiting his children regularly, a mother may try to stay nearby. The wish to facilitate father-child contact is another influence on the housing choices of women after divorce.

Being aware of the distinction between separation and divorce is important for understanding the housing needs of single parents. Their housing
arrangements are often very different before and after the actual divorce.
Separation is a transitional time with many ad hoc arrangements, including
housing. The housing circumstances for women during the separation
period may be quite misleading for understanding their long-term housing
circumstances and needs. The divorced father's long-term role in supporting housing (or not supporting it) becomes clear when the actual divorce settlement is made. The divorce often forces a new decision concerning housing. Many homes are sold within six months after the actual divorce settlement (that is if they are not signed over to the woman). Thus the stage of
dissolution, separation versus divorce, is a factor affecting housing moves
or strategies.[8]

Problems and Unmet Needs

Social Status and Housing Moves

Many of the difficulties and dissatisfactions expressed by women about
their housing as single parents are fundamentally related to the problem of
maintaining their social status. Research on social status in the United
States demonstrates the great importance of housing and neighborhood in
establishing a particular status level. In our kind of society, people acquire a
certain social standing or *rank* which is partially expressed and perpetuated
by where they live and the quality of their housing.[9] The problems of maintaining social status and potential changes in social status arise when
divorce occurs and complicate decisions about housing after divorce. This is
an underlying dimension in many battles over houses in the divorce settlements. If a women has a house in the marriage, she usually tries to keep it.
If the house is a higher quality and in a "better" neighborhood than she
could afford once she is divorced, which is almost always the case, she will
not give it up easily. If a couple owns a house, one of the first things the
husband-father discovers is that his wife is determined to keep the house.
Much more than the house itself is at stake—her own social position is partially at stake although she rarely expresses it in those words. Other considerations are stressed such as security, familiarity, comfort, wish to avoid
more "disruption," the children's best interests, and so forth. It is not only
the children's comfort which is of concern. Often a woman wants to keep
the house because she feels better remaining there and having the house is a
part of maintaining her own security, comfort, and place in society.

Many women, of course, do move and find they are dissatisfied with
their new housing in some respects. One of the problematic elements is a
lack of a status "fit" with the new single-parent neighborhood. The woman

looks around and compares her new housing and neighborhood to either her former marital neighborhood or, sometimes, the one in which she was raised. For lack of financial resources, women often find themselves in a lower-status neighborhood than that of the former location. This results in an underlying restlessness or instability in the single-parent housing situation. Until this status problem is resolved, there is the tendency to avoid putting down roots and really "feeling at home." Sometimes this manifests itself as a reluctance to "decorate" the apartment or make it look "homey." I have seen apartments with bare walls and the appearance that the woman has just moved in even though she has lived there for a year or more. Often a woman will say that the inside of her apartment is "okay" but the neighborhood "is not the best" or that it "is not my kind of neighborhood."

An analysis of status transitions in neighborhoods after divorce reveals quite a bit about the forces that press single parents to make additional moves. In the middle and upper-middle classes, the problem of ending up in a lower-status neighborhood after divorce stems largely from the lack of rental apartments in the type of neighborhoods they would prefer. Working-class women also have problems with neighborhood status. They often find themselves in run-down apartments in lower working-class neighborhoods instead of in the stable "safe," and "clean" working-class areas they prefer. They, too, feel restless and uncomfortable with their new surroundings. A working-class woman living in a transient, semislum area feels just as deprived and lonely as a middle-class woman who gives up her suburban home and moves to a small apartment in a working-class neighborhood.

Furthermore, women in all three class groups want to live in housing and neighborhoods that fit with their family life-cycle stages and their ages. Moving to a house or apartment that puts a woman among families at obviously different life-cycle stages leads to feelings of downward mobility or stepping backwards in time. For instance, if a middle-aged single parent is forced to live among young marrieds in a first-apartment or first-home neighborhood, she feels as if she has been "forced down." If a single-parent mother moves into a building with all elderly residents or all college students, she also starts feeling uncomfortable because she has little in common with the people around her. At every class level, people have conceptions of what is appropriate housing for a family like theirs at a particular stage in life. Feelings of success or deprivation are very much linked to those images or conceptions.

Social Isolation and Inadequate Transportation in the Suburbs

Suburban life is an isolating experience for must upper-middle-class women and also for most middle-class women who retain their homes after divorce.

They usually feel that their children are better off remaining in a familiar house and environment. Many of their new activities as single women, however, are outside their residential suburbs. They soon become involved in constantly driving back and forth to their own activities in the city or in other communities.

Another transportation problem that develops is the chauffeuring of children that goes with suburban living. This taxi service for children becomes a tremendous task for suburban single parents. Most parents work and simply are not available as chauffeurs. The children need rides to lessons, movies, shopping, and all the usual school events, and it is very demanding. Suburban homes are often situated so that it is a long distance even to reach the center of the local suburban community, and, of course, children want to go to the city too. Single parents sometimes feel they are "always sponging off someone" for rides for their children. Many single parents living in the suburbs become torn between the wish to stay and the desire to leave. "Free" time is split between taking the trash to the dump in the station wagon or "hauling around a million kids" and driving to the city for cultural activities or entertainment with friends. For the most part suburbia is still a couples' world and the single parent soon finds that she is left out of neighborhood gatherings for couples. Almost the only exceptions to this exclusion are middle-class women in their forties or fifties who have lived in the neighborhood for many years, who have large families, and have always participated in informal neighborhood gatherings with other long-time residents. Other women quickly find they are isolated socially.

Becoming "House Poor" and Facing Maintenance
Expenses

Another problem for women from professional, upper-middle-class (and some middle-income) marriages is that most find that the house they fought for in the settlement becomes a financial weight around their necks after a couple of years. They soon discover that it is hard to support an expensive suburban home and life style without the high (or fairly high) cash income that usually accompanies such a life style. Even if the exhusband provides substantial financial support, the house soon becomes very expensive for the women. Much of the problem is related to maintenance costs for the house: roof repairs, painting, caring for the yard, the furnace, and so on. Often single parents must let the exterior repairs and maintenance slip. They suffer financial strain and a good deal of worry, plus the social embarrassment of untidy property in well-kept neighborhoods. Middle-income and working-class women who manage to keep their houses on a shoe-string after divorce find home maintenance an especially severe problem. They are apologetic about the looks of their homes and are distressed, wondering whether they will be able to keep their homes after all.

Frequent Moves

Moving many times is often the fate of women from working-class marriages, especially women in their twenties and thirties. Two to four moves within the first three or four years is very common. At the lower economic ranges of this group, the exhusbands often have meager incomes and sporadic work histories. When the marriages break up, there are practically no resources and not many household possessions. Many women from such marriages move from one poor apartment to the next and live in poor neighborhoods. Perhaps the apartment is dark and dreary and needs repairs, or maybe the apartment is all right but up three or four flights of stairs in a rickety old building. Sometimes the housing conditions were poor during the marriage too; but this subsequent housing is truly poor.

The cases in which women feel they were victims of housing discrimination occur primarily with those of the working class. Some younger working-class women find that they are either forced out or unable to rent apartments because of their marital status. Some landlords see these women as financial risks; indeed, it is often the case that they do not seem to have an income or other resources when they seek an apartment. They may say, "I'm getting a job," but landlords remain skeptical. It appears, however, that these women are reliable renters; they dig in, get a job, work hard, and stay within their tight budgets. In the interviews, I was repeatedly amazed and impressed by their determination to support themselves and their success in managing their very frugal households. Their chief resource problems arise in that transitional period when they are forging out on their own, need an apartment, but may not have a job yet.

Living with Parents. This is common after separation or divorce but is a complex arrangement. Either temporary or longer term residence with their own parents is a housing strategy followed by many women. About half the women who move live with their parents at some point. It is often a crucial, financially necessary, transitional arrangement lasting from a month to a couple of years.

This living situation becomes a problem for the single parent for several reasons. Interference of grandparents (especially a woman's own mother) in childrearing is a major source of tension in this housing situation. Further, it results in lack of independence and privacy for the divorced mother. Once the single parent is living with her own parents, she finds they begin "taking over" both her life and the lives of her children. Women in their twenties and thirties are most likely to run into these conflicts with parents. They are usually rather embarrassed about negative feelings toward their parents because their parents provide them with tremendous help and support. In explaining their feelings, women usually go out of their way to make it clear that they are grateful to their parents but feel a strong need to be an independent adult. Living with parents also presents some social-status problems for single parents—it amounts to a dependency arrangement rather than an adult existence for herself and an independent identity for her own nuclear family. Because of these problems, most women try to get their own apartments as soon as possible.

Single Parents Abhor the Idea of Project Living. They do not want to live in some special "project" built to house "welfare mothers," "broken families," or "poor" people. The thought of living in a building that is seen as "that type of place" is rejected and scorned by single parents, even by those with very low incomes and who are on welfare. They resist any such housing with fervor. They speak in great detail about their dislike for such places, what they think about social workers who try to get them to projects, and sometimes, what they think about the inhabitants. This is not a rejection of apartments in general, or big buildings, or modern complexes or cluster apartments. It is a rejection of living in "projects for welfare mothers"—the imagery invoked includes "people who don't care about their children," "fresh kids," "disregard for property," "long, cold hallways." Women say, "Things are hard, but at least I didn't have to resort to that," or "I won't move in there."

Policy Implications

Design and Spatial Needs

Housing is a private matter for single parents, just as it is for two-parent families. Single parents do often try joint-living solutions to housing, but they usually are unsuccessful and unsatisfactory. The most common attempts at joint living are living with parents, taking in roommates, and communal-family experiments in which two families, several adults and children, or two single-parent mothers share an apartment or house with their children. These seldom work for several reasons. Grandparents interfere with childrearing as discussed already.

Furthermore, most families in our society live in separate dwellings and family dynamics, parental roles, parent-child relationships, and patterns of discipline are geared to living in a private housing unit. Most parents just are not able to tolerate much input from other adults regarding their childrearing. Single parents, similar in this respect to couples, seek a fairly exclusive role in the discipline and moral training of their children. Also, families are not geared to tolerate multiple sets of childrearing values and standards in one household. For instance, if the living companion is another divorced woman with her children and if that woman has different childrearing standards for her children, problems develop. Single parents do seek cooperative, supportive relationships with other adults and other families, but most prefer to live "in private dwellings" with their children. They are looking for housing solutions that maintain the integrity of the individual unit.

Inside their own apartments, many single parents, especially those of the working class, live with the problem of inadequate space for privacy and family living. It is not uncommon for a woman with one or two children to rent a small apartment and either spend her nights sleeping on a bed in the living room or give up the living room entirely, converting it to a second bedroom. One of the main fears of middle- and upper-middle-class homeowners with two or more children is the fear that they would not be able to afford a two- or three-bedroom apartment; this worry about adequate space in which to conduct orderly family living is another important reason for their attempts to keep their marital homes.

There is a great need for a *normalization approach* to single parent families and their housing. Single parents want their families to be viewed as "regular" families, not as anomalies in a world of two-parent families. This attitude also affects their housing aspirations. They want housing that is seen as appropriate for other regular families in comparable age groups, life-cycle stages, and occupational groups. Reference groups for single-parent housing are not other divorced families but regular, two-parent families at social levels similar to their own. They do not want to be segregated in a building along with a group of other divorced women and children or other families that need help. Single parents want to live in ordinary residential neighborhoods with various types of families. They seek housing that does not isolate them in special buildings or neighborhoods for problem or low-income families. For women who move from the former marital homes, the problem of not being able to find an apartment in the kind of neighborhood in which they feel personally comfortable is a repeated theme in dissatisfaction with housing. This dissatisfaction is a major underlying factor pressuring single parents to make additional moves in the future. They would like to have a condominium or a suburban apartment in a small building but rarely find such units in their old communities.

The hopes and dreams for housing held by single parents, in many ways, are similar to the aspirations of comparable two-parent families. Many women from working-class marriages still hope, or wish, that they might have their own homes one day. They gave up the marriages but not the dream-house goals of most blue-collar couples. Middle-income–single parents seem to have given up the idea of homeowning, at least they do not talk about it much. They talk about getting a better apartment and, in particular, one in a better neighborhood. Women from professional marriages who received a house in the divorce settlement plan to stay in it until the children have left home. After that, they look forward to apartment or condominium living; they are similar in their attitudes to two-parent families in this social group.[10]

Resource Needs

There is a need for some transitional housing security for single parents. Housing expense is a central issue in the financial problems for single parents after separation and divorce. Women who get a house in the settlement or who receive regular support from the exhusband start building their new income packages from a sound base. For the lower-income families, the absence of either a house or regular support is often a factor in the decision to go on welfare. A program to insure housing security in the first few years after the separation may provide a foundation for a stable, nonwelfare income package.

In the past, we have not paid sufficient attention to the role of the exhusband in subsidizing housing for certain groups of women. If the exhusband signs over a house in the settlement or if he pays his support regularly so that the rent is insured, an important part of the burden of supporting the family is taken off the single parent. If her housing is secure, she can usually piece together the rest of the income package without welfare. Women who own a house are often living on a budget with a rather low, and sometimes incredibly low, cash flow. Housing security is the key. Indirect housing support from the exhusband is not available through either housing settlements or regular support payments, however, to most women from working-class marriages and many middle-income women. Either there is no house or the exhusband does not pay.

Social-class differences in regularity and amount of support received are very pronounced, with working-class women being in a dramatically worse position than middle-class women, especially compared to upper-middle-class women. In the upper–middle-class, divorced fathers almost always pay their support regularly and in the full amount due. This means that the women are receiving a regular, reliable supplement to their family income every month. In sharp contrast, the large majority of working-class fathers do not pay regular support or not in the full amount due. They pay when they can and thus there is no regular income that the single-parent mothers can rely on to cover routine monthly expenses. Most working-class fathers do not have the money to pay. Furthermore, and this is a tough twist of reality, women whose exhusbands are ordered to pay the most, namely those in the higher classes, are by far the most likely to actually collect that support. Tables 2B–3 and 2B–4 in appendix B demonstrate this relationship between social class and receipt of support payments. Working-class women, in particular, need some transitional help. Many may then avoid being brought into the AFDC system. A nonwelfare, non-social work model is needed—an approach based on the idea that regular families in stressful special times need help. It could be designed to be time limited and transitional because (1) most single parents remarry so the single-parent family is, indeed, for most people a transitional stage; and (2) the first one to five years after the separation are the most stressful financially and the most unsettled in terms of direction and life style. The greatest needs are in the areas of rent support (including initial deposits), home-maintenance costs, and temporary mortgage support for women who may be able to keep their homes if they can get past the first year or so. It is during these first few years that help is needed. At that point most single parents have either remarried or have gotten on their feet financially and established a new single-parent life style.

Notes

1. A group of researchers at the Joint Center for Urban Studies of MIT and Harvard University are studying "Housing for Single Heads of Households," Martin Rein, principal investigator, funded by HUD grant number 4. In the first stage of that project, existing qualitative data bases were reanalyzed providing a foundation for a new set of interviews in three cities: Boston; Houston; and Rochester, New York. The interviewees include both female and male single parents, noncustodial divorced parents, and never-married singles (without children).

2. Susan Anderson-Khleif, "Divorced Mothers, Divorced Fathers, and Children: A Study of Interaction, Support, and Visitation in One-Parent Families," Ph.D. dissertation, Department of Sociology, Harvard University, 1976. A sample of twenty-six divorced fathers were also interviewed in the study for a total sample of $N = 76$. They were working-class, middle-class, and upper-middle-class fathers who did not have custody of their children. They were not the exhusbands of the women interviewed but were drawn from the same records and time periods as the mothers. (Findings on the circumstances of these fathers are not included since this chapter focuses on housing for single-parent mothers. A detailed discussion of the sample descriptions and methodology is presented in chapter 2 of the dissertation.) Both mothers and fathers were living in the Greater Boston area and in small towns in Eastern Massachusetts.

3. Richard Coleman and Bernice Neugarten, *Social Status in the City,* (San Francisco: Jossey-Bass, 1971), presents Richard Coleman's instrument for measuring social class which was employed in this study. Also, see

appendix 2 of Coleman's paper on "Husbands, Wives, and Other Earners," Working Paper no. 48 (Cambridge, Massachusetts: Joint Center for Urban Studies of MIT and Harvard University, February 1978), for Coleman's summary sketches of social class groups in the US; or see Richard Coleman and Lee Rainwater, *Social Standing in America* (New York: Basic Books, 1978).

4. Paul C. Glick and Arthur J. Norton, "Marrying, Divorcing, and Living Together in the U.S. Today," Population Reference Bureau (U.S. Bureau of the Census, 1977), pp. 36–37; and Norton and Glick, "Marital Instability: Past, Present, and Future," *Journal of Social Issues* 32 (Winter 1976):5–20.

5. Mary Jo Bane, "Marital Disruption and the Lives of Children," *The Journal of Social Issues* vol. 32, no. 1 (1976):103–117.

6. Heather Ross and Isabel Sawhill, *Time of Transition: The Growth of Families Headed by Women* (Washington, D.C.: The Urban Institute, 1975).

7. That is, these are patterns that are characteristic of the class groups included in the interviews: the working, middle, and upper-middle classes. The interviews covered a period of up to five years after the actual divorce, so these are the patterns observed within that time frame.

8. Furthermore, the need to take note of both the initial separation date and the divorce date is an important general methodological guideline for divorce research. For instance, if one is studying the effects of divorce on children, one must know the date the father (or mother) actually started living in a residence separate from the children. That initial separation may have been a long time before the divorce and thus the child was at an earlier developmental age and more time has elapsed that would be understood from the date of divorce.

9. Richard Coleman, "Seven Levels of Housing: An Exploration of Public Imagery," Working Paper no. 20 (Cambridge, Massachusetts: Joint Center for Urban Studies of MIT and Harvard University, 1973).

10. Susan Anderson-Khleif and Richard Coleman, "Public Responses to New Developments in Housing," Working Paper no. 26 (Cambridge, Massachusetts: Joint Center for Urban Studies of MIT and Harvard University, 1974), presents findings on postparental housing aspirations of different social-class groups.

References

Anderson-Khleif, Susan. "Divorced Mothers, Divorced Fathers, and Children: A Study of Interaction, Support, and Visitation in One-Parent

Families." Ph.D. dissertation, Department of Sociology, Harvard University, 1976.

Anderson-Khleif, Susan, and Richard Coleman. "Public Responses to New Developments in Housing." Working Paper no. 26. Cambridge, Massachusetts: Joint Center for Urban Studies of MIT and Harvard University, 1974.

Bane, Mary Jo. "Marital Disruption and the Lives of Children." *Journal of Social Issues* 32 (Winter 1976):103-117.

Coleman, Richard P. "Seven Levels of Housing: An Exploration of Public Imagery." Working Paper no. 20. Cambridge, Massachusetts: Joint Center for Urban Studies of MIT and Harvard University, 1973.

————. "Husbands, Wives and Other Earners: Notes on the Family Income Assembly Line." Working Paper no. 48. Cambridge, Massachusetts: Joint Center for Urban Studies, 1978.

Coleman, Richard, and Bernice Neugarten. *Social Status in the City.* San Francisco, California: Jossey-Bass, 1971.

Coleman, Richard, and Lee Rainwater. *Social Standing in America: New Dimensions of Social Class.* New York: Basic Books, 1978.

Glick, Paul, and Arthur Norton. "Marrying, Divorcing, and Living Together in the U.S. Today." Population Reference Bureau, U.S. Bureau of the Census, 1977, pp. 36-37.

Norton, Arthur, and Paul Glick. "Marital Instability: Past, Present, and Future." *Journal of Social Issues* 32 (Winter 1976):5-20.

Ross, Heather, and Isabel Sawhill. *Time of Transition: The Growth of Families Headed by Women.* Washington, D.C.: The Urban Institute, 1975.

Appendix 2A:
Social Class and
Housing

Table 2A–1 shows the strong relationship between social-class groups and whether women stayed in their former marital residence or moved to a different residence after separation and divorce. Overall, we see that only 26 percent of the women from upper-middle-class marriages made any housing move at all after the separation. In contrast, 47 percent of the women from middle-class and 55 percent of the women from working-class marriages moved to different housing after separation and divorce.

In table 2A–2 we see more specifically how staying in, or moving from, the former marital residence is linked to social-class levels and particular types of housing. Living in a single-family house versus living in an apartment is a central variable in the table. We see that women from middle-class marriages gave up the most single-family houses, 33 percent of that group gave up a single-family house and moved into an apartment after separation and divorce. They considered this a loss and unfortunate but a financial necessity. There is a sharp contrast in the housing of single-parent mothers from working-class versus upper-middle-class marriages. Seventy percent of the working-class–single parents were living in apartments by the time of the interviews (10 percent + 40 percent + 20 percent + 70 percent in the last column). In contrast 80 percent of the upper-middle-class–single parents were living in their own homes (67 percent + 13 percent = 80 percent in the first column in the table).

Table 2A–1
Whether Divorced Women and Children Moved from or Stayed in the Former Marital Residence, by Social Class

Social Class	Moved	Stayed	
Upper-middle-class women	(4) 26%	(11) 74%	$n = 15$ (100%)
Middle-class women	(7) 47%	(8) 53%	$n = 15$ (100%)
Working-class women	(11) 55%	(9) 45%	$n = 15$ (100%)
		$N = 50$	

Table 2A–2
Type of Housing Move by Social-Class Level

	Upper-Middle-Class Women	Middle-Class Women	Working-Class Women
Stayed in a single-family house	(10) 67%	(7) 46%	(5) 25%[a]
Moved from single-family to another single-family house	(2) 13%	(1) 7%	(1) 5%[b]
Moved from single-family house to an apartment[c]	(0) 0%	(5) 33%	(2) 10%
Moved from apartment to apartment	(2) 13%	(1) 7%	(8) 40%
Stayed in former-marriage apartment	(1) 7%	(1) 7%	(4) 20%
$N = 50$	$N = 15$ 100%	$N = 15$ 100%	$N = 20$ 100%

[a]One of these working-class women stayed in her own two-family house.

[b]This working-class woman moved from her own two-family house to her own single-family house (located right across the street).

[c]One working-class and one middle-class woman moved from a rented single-family house. All other references to single-family houses in this table are their own houses.

Appendix 2B:
Social Class and
Support

Table 2B-1
Support Received from Fathers, by Social Class

	Social Class		
Support Received	*Working*	*Middle*	*Upper Middle*
Father pays regularly and in the right amount	(3) 15%	(7) 47%	(13) 87%
Father does not pay, not regularly, or pays less than he should	(17) 85%	(8) 53%	(2) 13%
N = 50	(20) 100%	(15) 100%	(15) 100%

Table 2B-2
Whether Support is Actually Received, by Amount of Support Awarded to Divorced Mothers

	Amount of Support Awarded to Mothers		
Whether She Is Actually Receiving the Support	*$1,300 to $3,120 per year (n = 18)*	*$3,900 to $5,100 per year (n = 18)*	*$6,000 to $21,840 per year (n = 18)*
Yes: Regularly and in the Full Amount	(4) 22%	(6) 55%	(13) 93%
No: Not at all; Not Regularly; or Not in the Full Amount	(14) 78%	(5) 45%	(1) 7%
N = 43[a]	(18) 100%	(11) 100%	(14) 100%

[a]Seven mothers were awarded no support because the father's whereabouts were unknown or he was an alcoholic.

3

The Women and Mortgage Credit Project: A Government Response to the Housing Problems of Women

Donna E. Shalala and
Jo Ann McGeorge

In 1974 Congress enacted two important pieces of legislation: the Equal Credit Opportunity Act, which prohibits sex and marital-status discrimination in all aspects of the credit process; and section 303(b) of the Housing and Community Development Act, which was amended to prohibit sex discrimination in housing and housing finance.

Two years later, the newly elected President Carter named Patricia Roberts Harris as secretary of the Department of Housing and Urban Development. These unrelated actions by the legislative and executive branches of the federal government were fortuitous because they generated a new sensitivity to the housing problems of women.

One of Secretary Harris's priorities was appointing women to managerial positions where they could have an impact on policies and programs. For those women beginning work with the Office of Policy Development and Research, the recent credit legislation spurred an interest in the housing situation of women. They were well aware of the incredible rise in the number of women in the labor force and the changing American family; that is, the growth in the number of two-earner husband-wife families as well as the dramatic increase of female-headed families. What was not known was how the changing role of women was reflected in the housing market.

As HUD's Annual Housing Survey of American households and the department's many housing programs became familiar, a startling dichotomy was evident: in this country we have, in essence, a dual housing market. First, there is the private market, in which the majority of homeowners are male. Of the 48 million owner-occupied households in the United States, only 18 percent are owned by women. Moreover, almost half of these women homeowners are sixty-four years of age or older and, one may presume, are homeowners as an unfortunate corollary of widowhood.

Public housing, on the other hand, is a market in which the overwhelming majority of households are headed by women. Because so high a percentage of senior citizens are women, even the housing programs for the elderly serve a female constituency. With the exception of Federal Housing Administration (FHA) and Veterans Administration (VA) programs, federal housing programs are essentially women's programs.

The large number of women who must depend on public housing is a bitter comment on women's low economic status. While many women live in poverty or are part of the working poor, there is a growing number of economically independent women whose incomes clearly indicate homeownership as a realistic option. Moreover, for women whose incomes are on the average only three-fifths that of men's incomes and who are struggling to provide adequate housing during a period of double-digit inflation, homeownership is a very important option. The same inflation that erodes the value of conventional savings has made housing the most rapidly appreciating form of investment readily available to the average consumer. Property values have appreciated at roughly 10 percent per annum nationwide over the past several years; in some markets, the rate tops 20 percent. Added to appreciation is the value of the special tax shelter that the federal tax code provides through the deduction of mortgage interest and property taxes, the exclusion of implicit rent from the taxable income of homeowners, and the exemption of capital gains taxation on the proceeds from reinvestment sales. As a result, the rate of return on a dollar invested in housing can range from 18 to 22 percent per year. For many of the millions of single women and women who head households, entry into the mortgage market clearly would be economically advantageous.

Why were women not undertaking homeownership in numbers commensurate with their presence as single, widowed, and divorced members of the labor force? Sex discrimination was one possibility. Until the Equal Credit Opportunity Act (ECOA) and the Fair Housing Act were enacted in 1975, discrimination against women in the granting of credit was not only legal but also accepted as a matter of sound business practice. Conventional wisdom among mortgage grantors held that women's incomes were less stable than men's because their work patterns tended to fluctuate with marriage and children. Traditionally when women worked outside the home, they usually did so until they married or had children. Because few women were permanent members of the paid labor force, women generally were not considered good credit risks nor was their income considered stable. HUD had commissioned a 1975 study, *Women in the Mortgage Market,* which demonstrated that prior to ECOA, mortgage lenders consistently discounted married women's incomes by 50 percent and were reluctant to lend to single or divorced women especially when they were of childbearing age. Had the legal ending of credit discrimination ended these practices? It was a question that required an answer.

While empirical evidence was needed to confirm or refute that sex discrimination in mortgage lending was inhibiting homeownership for women, contacts with innumerable representatives from savings and loan associations, banks, and regulatory agencies suggested overt discrimination was no longer an acceptable practice. At the same time, lenders seemed to have little awareness of the fundamental changes in women's lives that had created a new "female market." Few lenders seemed to comprehend that it was in their own best financial interests to actively market the growing number of economically independent women who were making housing decisions for themselves and often for families as well. Perhaps the lending industry needed some "consciousness raising" on the realities of women's lives today as an incentive to encourage women to enter the mortgage market.

That women needed encouragement was evident. Studies such as the *Ms.* magazine survey on women and money revealed that although women were financially responsible, they admitted they lacked financial expertise and had inhibitions about investing their money. Other studies confirmed that women are often "immobilized with fear" about the "money game" because of their limited knowledge and experience. Clearly a significant contribution to low homeownership rates among women was the attitudes of women themselves. Women needed to know their rights under the law and the housing options available to them. And to overcome any fear about investing their money, they also needed to know the basic steps involved in mortgage credit.

In raising the question of why women were not entering the mortgage market in numbers reflective of their incomes and status as heads of household, three possible problem areas needing attention were identified:

1. There was no empirical evidence on sex discrimination in mortgage lending following the ECOA and Fair Housing Act;
2. There was a lack of awareness in the lending industry about the mortgage market potential of a new female market; and
3. There was a lack of information among women about their housing options and the basics of housing finance.

The next step was to design a program that would initiate a solution or solutions to the problems. The Women and Mortgage Credit Project was thus conceived: a two-year effort to facilitate the entry of women into the mortgage market through research and a national public-information campaign.

First, to ascertain the extent and degree of sex and race discrimination (if any) in mortgage lending, HUD awarded a contract to Harvard University for some basic research on mortgage lending practices. Through analysis of existing or newly developed data on the experience of people who actually applied for mortgage lending, the study was designed to examine the accessibility to mortgage funds by women vis-à-vis men and by blacks vis-à-vis whites. This study is the first comprehensive examination of mortgage-lending practices since passage of congressional legislation outlawing unequal treatment of women in the field of credit. From a preliminary draft of the findings, it appears that the legislation has been effective as there is little or no evidence that women are discriminated against when they actually apply for a mortgage. But the report cautions that examining applications cannot measure any "discouragement" or "steering" practices that, in effect, deter a woman (or black person) from actually filling out a mortgage-credit application.

The second area of concern was lender attitudes and perceptions. The Office of Policy Development and Research is working to raise the consciousness of bankers and savings and loan officials, but on their terms; hard data, not rhetoric, is being used. Thus the realities of women's lives are presented: their stable work patterns, their incomes, their independent life styles.

As evidence of women's credit worthiness, factual testimony from business executives is given on the reliability of women as credit risks. Statistical projections are used to counteract any attitudes that the situation of women today is somehow a temporary aberration—real but transitory. For example, at the turn of the century, the average life span of a woman was forty-seven years, eighteen of which were spent in childbearing. Today, a woman's life expectancy has risen to seventy-seven years with only ten years involved in childbearing. This means that for the first time in human history, the major part of a woman's life is no longer confined to her biological role as childbearer. Women will be spending most of the thirty years they have added to their life span in the labor force.

Or consider this example: the feminization of the labor force is a trend that will continue as increasing numbers of women combine the role of spouse and parent with the role of wage earner just as men have always done. Labor-force participation rates and projections as contained in figure 3-1 graphically substantiate this assertion.

The overall message, however, is that working women of the 1980s are a rich new market available to American business, and companies that best understand the new lives and new needs of their women customers will be the ones best prepared to generate the most profitable sales from this virtually untapped market. When printed in a brochure, such facts will be distributed to individual lenders and to their national association meetings throughout 1980.

The third component of the project, an educational outreach to women, is truly the heart of the effort. To assure that the women who were reached would be representative of all women, sixteen cities across the

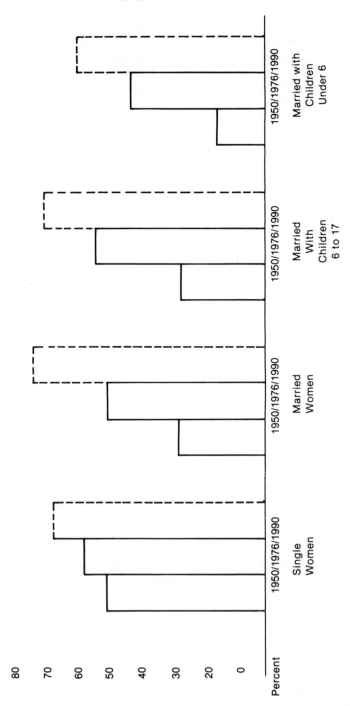

Figure 3-1. Growth of Labor-Force Participation Rates of Women by Family Status, Projected for 1990.

country were selected on the basis of their diversity in size, racial and ethnic groupings, housing markets, and geographical characteristics. The Office of Policy Development and Research contracted with BLK Group, Inc. (a women-owned management and consulting firm) for overall management of the grass-roots campaign. BLK visited each of the sixteen cities where they presented the project to women's groups and local officials and chose a local coordinator. (To further assure representation, BLK subcontracted with Lourdes Miranda and Associates, a Hispanic woman's firm, and the National Council of Negro Women.) Each of the coordinators was brought to Washington by BLK for a week's intensive training in conducting workshops, which they held for all interested women in each of their cities.

The workshop agenda included credit histories, credit rights under the law, the pros and cons of homeownership, housing options (single family, condo, co-op, mobile home, and so forth), the pros and cons of various mortgage instruments, how to compute what is affordable, and the step-by-step procedures—from application to settlement closing costs—involved in acquiring a mortgage. Coordinators ran workshops through June 1980, and it was anticipated that hundreds of women became more knowledgeable from this training and the information they acquired will spread by word of mouth to many more women.

For those women who do not live in the target cities, information packets were prepared that include an annotated bibliography on housing and mortgage credit. Each listing has an address and the cost, if any, of the item. BLK sent out thousands of these packages and the demand remains high.

The League of Women Voters, which has received a grant for educational work with women, has selected ten local leagues for pass-through grants. These leagues are conducting workshops, holding brown-bag seminars, appearing on local television, and visiting local lending institutions as they carry the message of the Women and Mortgage Credit Project. In addition, the league will make a special effort to reach displaced homemakers.

Finally, to reach a national audience of women and lenders, the Office of Policy Development and Research contracted with Hager, Sharp and Abramson, a woman-owned and operated public-relations firm, to design a national multimedia campaign directed to both the female audience and the lender audience. They prepared radio and television public-service announcements, newspaper ads, and feature stories promoting the entry of women into the mortgage market.

It has long been a truism that "the best laid plans of mice and men gang aft agley. . . ." We now know the best laid plans of women are equally subject to going awry. When this project was first conceived, interest rates on home loans were around 8 percent. By the time the first workshops began, mortgage rates had soared into the 11 to 14 percent range. Inevitably criticisms were heard. "Why are you encouraging women to buy homes when their addition to the mortgage market will just increase competition for scarce money?" "Why are you encouraging women to buy at this time when interest rates are so high?"

The response to the first criticism is to assert strongly that women should not be denied access to their share of the mortgage money just because those funds are scarce today. Women should not remain on the periphery of economic activity in housing whatever the state of the overall economy.

The second response is to point out that just as no one could foresee what interest rates would be a year after the project started, no one can foresee what they will be a year after it ends. Women who decide that home-ownership is an option they want to exercise will not be pouring into the mortgage market immediately following their workshop training. It takes time to find a suitable place and time to acquire a down payment. But by learning about mortgages and housing, women will be better prepared when mortgage markets begin loosening up.

What we set out to do at the Department of Housing and Urban Development was to use our feminist enthusiasm to take the first positive steps toward advancing women's participation in the mortgage market. We are contributing to a process that gives women the information they need to exercise all the housing options available to men. At the same time we are encouraging a more receptive mortgage marketplace should women decide to enter it. Our optimism that HUD's Women and Mortgage Credit Project is indeed a major beginning toward resolving the housing problems of women is matched by our delight in contemplating a new response to a tired cliche. For those who assert "A woman's place is in the home," we can respond, "Fine! It just well may be her own."

4 The Woman's Building: Physical Forms and Social Implications

Sheila Levrant de Bretteville

As a center for exploring woman's culture and presenting it to a participating public, the Woman's Building is the site of connection and optimism. Caring interdependence and personal connection to the material world are enhanced by extension into a large, public context. Traditionally restricted to the private house and considered dysfunctional as a professional system, the environments women create have now inspired a bold public structure: the enlarged physical space of the Woman's Building provides a new place for the illumination of women's relatedness, a place constructed to expand with our own growth. The Woman's Building provides a social and physical place in the public world in which women can reevaluate and re-create their gender identity, crossing boundaries of age, class, race or ethnic origin. Here, acts of self-definition are transformed into courageous involvement with society as a whole.

During the four years of its development, the Woman's Building has housed a variety of private and collective enterprises. Filling first the defined space of a two-story unused art school and then defining the interior space in a three-story warehouse, the Woman's Building has been the locus of national conferences, local workshops, and classes, welcoming joyous celebrations, serious study, protest, accidental and planned conversations. Visiting, looking, and milling are invited as well as active participation in existing programs and the invention of new ones.

The wave of feminism in the late nineteenth and early twentieth centuries provided the Woman's Building with its name as well as with antecedents for its physical presence. In the space between domestic and business life, many groups developed the cooperative, caring, and socially responsible surroundings that had been limited and isolated in the private home and were now needed for women's activities. Despite differences in political orientation, the collective kitchens of the Cooperative Housekeeping Movement, the urban Settlement Houses, Women's Clubs, and the Woman's

The Woman's Building and this article about its physical life could not exist without the caring community of women practicing "the gentle art of mutual aid." In particular I am grateful to Dolores Hayden for having suggested that a record of the Woman's Building be included in this book and for providing me with criticism and comfort while I put some of the work that has been such a major part of my life into words.

Building at the 1893 Columbian Exposition in Chicago are nineteenth-century structures which the Woman's Building (1973 to the present) can claim as its history.[1] In the Community Gallery we have painted, with pride and irony, "We have such an organization as has never existed before . . ." a phrase from 1893 Woman's Building catalog.[2]

In the 1960s and 1970s, women gathered together again to focus on many of the same needs for discovering and sharing experience and information. Essentially three types of physical spaces were utilized for this feminist activity: livingrooms, kitchens, and studios in private residences; storefronts and offices in commercial buildings; and classrooms and studios in academic institutions. The imposing regularity of these structures often contrasted with evolving feminist values. Few women's groups in Los Angeles were neighborhood based. Many consciousness-raising groups contained women who came from all over the city to weekly meetings held alternately in each other's homes. But when some groups became committed to working together—providing services and information as self-supporting rather than as after-hours activities—they found the need for more public space.

The Feminist Studio Workshop Constructs the Woman's Building

In the winter of 1973 Arlene Raven, an art historian; Judy Chicago, an artist; and I, a designer, formed an educational, nonprofit corporation, Feminist Studio Workshop, Inc., for the purpose of starting an independent environment in which women in the arts could work. The first designed expression of our alternative environment was a brochure that brought together our professional skills and announced the creation of a new working context, the Feminist Studio Workshop (FSW). The name and brochure gave form to our values and goals before we had begun to determine the physical expression of the FSW in terms of place.[3] We envisioned a studio/gallery, insular during the personal exploratory process but opened periodically to the public for exhibitions, performances, lectures, and discussions. When the first thirty-two women arrived from all over the United States to be members of the Feminist Studio Workshops, we met in a private home while we negotiated with the California Institute of the Arts to lease the vacant Chouinard art-school building. Before spring of 1973 attempts had been made to rent the building for artists' studios. I proposed to Cal Arts that they lease it to us because we had the commitment of five existing women's groups and businesses and had encouraged the creation of three more who had chosen appropriate spaces and rents.[4] The women artists' movement[5] as well as the growing number of women's groups offering services to the public allowed us to acquire the building without capital from the FSW while changing plans for the building. Now it was to be used not only by individual artists but by a larger community.

We again launched a naming and graphic process that established the group. In the Woman's Building's first poster, I provided a diagram of the Woman's Building's values: our egalitarian and participatory intentions were expressed by the matrix of the actual building's facade. The eight equal bays punctuated by spandrels provided each of the womens' groups that comprised the Woman's Building with equal amounts of space within which to define ourselves. On our poster, women joyously ran toward the entrance above which "the Woman's Building" was highlighted, acting out the desire that the Woman's Building would attract wide participation. We expressed our gratitude and connection to the past as well as our commitment to the future:

> The great work of the world is carried on by those inseparable yoke-mates man and woman, but there are certain feminine touches in the spiritual architecture which each generation raises as a temple to its own genius, and it is as a record of this essentially feminine side of human effort that the Woman's Building is dedicated. Now, in 1973 a new Woman's Building has opened its doors in Los Angeles. Established by women, run by women, this building houses a multiplicity of women's creative efforts, illuminating women's art, communicating women's experience. We invite you to come and participate in the activities and spirit of the Woman's Building.[6]

Growing

Problems arose because of unequal participation and responsibility. From the time the lease was signed until the sale of the building in July 1973, the actual patriarchal owner was generally forgotten and all assumed the ultimate responsibility was that of the FSW, Inc.[7] Upon appropriation of the Chouinard building as the Woman's Building, we created a tenants' union named the Board of Lady Managers after the governing body of the 1893 Woman's Building. Within the first year it was clear that participation in decision making and its consequent actions varied greatly.

The groups at the building planned activities that generally took place only within our own space. Autograph parties organized by Sisterhood Bookstore were a notable exception and often attracted hundreds of people. Generally, "the Woman's Building should . . ." was heard often enough at Board of Lady Managers' meetings to indicate that most residents were having difficulty realizing there was no one to take care of the social, economic, and physical life of the building just so we each could do our selected work. The Woman's Building was its participant groups.

The Physical Plant at the Grandview Site

The first Los Angeles Woman's Building tended to expand our possibilities as well as to reinforce our difficulties. The building's space was organized into two stories of discreet units entered off a hallway lining a courtyard. In plan it resembled a "C" with the entrance along the base. The spaces with windows and doors to the courtyard allowed users to know of other activities and opened the possibility of mixing space. However, entering from the hallway, particularly for those groups utilizing the rooms off the corridor, enabled any unit to be occupied by its constituency without much mingling. Womanspace galleries and Sisterhood Bookstore could be visited without encountering other exhibitions to some extent. This privatization of space isolated the groups and their respective publics. The entrance corridor hid the existence of the shared space—the courtyard—and further limited an understanding of the organization be detracting from the sense that these parts did contribute to a larger whole. Had we been able to enter from the courtyard where the names and organized spaces of participant groups could be understood, this primary awareness of context could have been created.

The number of spaces available in the building had initiated our search for groups to fill them. Now they reinforced a visitor's sense of the abundance of women's creative work. A review in the *Los Angeles Times* (3 May 1974) announced, "Contemporary art continues lively in the cheerful, active ambience of the Woman's Building . . . exhibitions squirreled into every corner." The grand opening in November of 1973 brought 4,000 people together and charged us all with the possibilities our accomplishment evoked. Each group attracted a constituency that mingled with others in the courtyard and squeezed through corridors to see what was going on elsewhere in the building. The Woman's Building had effectively brought together members of the art community, the feminist community, old students who had used the building during its Chouinard life, friends, family, associates, and acquaintances of all who participated as well as those who had heard about it through the media.

At the height of the second wave—hopefully one of many peaks in a growing movement—local people as well as those visiting Los Angeles began to contact the Woman's Building managers to schedule performances. Attendance at the monthly exhibitions and at the lectures, rallies, dances, and autograph parties provided a regular indication of the continued involvement of what seemed to be an ever-growing, participatory community. There was a sense of abundance, multiplicity, and support. And the beginning of strain.

To some extent we did not acknowledge difficulties. Rather than diminish our confidence and energy we escalated our commitment and activity.

We began by making the Woman's Building's needs clearer to our participating public. In the entrance corridor which I had thought would have been "taken over" by successive artists and made into a changing welcoming environment, I designed signage that would look accomplished and professional yet could be painted by anyone at the building. Leaving the wall space free for changing uses, high up along the entire edge of the entrance corridor, in soft colors but bold letters, we painted, "Welcome sisters and friends, to the Woman's Building. Support the Woman's Building." Over the donation box and membership cards appeared "Help provide these and other activities," and over the list of resident groups followed "with a new home." The last word "home" was over the entrance.

By the fall of 1973, a representative Building Search Committee had been formed. The FSW changed. Some groups and individuals left; more became involved. While Judy Chicago withdrew to do her own work, starting a large art project within her home studio, Arlene Raven and I placed more of our creative and professional energy into the Woman's Building while continuing to give lectures and contribute to feminist programs in other institutions. We left Cal Arts, bringing colleagues with us to teach in the FSW. A poet and novelist, Deena Metzger, and I had developed a deep, working friendship when we "realized that woman's work corresponds to a particular organization of time and space and to a frequent reference to the immediate and the everyday."[8] Ruth Iskin, an art historian, had come to Los Angeles and worked as a director of Womanspace and an editor of *Womanspace Journal* until both dissolved in June 1974. Suzanne Lacey, a performance artist, and Helen Alm Roth, a printer and graphic artist, had been students in the Feminist Art and Women's Design programs. These feminist artists and teachers became the collective teaching staff of the FSW. From September 1974 through June 1975, Edie Folb, a linguist, joined us, contributing her skills and being nourished herself by the support community for the Woman's Building. It was an extraordinary year: we initiated an extension program of classes and workshops that would involve new students and teachers, as well as a series of national conferences in design, writing, performance, and film and video. It was the students and staff of the FSW who most often took leadership and gave form to extensions of the Woman's Building. Three of the four groups created to coordinate conferences were organized by FSW staff. FSW students participated in these work groups to aid staff in the preparation of exhibitions as well as to organize exhibitions of their own. Between the departure of a tenant group and its replacement, the creative and committed energy of FSW members filled the gap—provisionally, we thought.

The FSW began to share what we were doing by giving lectures, organizing exhibitions, and running educational workshops. Within the Woman's Building and in educational and professional institutions

throughout the U.S., we made the attitudes, processes, and work of the
Woman's Building known. Deena Metzger named our tone "conversa-
tional" after the dialectical reciprocity she was finding in women's words.
Arlene Raven articulated art's function: "to raise consciousness, invite dialogue and transform culture." I called our process "the gentle art of mutual
aid," a phrase taken from an early twentieth-century article on female
involvement in urban reforms.[9] Finally, as we were about to move to the
new building we defined our intentions, naming our institution "a public
center for woman's culture."[10]

Moving

Taking our activities out of one building and moving them to another
forced us to confront the problems of our entrepreneurial style based on
vision, graphic expression, physical manifestation, and public participation. If we were to continue, we needed a thorough understanding of our
economic position, greater sharing of the responsibilities (and ambiguities)
of leadership, and increased public involvement in our activities.

Few people understood that the Woman's Building had been created
without large gifts or grants from private individuals, corporations, or federal and state agencies. Project grants had been received but economic support for the ever-increasing administrative strain was, and continues to be,
lacking. There was little initial capital. The FSW itself was started with $100
from each of its founders, paying for the brochure which channeled the
interest aroused by our writings, lectures, classes, and work. Similarly, we
imported an exhibition of the design work of Eileen Gray from England
with borrowed money, which we could only pay back when we had received
the fees from the participants in the Women in Design Conference. This
pattern of moving through need to public participation and recognition,
with funds just barely keeping up, could not be repeated again and again
without strain. The size of the building and the quality of our work required
substantial financial resources; in reality, we had feminist energy and no
money.

During the eight months of searching for a new home, the physical and
economic situation at the Woman's Building remained ambiguous. Several
component groups dissolved or withdrew. Stated reasons ranged from an
inability to attract customers at our location—the Grandview site was in a
busy working-class neighborhood on the east side of town—to political,
professional or personal differences, often within the constituency of the
particular group. For Womantours, Gallery 707, Los Angeles Women's
Union, and the National Organization for Women (N.O.W.) it seemed

easier to carry on work in an individual office than to share the additional problems and work that our community required. While we had originally been able to pay the monthly rent with the cumulative sum paid by residents, the loss of groups made it necessary to actively search for replacements.

While we were not confident about our ability to draw up a long-range fiscal plan, we met our immediate needs by coordinating our first large-scale, fund-raising event. Cheryl Swanack, a second-year FSW student, and Kate McDonnough, member of a new resident collective at the Woman's Building, the Women's Switchboard, organized "Building Women," a concert by Margie Adam, Meg Christian, Lily Tomlin, Chris Williamson, and the Alice Stone Ladies Orchestra. They raised $6,000 to move our activities to a new Woman's Building.

Finding the right building was not easy. We wanted square footage comparable to that of the Grandview site. We needed public performance space; women's music had made the move possible, and our performance space at Grandview had been the major source of rental fees for performances despite the lack of professional lighting, seating, and sound equipment. The commercial businesses such as Sisterhood Bookstore and Womantours Travel Agency needed easy street access, preferably on the first floor. The Women's Graphic Center also needed their space on the ground floor to accommodate heavy presses and paper delivery. Office space was required for the administrative functions of the building as well as for professional services rendered by individual therapists and attorneys who planned to move into the new Woman's Building. Appropriate spaces for a café, exhibitions, and classes were needed.

The symbolic requirements had become clearer also. Our space could not be private if we were to be seen as an effective participant in the public sphere. The building would have to be a discernable unit, not embedded in other structures that could limit the value or scope of our work. We valued qualities designated female and generally relegated to the home, such as mutually supportive relationships, and we knew they were needed to humanize professional work in society at large. We therefore would not tuck women's experience for forms away again in a residential neighborhood. Our space would have to be accessible to as broad a public as could be found in a city where neighborhoods tend to be homogenous by race, economic wealth, and often political and professional affiliation.

We looked at automobile showrooms and body shops, churches, fire stations, and small factories, seeking a combination of large performance and gallery spaces, storefront commercial spaces, classrooms, and offices. We found absolutely nothing we could afford until June 1974, the deadline for our departure from the Grandview site. Thus many sisters and friends moved us to Spring Street.[11]

The Physical Plant at the Spring Street Site

The difficulty of the move threatened to destroy the young institution, and while the Spring Street building offered a home and some new possibilities it also had several severe drawbacks. The most positive characteristic was that we paid only five and one-half cents per square foot for 18,000 square feet of space; we had paid three and one-half cents per square foot at the Grandview site but had seen no other buildings for under eleven cents per square foot.

The Spring Street building was a three-story red brick structure, easily discernable as a unit, fenestrated on three sides, and with an exceptionally dignified portal. Orginally designed in the 1920s as the administrative offices of the Standard Oil Company of California, it had been converted into a warehouse in the 1940s. Virtually all the marble had been ripped off the floors and the internal walls had been removed. The central core that was originally filled with natural light from a skylight in the center of the roof had been filled in. We now had three floors of undifferential space except for regular steel and wood columns. The construction materials had positive associations; the wood floors were considered more natural and warm than the concrete construction of the previous building. Loading docks, ten-foot ceilings, an elevator, and particularly the natural light that flooded the spaces from the many large windows on two sides of the building fulfilled some practical and inspirational needs.

The location of the building brought some positive but mostly negative response. Although it was situated between diverse ethnic groups (opening a possibility of new participants from groups previously uninvolved in building activities), the immediate neighborhood is industrial. Although there are active areas nearby—the old city center, Chinatown, Little Tokyo, a Mexican-American community just across a foot bridge—the street was generally unfrequented. The unfamiliarity of the site promised to make the building difficult to find and visits preplanned. This isolation could be misconstrued to mean that contact and interrelationships were not wanted. It threatened the business aspects of the building. The building itself drew few negative responses, although the facade was somewhat formidable, and there was no easy access to nature despite the fine view of Elysian Park.[12]

Designing Process

Cleaning was the first step in a process designed to prepare the physical space for our use and repair the emotional disorientation caused by the difficulty in finding and accepting the new home. To rebuild our community and restore our optimistic spirit, the design and construction process had to be as inclusive as possible. In four months over 2,500 people helped build this Woman's Building.

Ideally we would have worked together in the undifferentiated space, perhaps putting up provisional canvas walls as we defined space through use over time. This utopian vision was adjusted by urgent needs for spaces in which to work. Thirty years of warehouse grime and total lack of definition were not evidence of the building's capacity for inspiration. We hoped to manage space so that various groups could appropriate it for brief periods without "permanently" owning an area. This appeared to be a precarious model demanding extensive outreach by the scant administrative staff. But when residents left or dissolved we accepted the challenge. Groups housed elsewhere could now begin to participate in program development by planning events to take place in the new buildings. We would share what was built according to similarity of function, choosing to rigidify as few spaces as possible. Lack of money for abundant materials made a fine rationale for building as little as possible. Few of our needs were so specific as to limit facilities to one group. Even psychologists and lawyers sublet their offices for night classes.

Those businesses who remained with the Woman's Building through the transitional period had been extraordinarily patient, but now they needed to move in and start earning money. The revenue-producing office and store (as well as the performance space) would have to be readied immediately. Needs for privacy and security had been aroused by fears of the new neighborhood. Lack of experience with an open plan or with defining one's specific requirements closed off more areas than might have been if we had taken more time for interaction and discussion with open spaces in the new setting.

Everyone anyone already knew or had just met was encouraged to come down and join in the work, literally building connections. Sharing the cleaning, scraping, patching, sawing, hammering, taping, and painting recreated our community. It is perhaps through this mass participation in building that we have most completely actualized our intentions of bringing together people from all areas of the city, all ages, classes, races, and ethnic origins. Each built a personal connection, seeing the impact her work had on the quality and use of the space as well as on the community among participants. The teaching staff of the FSW and the administrative staff of the Woman's Building shared the responsibility of organizing tools and work while building alongside the other workers.

Intentions, Forms, Contradictions

In designing the space, the emphasis was on generous open forms for conversation, protest, and celebration. Again, there was a utopian model: spaces in which to meander, an active field for personal, professional, and cultural interaction. The area along the periphery was to be an indoor street, bringing the public space inside and diminishing the separation between inside and outside that tradition and the formidable facade set up. Initial demands by individuals for "my" window rather than any ideas about office landscaping meant that natural light would have to be part of the shared public environment. All new walls facing the windowed exterior walls were kept to eight-foot-high partitions which we intended to glaze, reducing noise, when we had the funds. Efforts were made to encourage windows in some of these walls to reinforce the street associations and make it even more possible to know what was going on inside from the outside.

By keeping the density at the building's center we hoped to facilitate an easy understanding of the whole container that would encourage an exploration of its parts. Specific spaces on the first and second floors grew off ten-foot-high backbone walls constructed along the existing wood columns ringing the center of the building. Leaving the steel columns free in space and attaching the walls to the wood columns, which made stud wall construction easier for the newly initiated, a sense of continuity from floor to floor was maintained despite the different choices on each floor regarding where to draw a wall. Decisions about which side of the wood columns would receive a wall were determined by the gallery spaces' need for an uninterrupted neutral background. It was decided to leave the third floor completely open—6,000 square feet of skylit space.

Due to limited time, money, and materials, coupled with the intention of leaving space open to future definition, some plans and needs remained unfulfilled. Since the opening on 13 December 1975 the pleasure and variety in the use of the open space, as well as the continuous shortage of funds, inhibited new construction.

On the second floor, the full-height wall wraps around to define a gallery space in which a storage area was constructed by enclosing one set of columns. This provides more wall space and divides the gallery into two parts; a more private and protected internal space at the central core and a wide gallery hall that connects the two stairways. Along the backbone wall facing the windowed exterior walls, two small spaces (50 to 100 people) were constructed for classes, meetings, readings, and so forth. These were considered only two in a possible series of spaces to be built off of the backbone wall on this, the quiet floor. Now it seems unlikely that more will be built. We have become accustomed to the variety of events that have occurred in the places that have been left open; the generous circulation spaces allow art work to be experienced to and from anywhere on the floor.

The first floor was the most defined by specific programmatic needs and code requirements. As on the second floor, the commercial spaces were created off the ten-foot fire wall that separates the Women's Graphic Center in the back from the commercial offices and welcoming entry in the front of the building. An indoor street was created outside the more specific spaces with eight-foot-high partitions facing the exterior windowed walls.

These eight-foot walls have begun to be glazed for sound and security clo-
sure though we asked the renters of these spaces to fenestrate the wall and
door if possible. Originally I had hoped to enclose Sisterhood Bookstore
with only a protective sliding grate that would be pulled back during their
business hours. This was more threatening than the window-storefront suggestion they originally rejected, so a solid wall was built; however, I have
been trying to find someone who would like to paint a trompe l'oeil view
into the bookstore. The space adjacent to the bookstore was rented by two
women as a gallery after the travel agency withdrew, having found its
interim space quite comfortable. The new residents chose sliding glass
doors, making the exhibited work visible even when they were closed.

Naming has been an act of intention and hope at the Woman's Building, affecting how it has been seen and used. Calling the circulation spaces
on the second floor the "Street Gallery" helped users see this space as an
indoor street while encouraging performance and art work to be placed
there. Naming the enlarged circulation space "Environmental Gallery" virtually evoked inventive walk-through installations. Naming our place "the
Woman's Building" links us with the first wave and a worldwide exposition
space in which women's work is honored. During the two years at the
Grandview site, the building had overlapped many more uses with the
women's centers, providing services and a meeting place.

Needing to make our orientation clearer, we enlarged our self-definition and stressed our desire for inclusive participation. Knowing that people
coming to the Woman's Building were unsure of what it was they were visiting, we made an explicit welcoming area in which each visitor would be
warmly greeted: behind her the wall opens out and is painted as if bathed in
warm light, and in large clear letters we state "the Woman's Building, a
public center for woman's culture, welcomes you." We have found in five
years at the Spring Street site that people understand us as an independent
cultural institution focusing on the social and artistic expression particular
to a class of people—women—with the intention of making that experience
and expression available in a public setting to as broad an audience as we
can reach. While many of the creations in this environment have evoked the
nurturant and soft aspects of female experience, the value and caring of
women's conversation, there are no spaces yet in the building that feel like
nests; not enough soft materials have been added to the open, spare construction. These materials need to be used not only in artwork but in furnishing. The white walls are regularly transformed during exhibitions providing a screen onto which diverse aspects of women's experiences are regularly projected.

The program at the Spring Street site has been hindered by economic
problems. The strangeness of an industrial neighborhood in an unfamiliar
part of the city has reduced the number of people who come to the building

on days when there is not a particular large-audience event. This lack of ongoing foot traffic has made it difficult for the bookstore and café to schedule their time at the building so as to make their businesses economically viable. The three women who ran the Bookstore also maintained one on the opposite side of the city and engaged in various political and therapeutic activities as well. The strain was too much. Sisterhood Bookstore left in March 1977. Their space was then rented as the editorial offices of *Chrysalis* magazine. The café owners gave up in May; the café was revitalized and reopened as "Val's Café," with open hours coordinated more efficiently with the Woman's Building's peak times and events, but since 1979 it has been underutilized. We have been fortunate to receive CETA money enabling us to add staff and extend our learning-by-doing educational programs to those who could not attend without being paid. And we are creating structures, such as an advisory board and active committee, which invite new people to bring their ideas and work.

Idea-Hopes and Actualities

A painful and productive tension exists between space built with ideal goals and the actual human processes of the place. Susana Torre calls this "the paradox of architecture, an act forever striving towards the realization of an ideal, while as a product it is forever eroded or modified (depending on the view taken) by new social or personal events and by the changing desires of the occupants."[13] As the creators of the space are also among the users, there is the potential for a synthesis between the material aspects of the Woman's Building and the organization, the passion, within it.

With continued growth could come the economic power to build a roof garden for eating and enjoyment of the view of Elysian Park, the trains, and Los Angeles, the city in which we work. Behind the Woman's Building on Spring Street, between it and the railroad tracks, is a plot of land presently used for junked cars. We could acquire it and cultivate a garden of flowers, fruits, and vegetables. And given the proximity to the railway, we could bring a caboose from the track alongside the building to act as a place for children to play and work while their friends and parents were at the Woman's Building. Since the caboose would use the limited parking area and because more parking space is needed during large openings and performances, the parking lot next door might be obtained on a permanent basis for mass parking.

More electricity could be brought into the building and up to the roof so that we can be seen from afar, as well as to light the parking areas so women will be less fearful that they or their cars will be attacked. We could fly balloons or kites and invent non-energy-wasting ways to extend into the physical environment around the building. Presently our physical environment ends at the exterior walls, yet the women inside have created numerous outreach programs in other institutions around the country. We have not as yet put a large sign on the Woman's Building's exterior—perhaps an expression of our confidence in making interior space but not in changing the dominant culture. As this internalized emphasis is contradictory to our purpose, some of these fantasies are important steps in institutional self-actualization.

In 1980 the lease on the Spring Street site was up and we had the choice of renewing the lease, getting a new building, or having a crisis like that of spring 1974. Economically and emotionally, renewal would probably be best. The Woman's Building is so much our home that some of the initial advantages which had been obscured by difficulty are now being enjoyed. The possible revitalization of the downtown area may bring even more people to our part of town, particularly if we can get minibus service from the nearby tourist and ethnic centers to the Woman's Building. A planning committee might find a building that we could buy or get another building for little or no money through a municipal program as yet undiscovered. But a crisis situation could easily develop, particularly if the overextension of staff repeats the pattern of dealing with problems on a day-to-day basis without an active five-year plan. Present efforts in such planning are still new.

The quality of communication at the Woman's Building provides a loosely organized community able to respond quickly to long- and short-term issues affecting us.

The larger physical environment of the Woman's Building—in comparison to the private home, studio, office, or storefront—has acted as a vehicle for physically uniting diverse aspects of the community, bringing women together at the same time in the same place. In the 1970s a series of fragmentations have made this progressively more difficult, though recent threats to the Equal Rights Amendment, gay rights, and racial integration may provide a new wave of combined activity. Fragmentation and re-ghettoization cannot be halted by the sheer physical presence of the Woman's Building, but our very existence, stated goals, and inclusive accomplishments imply an alternative.

It almost appears to be a physical need for people to see others like themselves represented at the Woman's Building in order to accept the Woman's Building as their place. Members of the FSW have created numerous in-house and outreach programs that provide various groups with a familiar content in the hope of wider participation by members of diverse ethnic, economic, and political groups. Among such programs initiated in 1980 were "Las Venas de la Mujer," an environmental exhibition and celebration of Chicana culture; "Not as Sleepwalkers," theatrical readings created from a journal workshop composed of elderly women and FSW students; "New Moves," scholarships to the educational programs at the Woman's Building for disadvantaged women; as well as lectures, performances, and exhibitions for those attending professional conferences in Los Angeles (such as the College Art Association and the American Humanistic Psychologists). Maintaining the connections created by these events requires continual work. By having access to a greater variety of images of women and their lifestyles, we are better able to conceptualize what is happening in our own lives. Each group lacks a range of images and creates out of what is available to it. By bringing together the variety of expressive forms, each articulating the wide-range as well as the shared experiences of women, the Woman's Building gives us all more space in which to create new possibilities for ourselves.

Despite the inclusive intentions enacted in outreach programs and reiterated on the walls and in the printed matter of the Woman's Building, the largest constituency at the Woman's Building has ranged between early twenties and late thirties in age and has been essentially homosocial and homosexual. Fears of the most consistently committed group of workers at the Woman's Building have laden the job of involving people whose lifestyle and sexual preference is more easily accepted by the dominant culture. An understanding of the contributions of gay women to society as a whole must be acknowledged. The heterosexuals' fears of homosexuality must be shared if we are to have the full complexity and variety of women's experience honored and visible within the Woman's Building and in the society we intend to transform.

The orientation, accomplishments, and difficulties of this Woman's Building can provide a useful model for women elsewhere who might create a new independent cultural and feminist institution. As the goal of this institution is to project woman's culture into the public sphere, the more women can group together to locate and create this culture the more likely it is that we can have a positive impact on society at large.

While claiming no moral superiority or greater sensitivity for women, I am suggesting that the society has devalued the attributes it has assigned to women, so that successful women (in terms of recognition and economic security) have had to shed those very abilities that make them most human and that might provide for more practice of "the gentle art of mutual aid" among workers. While several colleagues and I at the Woman's Building have located some of the forms of woman's culture[14] and called those interactional modes and formal expressions that are repeated among women everywhere as woman's forms, our goal is not to isolate these phenomena and honor them in order to set up further inequities and boundaries; rather we would have the basic values of these modes and forms be attractive and usable by that same broad audience that we keep reaching out to from the Woman's Building.

Barbara Meyerhoff, an anthropologist, tells of shamans in other cultures who enact the human will of their tribe to change a mountain that has not altered perceptively for centuries. In symbolic and actual ways the Woman's Building affirms the importance of our shared culture as women, contributing to our personal strength to move the patriarchal mountain.

Notes

1. For more information on nineteenth-century alternatives see Dolores Hayden, "Redesigning the Domestic Workplace," *Chrysalis* no. 1 (February 1977):19–29.

2. The full quotation that you see as you arrive at the second floor's Gallery space establishes the extramaterial benefits of exhibiting women's work:

> We have such an organization as has never before existed of women for women. Women's thought and sympathy have traveled to us along the slender imperishable thought railway. Our building is like the terminal station of a vast city, where the iron rails come together from north, south, east and west. The freight that our railway has brought is very precious. The exposition will thus benefit women, not alone by means of the material objects brought together, but there will be a more lasting and permanent result through the interchange of thought and sympathy among women of all countries, now for the first time working together with a common purpose and an established means of communication.

3. For a discussion of feminist form language as expressed in built and graphic work, see S.L. de Bretteville, "A Reevaluation of the Design Arts from the Perspective of a Woman Designer," *Arts in Society* (Spring/Summer 1974):115–124.

4. The following is a list of tenants comprising the Woman's Building from 1974 to 1977. Such a list demonstrates the changes in permanent rentals but does not show the growing involvement of diverse groups and individuals using the space for films, classes, rallies, and so forth. It does indicate the difficulty in prolonged relationship of both the members of the group and the group to the whole. An asterisk (*) indicates groups that dissolved.

October 1973

The Feminist Studio Workshop (FSW), an educational and support community for women, including the Women's Graphic Center

*Grandview One and Two, a collective of forty-three women artists (changed membership and renamed itself Double X in 1976

*Womanspace, previously run collectively for a year as an art gallery and performance space in a storefront

*Gallery 707, previously situated in the owner's private studio Sisterhood Bookstore run by three women who had another store

*Association of Women's Presses (AWP), never quite existed

*Los Angeles Feminist Theatre (left after three months)

Susan Kuhner, therapist

October 1974

The FSW Women's Graphic Center and Center for Art Historical Studios

Women's Liberation Union, an activist community group

*Women's Switchboard, a telephone referral service

N.O.W., Hollywood chapter (moved to an office in Hollywood)

Womantours, a travel agency run by Estilita Grimaldo

Susan Kuhner, therapist

The Extension Program

Sisterhood Bookstore

October 1975

FSW The Women's Graphic Center, the Center for Art Historical Studios

The Extension Program

Sisterhood Bookstore

Canis Gallery

Susan Kuhner, therapist; Johnnie Zeutlin, therapist; Bobette Fleischman, lawyer

5. For a discussion of the growth and accomplishments of the Los Angeles women artists' movement see Faith Wilding, *By Our Own Hands* (Los Angeles: Double x 1977).

6. Catalog to the Woman's Building of the World's Columbian Exposition, Chicago, 1893.

7. Several times efforts were made to redistribute leadership. Upon Judy's departure, Arlene and I offered to equalize the legal and actual responsibility for the Woman's Building among individuals and groups participant in the women's community. While no one seemed to be willing to make that level commitment and responsibility, we renamed the corporation Women's Community, Inc. to enable it to be a descriptive and legal umbrella. The corporate officers are still Sheila Levrant de Bretteville (president), Arlene Raven (vice president), Judy Chicago (secretary and treasurer). We were designated by the pulling of straws. Although we were working in equal partnership when we formed the nonprofit corporation, the format of legalization imposed its own token hierarchy. I have often thought that this naming had a quality of self-fulfilling prophecy easing Judy's withdrawal, my extraordinary responsibility during the second year and the move, though there is now a collective, horizontal spread of leadership among more people than before, more division of labor but an equalization of commitment and responsibility.

8. For a presentation of the forms of woman's culture see Deena Metzger, "In Her Image," *Heresies* (June 1977):2-11.

9. Caroline Hunt, "Women's Public Work for the Home an Ethical Substitute for Cooperative Housekeeping," *The Journal of Home Economics* vol. I, no. 3 (June 1909):574-576.

10. During the second year of the Woman's Building at the Grandview site, much of the income came from dances. The building was becoming a hang-out, and the social function was obscuring the cultural functions of the building. We wanted to keep the Woman's Groups as a meeting place for all women and one that would express the togetherness in artistic and political activity. To make our focus clearer we enlarged our institutional self-description, emphasizing the public participation and expressive nature of the emphasis. We requested that those organizing dances and renting the performance space consider making the celebrations informational and cultural as well as social. There was resistance to this suggestion as the creators of the event felt even the naming of the dance for a woman past or present was extraneous to their goals and a burden. One concert dance was held, however, called "flying." During the week prior to the concert dance, poetry readings and films were scheduled in which the metaphor of flying appeared in diverse forms of women's work.

11. While searching for a building that was underused but near if not in a public setting, Cheryl Swanack and I found our present structure. Although Cheryl had seen it before, she had discounted it as a possibility because of its limitations. But now, when no agent or individual had found anything that fulfilled even half our program, we responded to this building's potential, especially as it was already the month in which we were to move. As officers of Women's Community, Inc., Arlene Raven and I

signed the five-year lease agreeing to pay $1,000 a month in rent. Although the owner was not interested in selling, we have first option to buy. With the help of many sisters and friends the contents of Grandview were moved to 1727 North Spring Street.

12. There were additional problems that threatened the use of this building that were encountered while getting building permits. Fees, requirements, and new laws are applied when a building's designated use is changed. Building, fire, and electrical inspectors have certified that the building is up to code for a manufacturing company, the registered designated use we have continued. As it is impossible to change the designation to 'public' without getting a variance, future ownership would seem to be ruled out.

13. Susana Torre, ed. *Women in American Architecture: A Historic and Contemporary Perspective* (New York: Watson-Guptill, 1977), p. 198.

14. See note 8.

Part II
Community

The local community is a soil that can nourish and support human efforts or discourage and depress them.

In "Women and Children in a Planned Community" Suzanne Keller explores the neglected needs of women in a community planned to provide some of the benefits of suburban living. Outmoded ideas (and design) about the social, economic, and personal goals of contemporary women make such communities less responsive and nourishing than they could, and should, be. The author points to a range of women ill-served by the planners' traditional models of family life and sex roles.

Ilene Kaplan examines women's satisfactions with the physical and social features of a planned community in "Family–Life Cycle and Women's Evaluations of Community Facilities." She notes patterned variations over the life course and proposes the family–life cycle as a significant tool for planning. In this research, satisfaction with community services was greatest at two points in time: in the early years of married life before the arrival of children and in the later years after the children had left home.

In "The Life Space of Children" Sarane Spence Boocock looks into the activity patterns, responsibilities, and satisfactions of children with their neighborhoods and communities. She suggests the possibility that current land-use patterns "may inhibit the behavior of" children in "major ways," and that an environment suitable for children may not be so for adults. Planners, designers, and architects need to be sensitive to such incongruities of needs and preferences and include this multiplicity of goals in their images of community.

Chapter 6

5 Women and Children in a Planned Community

Suzanne Keller

Ever since Clarence Stein and Henry Wright created their "garden city" of Radburn, new communities have been viewed as gateways to a better life for contemporary Americans. Their comprehensive designs of facilities and services, within relatively easy access of homes and neighborhoods, were not only to meet the varied needs of their residents but also to provide a sense of togetherness and belonging.

These commendable goals, research has shown, are easier to state than to achieve, for while new communities do provide numerous benefits, they also neglect the needs of important segments of their inhabitants. Chief among these are the women residents whom planners still tend to view largely in their traditional roles as wives and mothers happily focused on home and neighborhood, while husbands and fathers are away in the big city earning a living for the family. This idyllic image, however, does not fit the reality of most women's lives.

Another group typically ill-served by planned environments consists of those passing through the no-man's land of adolescence, otherwise known as the difficult age, for whom planned communities often spell lack of privacy and boredom.

In this chapter I will summarize the main findings of an in-depth study of one planned community in regard to each of these important populations. The community in question was the first planned unit development in the state of New Jersey which I explored during the first five years of its life.[1] A large-scale survey of 930 households, as well as lengthy interviews with 250 adults (three-fourths of them women) and 80 adolescents, provide the empirical data for this chapter.

The samples interviewed represent a cross section of the 12,000 residents living in a mix of townhouses and condominiums as to neighborhood, house type, education, family status, age, and income.

The residents resemble the typical residents of other planned communities in being young (one-half under thirty years, eight-tenth under thirty-five years), highly educated (the majority had attended college), and native-born offsprings of native-born parents. They come to the community from other parts of New Jersey (37 percent) and from New York City (46 percent) in search of space, a good environment for their children, and that insignia of economic and occupational success—a house of their own.

The men typically commute to jobs in business and the professions and family incomes were already well above the national and the New Jersey average with more than eight-tenths of these households earning $15,000 or more annually in 1974. Thus the sample represents the proverbial third generation (though native born, eight-tenths had a least one foreign-born grandparent) who had experienced upward mobility by means of educational and occupational achievements for the men and marriage for the women.

The large majority of the residents are married (93 percent) and have one (31 percent) or two (40 percent) children under age five. The majority also are new homeowners for whom the move to the community represents a positive step in their lives and especially in the lives of their children.

While the majority of husbands worked outside the community, the majority of wives stayed within its borders. Although most of them had held jobs before moving to the community, only three-tenths were jobholders at the time of the interviews. Their reasons for discontinuing were, first of all, maternity, and secondly, the move itself. Most expressed some hope of taking jobs in the future, but few had a specific date in mind. Domesticity had become their prime occupation.

Having heard so much about the home that runs itself, it may come as a surprise to note the great concentration on the home as a locus of activities and the amount of household work these women do daily. Most of them did all their own cleaning, cooking, ironing, mending, washing, and food shopping. Some had sporadic help from husbands (30 percent) and a few (8 percent) had paid household help.

Specifically, more than eight-tenths cook every day, making frequent use of frozen foods and of TV dinners less frequently; two-thirds regularly do the dishes, with the remainder receiving some help from husbands and, to a lesser extent, from their children; four-fifths do their own ironing; virtually all do their own laundry (only half approving of the laundry's present location); more than one-half clean their own windows. In addition to this daily routine they also frequently entertain informally and the large majority have overnight guests every few weeks or months.

As for households, so for childcare. It, too, falls virtually exclusively on the women's shoulders. This may be why eight-tenths of the women describe themselves as being harassed, overworked, and more than occasionally pressured. At the same time, however, a sizeable number (three-fifths) complain of being bored and having too little to do besides staying in the house in the company of their small children. Thus it seems that most of the women are alternately overburdened and underoccupied.

Asked what they considered the best and worst times of day, the great majority opted for evenings as the best time (65 percent) either because their husbands were home then (27 percent), they were less busy (20 percent), they had time to themselves (20 percent) or they could go out for amusements (20 percent).

Supper time (40 percent) and mornings (35 percent) were leading candidates for the worst times of day, the chief reasons being the hectic pace, fatigue, and demanding children.

Demanding children may explain why more than eight-tenths of the women favor childcare facilities in the community. This is surely a remarkably high endorsement by this middle-class population that has traditionally been opposed to such inroads upon a mother's exclusive role in childcare. Moreover, most favor such facilities for any women who wants them (70 percent) and only a minority (25 percent) would confine their use to employed women. There is, furthermore, agreement that both sexes should staff such centers which should be open all day (52 percent) and during the evening hours as well (23 percent). The reasons given for favoring day-care centers include benefits for working mothers (34 percent), freedom for mothers to do other things (17 percent), and general psychological benefits (14 percent).

The desire for day-care centers, which is shared by husbands, distinguishes these women from previous generations and constitutes a break with the tradition that made full-time, individual, exclusive childcare a sacred obligation for their mothers and grandmothers.

This important exception aside, however, these women do not depart markedly from tradition. Indeed, their dream is the familiar one of a house of their own, marriage, children, neighborliness, and material affluence. These are no dramatic changes in the domestic division of labor nor in traditional priorities, with the men earning a living for their families and the women giving up jobs to take care of husbands, homes, and children full-time.

Since the women chose to move to this community, it seems that its general design was to their liking and they were in that sense preselected for living there. One question of interest, then, is whether there are any differences in work and household patterns by generation. A look at the one-fifth of women who were young (under twenty-nine years old) and well educated (all had at least a college degree) suggests no striking generational differences.

The data show the young women to be quite in line with the sample as a whole: 96 percent were married, 60 percent already had one child, and another 20 percent had two children. Two-thirds, moreover, intended to have at least one more child, thereby achieving the community's two-child norm.

As was true for the older as well as the less educated women, only a minority (one-fourth) of the young women currently hold jobs, one-half of these part-time, and most of them locally. All had held jobs in the past and nearly all (nine-tenths) intended to do so again in the future though only one-half had a specific date in mind. And like the older, nonemployed women, the young women, too, gave up their jobs because of maternity.

They spend their days on housework and childcare feeling alternately over-worked or underemployed and bored.

Both generations of women are also alike in their concentration on home and children. More than half, for example, spent the previous day on housework, meals, cleanups and nonrecreational childcare. This is far more time than they spent in conversations with their commuting husbands as only one-tenth spent as much as an hour and another tenth, two hours, in such conversations on the previous day. Given their traditional domestic preoccupations, it is therefore especially noteworthy that the large majority of women of all ages strongly endorse the availability of daycare facilities for their children. It is equally noteworthy that these were not anticipated or planned for.

Before considering the women's criticism of this community, the perceived benefits are examined. The majority appreciated a number of features: the scale of the community, the other residents, the benefits to their children, especially the open spaces and safety, and the house itself. Although they would have like to make some changes in layout and design, by and large they were pleased with the move, their houses, and their neighbors.

From the beginning, however, there was a sizeable group that suffered from loneliness and boredom within the community and from inadequate access to jobs or diversions outside it.[2] Of the two, boredom affects women more than loneliness. Nearly one-half said they were bored frequently (daily to several times a week) and only one-fourth, never. Moreover, younger women experience boredom more frequently (35 percent of women under thirty years) than do older women (16 percent of women thirty-six and older) and women with children more than women without (47 percent versus 33 percent). Since both older women and childless women are more likely to have jobs that absorb their time, this highlights the special needs of the house-bound women with young children.

Employment does indeed turn out to be an antidote to boredom. Twice as many housewives as employed women say they feel bored very often (33 percent versus 17 percent, $X^2 = 0.155$). And women employed full-time are least bored of all, with eight-tenths versus two-thirds of those employed part-time saying they are rarely or never bored.

As for loneliness, one-third admitted to feeling lonely at the time of the interview, two-fifths said it was hard to meet people like themselves in the community, and one-seventh did not yet feel part of it and had no close friends there. Indeed, the majority had experienced loneliness at sometime (34 percent were lonely now; 27 percent had been lonely at first; and 39 percent had never been lonely).

Contrary to what one might expect, moreover, having children does not protect one against loneliness unless, perhaps, one has a large number which very few in this community do. Childless women experience less lone-liness than women with one or two children (table 5-1).

The youth of this community have unique problems and share some with their mothers. Of the eighty adolescents interviewed, most were clus-tered in the thirteen- to fourteen-year-old category, though they ranged from eleven to seventeen years.

It has often been noted that preteenagers and adolescents are among the more disgruntled and least satisfied residents of new communities. This is due not only to the generally stressful nature of this particular stage of life but also because new communities are so often oriented primarily to young adults and very young children, leaving the older child relatively neglected and deprived.

The move was seen as a rather positive experience for the large majority (85 percent), who thought that their lives had changed for the better in terms of more activities, new friends and more freedom. And since, at that age, most readily made friends in the new community, they began to feel part of it within a fairly short time. In contrast to their parents, moreover, they were far less spatially confined, the majority (nine-tenths) drawing on the entire community for their social contacts. Their parents' friendships, on the other hand, were confined to neighbors very close to home; one-half to the street and one-third to the quad in which they lived.

The youngsters also appreciated the community for its openness and safety, but they voiced strong complaints on other grounds. The lack of transportation facilities, not enough recreation, and inadequate shopping all loomed large in their minds, with the girls more dissatisfied with shop-ping and recreation, while the boys stressed the absence of adequate space for various athletic activities.

Both boys and girls complained about the absence of public transporta-tion to get them to desired athletic, cultural, and social events outside the community. Many had come from urban settings that had public transpor-tation and a great many activities within easy reach which they could get to on their own. In the present community they could walk and bicycle to vari-

Table 5-1
Reported Loneliness in the Community

Number of Children	Percent Never Lonely
None	47 $N = 45$
One	30 $N = 63$
Two	40 $N = 77$
Three or more	56 $N = 9$

ous sites, which they did to some degree, but this proved inadequate for great distances, if they had to carry along cumbersome equipment, or in inclement weather. On all those occasions, either mother, the chauffeur, was called on, or they simply did without but not without some resentment.

One facility that was keenly missed was a teen center of their own at which they could gather away from the watchful eyes of the adults. Given the skewed age distribution of the new community population, heavily weighted with young couples and toddlers, adolescents cannot count on the critical mass necessary for their social life which seems to require both anonymity and visibility for maximum success.

All in all then, not being very numerous in the first generation, older children and adolescents tend to get shortchanged in a number of respects important to them.

In appraising this unfinished community basically designed for other age groups, they stress feelings of relative deprivation with regard to special facilities of interest and community support. High on the list of grievances is the lack of enough things to do in the community, a sense of being cut off from other communities, and their not having a place of their own.

Of further interest to planners is the focus of most youthful complaints on design aspects of the community, including its impact on their social and recreational life. The adults are seen as reluctant and often hostile compatriots who tend to monopolize the desirable spaces for their own benefits. Hence the persistent refrain of the young that there is nothing to do and no place to go and no one who cares about them. Their complaints are particularly pronounced in bad weather and in the evening hours since the community was basically designed for daytime and good weather.

Ironically, all that open space for which the parents left the crowded city is experienced by their children as too confining by its lack of activities, variety, and excitement. By contrast, the cities left behind emerge in retrospect as havens of freedom and mobility.

These findings are not confined to this one community. They are corroborated by a number of other studies both within and outside the American setting.

For example, in their careful comparison of thirty-six communities, of which seventeen were new communities, Burby and Weiss found that, as regards the younger children, although child play areas are the most ubiquitous feature of new communities, most children did not use them.[3] They preferred to play in their own or a neighbor's yard or in the streets and parking areas. Similar preferences were evident in the community I monitored.

As for youngsters aged fourteen and older, the majority was not satisfied with the organizational activities and programs; did not feel that there were enough good places to get together with friends; and did not rate their teen centers very favorably. They also note a discrepancy between the parents, who generally rated such facilities highly, and the youngsters, who did not.

In this connection, there is Richard Dattner's observation that although children are "the most deeply affected group of users of play facilities, they are at present least able to influence the design of their environment."[4] As for parents, although they obviously have a great interest in successful play facilities and will "go through great lengths to provide a good environment," the problem is that either they too are not consulted or they seek to satisfy their own personal needs in the name of providing for their children. In this view, the group that has the greatest influence of all are the city officials with money and decision-making power who are also, however, "least affected by the results."

There is also the study of a British housing estate in a working-class area, which noted that the children "were exposed to constant repressions and frustrations and the working of a system which was inconsistent and capricious." The result was "marked hostility" to the adults and to the environment.[5]

A comparative study of a Swedish and an American suburb found complaints similar in tone and context to those we have reviewed in the American community.[6] Youth complained that activities were too supervised, too hard to get to in the evenings, and the environment too unstimulating. Lack of transportation was also mentioned, as were monotony and boredom.[7]

Finally, noting that New Towns are boring to children, C.A. Doxiadis cites a German study that found that "children gauge their freedom not by the extent of open areas around them, but by the liberty they have to be among people and things that excite them and fire their imaginations.[8]

Thus there is cumulative evidence that the designed environment leaves much to be desired for children and youths in planned communities. Access is one problem, inadequate public transportation, recreational and cultural activities are others. A lack of participation in the design is yet a third.

I agree with Dattner's observation that every environment is a learning experience, even a poorly designed one.[9] In his view, the lessons learned in all too many planned environments by the young residents are negative ones. He mentions, among the specific lessons, the idea that the young do not matter as individuals but only as a category, thereby being forced to yield their individuality to uniformity and standardization. In addition, the young learn that they can have no constructive effect on the fixed and immobile environment because they seem to be able to change it "only in a destructive way,"[10] and all too often they learn that the adult-made world is dull, ugly, dangerous, and "empty of sensuous satisfactions."

In endeavoring to make design responsible to human needs, the planners' chief limitations appear to be their definitions of such needs and of the residents who exemplify them. This is evident, in this instance, in regard to youth and the adult women.

The ideal women for planners are of a single social type: that of the young, unemployed housewife with young children. This leaves all other ages and types—the jobholding woman, the back-to-school woman, the part-time mother, the exmarried, and the unmarried—at a distinct disadvantage. Not surprisingly, these neglected types are particularly discontented with what planned communities have to offer.

However, even the planners' focus on the traditional housebound wife and mother is proving to be too narrow. For while women may give top priority to the care of children and households, this does not preclude their having other interests and needs as well, for variety and diversion, and for interesting activities, including employment and education, close to home. An environment offering well-designed houses but no interesting collective spaces, no engaging panorama of terrains and activities will be inadequate even for the women whose needs the planners supposedly try to address.

Data from the present study suggest, moreover, that planners may be underestimating the impact of contemporary change on women's roles and self-perceptions. Today, even traditional women are more demanding and more modern in their tastes and expectations than planners acknowledge. One striking example from the present study concerns the nearly nine-tenths of the residents who are in favor of day-care facilities but have no such facilities available or planned for. This would support one frequent claim that planners are not always in step with public sentiment. Similarly, the majority of women hopes to find part-time employment near their homes in the future, but no currently ascertainable policies exist to make such hopes a reality.

It is also noteworthy, in this era of high divorce rates, that the aftermaths of divorce were not considered when designing the community; there are few apartments, especially reasonable ones, little local employment, and no public transportation except for the special morning and evening commuter buses that carry the men, and some women, back and forth to outside jobs.

Evidently, the single-parent household, which is often one outcome of divorce, is at odds with a community planned primarily for intact families with young children. But can one assume that such typical occurrences as divorce and single parenthood will somehow pass this community by?

The design of this as of so many other planned communities suggests as much. For it rests on an implicit model of the family whose members are forever young, domesticated, and content with the existing scheme of things, whose children never grow up, and who remain outside of the turmoil and changes that beset the general population. Such a model leaves important minorities ill-served, including the childless, the full-time employed mothers, the single parents, the divorced and the singles—all of them present in this community but not recognized, hence not adequately provided for. If we would build sound communities in the future, we need to expand our conceptions of who is to live there.

Notes

1. The study was carried out over a fourteen-month period (1974–1976) under direction of the author with the aid of an interdisciplinary team of social scientists, architects, and photographers. Its findings are available in a lengthy report submitted to the National Science Foundation whose generous support is hereby gratefully acknowledged. See Suzanne Keller, "Twin Rivers, Study of a Planned Community," report (NSF Grant G141311, 1976).

2. Suzanne Keller, *Women in a Planned Community,* Land Policy Roundtable Basic Concept Series no. 101, (Cambridge, Massachusetts, Lincoln Institute of Land Policy, 1978).

3. Raymond J. Burby, III and Shirley F. Weiss, *New Communities USA* (Lexington, Massachusetts, D.C. Heath and Co., 1976), pp. 232.

4. Richard Dattner, *Design for Play* (New York: Van Nostrand, 1969), p. 4.

5. L.E. White, "The outdoor play of children living in flats: an enquiry into the use of courtyards as playgrounds," in *Environmental Psychology,* Harold M. Proshansky, W.H. Ittelson, and L.G. Rivlin, ed. (New York: Holt Rinehart and Winston, 1970), pp. 235–258.

6. David Popenoe, *The Suburban Environment* (Chicago: University of Chicago Press, 1977).

7. Ibid., pp. 135, 138. By contrast, no such boredom was found among the Swedish youngsters who seemed to be content with the community and what it had to offer. Possibly the ready accessibility of Stockholm and the existence of adequate recreational facilities, including a teen center, account for this.

8. C.A. Doxiadis, *Anthropopolis, City for Human Development* (Athens: Athens Publishing Center, 1974), p. 92.

9. Dattner, *Design for Play,* p. 37.

10. Ibid., p. 7.

6

Family Life Cycle and Women's Evaluations of Community Facilities

Ilene M. Kaplan

Although as early as 1947 Wirth predicted that community life would become an important issue in family studies, very few studies have focused on the responsiveness of communities to the needs of women in their family roles. Most traditional community studies are descriptive, even prescriptive, with regard to family life and the roles of women.

The study of Middletown by Lynd and Lynd (1929), one of the earliest and best known, contains extensive descriptions of married life, childrearing, and housework (and includes an entire chapter on housing) but does not examine women's uses of community facilities or their evaluations of their homes and community. Warner's study of Yankee City (see 1963 edition) is subject to similar criticisms, as is Seeley's (1956) study of Crestwood Heights. The latter does, however, present at least a provisional account of the functions that a house provides for the family, although it does not examine how women's uses of the house change with regard to family life nor does it extend the discussion to uses of community services and facilities.

The work of Young and Willmott (1957) marks the beginning of a major change in the research questions being asked by sociologists. In *Family and Kinship in East London,* an early project of the Institute of Community Studies, Young and Willmott focused primarily on the relationship between family life and the community, thus representing the beginning of a merging of the research interests of sociologists and community planners. This chapter builds on this and related works; it utilizes the family-life cycle as a scheme for analyzing women's uses and evaluations of facilities in a planned community.

Women, as well as family members in general, must respond to both internal family demands and the expectations and demands placed on them by the larger society of which the family is a part. For example, women with children will obviously require different services from those without children and those with preschoolers will face different problems from those with teenagers. This includes transportation facilities, job opportunities in or near their community, and meeting places. As women's roles expand beyond the family environment, the community increasingly will be called on to help provide some additional services, such as recreational and educational facilities, childcare centers, and quick and convenient shopping fac ties. The latter may be particularly appreciated by working women who must allocate their time between job and family.

It seems then, that planners' awareness of changes in women's needs should be a crucial part of the design process. Indeed, the success of community planning will depend, to a rather large extent, on the sensitivity of planners to anticipating women's needs. The family life cycle provides a scheme to assess such changes.

Women and the Family Life Cycle

The *family life cycle* depicts the family as it passes through critical periods, or *stages,* of development. These stages are marked by events such as marriage, birth, growth of children, and the "launching" of children. Specifically, the family life cycle refers to developmental changes in the family with regard to size, structural arrangements, age composition, and roles of family members.

Contemporary work on the family life cycle draws from early developmental models such as those of Sorokin (1931), Kirkpatrick et al. (1934), and Bigelow (1942). In more recent times, Rodgers (1962) constructed a complex twenty-four-stage model based on the assumption that a new stage begins whenever there is a major change in the family role complex.

Duvall (1957, see revised edition 1977) devised an empirically more manageable model based on the activities of the married pair and the age and school placement of the oldest child. This construct, which depicts the family as passing through eight stages, is the basis of most of the recent empirical research on the family life cycle.

The transition to each successive stage of the family life cycle entails new responsibilities arising from individual and family growth, the demands and expectations of others, and cultural pressures. Such responsibilities are referred to as *family developmental tasks,* which Duvall (1977, p. 177) defines as,

> A growth responsibility that arises at a certain stage in the life of a family, the successful achievement of which leads to present satisfaction, approval and success with later tasks—whereas failure leads to unhappiness in the family, disapproval by society, and difficulty with later family developmental tasks.

For the purpose of conceptual clarity, some of the major family developmental tasks, particularly as they relate to women, will be briefly reviewed for each stage of the family life cycle. The reader should be aware, however, that the life-cycle model is an idealized sequence based on societal assumptions and expectations and, as such, is subject to the same weaknesses as other ideal constructs.

Stage 1: Young Married Couple without Children

The family developmental tasks during the first stage of the family life cycle, a period which normally extends from one to two years, may be described under the rubric "setting up house" and include locating and furnishing a home and establishing comfortable and compatible shared living arrangements. Although both the husband and wife can continue to pursue interests and activities established before marriage, their primary concerns and leisure activities are home oriented (Rapoport and Rapoport 1975; Sillitoe 1969).

This stage marks the foundation of family life, during which the couple must arrive at decisions concerning division of labor in the family, whether or not to have children, and, in general, allocate mutually acceptable roles and responsibilities.

Stage 2: The Childbearing Family

The childbearing stage marks a major change in the structure of the family; it adds complexity to the family structure by expanding the number of relationships and adding a new generation, as well as the tests of parenthood. The major family developmental tasks at this stage include providing adequate housing arrangements for the expanding family, meeting the increasing financial costs of the growing family (particularly the costs associated with childbearing and increased expenditures on food, clothing, and household furnishings), and allocating new responsibilities associated with childrearing, such that family stability is maintained.

Stage 3: Preschool Stage

The preschool stage of the family life cycle begins when the oldest child is about two and one-half to three years old and ends when the child begins school. Kirkpatrick (1963) notes that during this stage, women confront various situations that pit family against community loyalties; restrictive and intensive relationships against extensive, casual associations; and childrearing responsibilities against other, self-expressive activities. A major concern of mothers at this stage is to reconcile their responsibilities to their children and to themselves.

Recent trends indicate that the proportion of preschool children enrolled in nursery schools has been increasing. In 1964 about 25 percent of children between the ages of three and five were enrolled in nursery or kindergarten classes; by 1973 the figure had risen to over 40 percent (U.S. Bureau of the Census 1974). Awareness of these trends on the part of planners should contribute to the success of the communities which they design.)

Stage 4: School Stage

The maturation of children means that there will be more shared activities in which the family as a whole can participate (Sillitoe 1969). In addition, since children now spend much of their time outside the home, mothers have time to rejoin the world of adults and many women now enter the labor market or resume interrupted careers.

Until the 1940s, most women left their jobs when they were married or at the latest, when they had children. Since then there has been an increased participation in the labor force of married women over thirty-five years old whose children are of school age. More recent trends indicate that many mothers now remain employed or begin careers even before children start school. Thus the labor force participation rate for married women who have children under six years old was 42 percent in March 1978. This represents an increase of eleven percentage points over the decade. (U.S. Bureau of Labor Statistics 1979). This is consistent with the aforementioned rise in the number of preschoolers attending nursery schools. Thus nearby employment opportunities during these family stages should be particularly appreciated by these women.

Stage 5: Families with Teenagers

This stage is marked by the loosening of family ties and the emergence of altered parent-child relationships. Tensions can develop over such issues as rights, privileges, and responsibilities of family members (Duvall 1977). Privacy, the appearance of the home, and the uses of the telephone and bathroom provide potential points of conflict (see, for example, Butler 1956). Problems regarding space and the use of the home should be of interest to the planners and designers of communities for families at this stage.

Stages 6 and 7: Families Launching Children and Empty-Nest Families

The launching stage marks the beginning of a transitional period for husbands and wives and a period of role transition from adolescence to young adulthood for children. A primary developmental task during this stage is for parents to accept and encourage their children's independence. Women must begin to accept the departure of children and the loss of the active role of parent, particularly those who are not employed and have been involved primarily in home-oriented activities. Although active parenthood comes to an end, other activities may occur, especially renewal of the couple relationship and increased involvement in community affairs. Postparental couples turn to each other for companionship and now have more time for shared activities (Hayes and Stinnett 1971; Sussman 1955).

Stage 8: Aging Families

This stage of the family life cycle begins when the employed family members reach retirement. The major family developmental tasks at this stage include adjusting to a retirement income and generally providing for the well-being and health of the aging couple. Maintaining close family ties is also important during this stage, as is physical mobility.

Family Life Cycle, Women, and the Community

The existence of a relationship between the family life cycle and community life has been suggested in previous studies. Morris and Winter (1975) assert that family members judge the adequacy of their housing by standards that are appropriate for different stages of the family life cycle. Rossi's (1955) study on why families move suggests a direct link between the family-life cycle, housing needs, and residential mobility. The results of his study indicate that the most important factors that influence a family's decision to move are dissatisfactions with the amount of space in the home, the neighborhood, and the costs of rent and maintenance. Such dissatisfactions reflect changes in the needs of families which are concomitant with changes in family development. Notably, the most mobile families are those in early stages of the family-life cycle—periods during which families are experiencing the greatest amount of growth. Similar patterns of residential mobility have been found repeatedly in more recent studies (Long 1972; Speare 1970; and Hill et al. 1970). In addition, spatial considerations, propensity toward home ownership, dwelling type, location preference, community satisfaction, and social interactions within a community have all been linked to the family life cycle (for further discussion see Kaplan 1980; Michelson 1977; Foote et al. 1960; and Rossi 1955).

Method of Study

The study presented here is a secondary analysis of data collected during a large-scale study of Twin Rivers, the first Planned Unit Development in the state of New Jersey (Keller 1976). The Twin Rivers project examined residents' reactions to the design of spaces and facilities, the role of spatial organization in social life, and people's modifications of the built environment. The community, with a population of approximately 14,000 residents, is divided into four quadrants, or *quads,* each of which is identified in the community by a number (that is, I, II, III, IV). Although the vast majority live in townhouses, residents have the choice of living in townhouses, detached homes, apartments or condominiums. For the most part, the community is comprised of families with young children.

Although the general characteristics of Twin Rivers residents have already been discussed in chapter 5, a further examination of the housing and employment profile of the women, grouped according to stage of the family-life cycle, provides an interesting starting point for the analysis of women's uses and evaluations of community facilities.[1]

Housing and Employment Patterns

A breakdown of the housing types of women at different stages of the family life cycle provides information as to who decides to live where in Twin Rivers (table 6–1). Not surprisingly, the selection of house type seems to be strongly influenced by expanding and contracting family stages. Thus the majority of women in smaller family units (that is, young marrieds without children and empty-nest families) do not live in townhouses or detached homes but in the smaller housing units in the community, such as apartments and condominiums.

The employment profile of the women in Twin Rivers, according to stages of the family life cycle, also offers some interesting insights into community life, particularly with regard to women's expectations for employ-

Table 6–1
Women's Housing Types According to the Family Life Cycle

	Family Stage (percent)				
Housing Type	Young Married (n = 25)	Preschool (n = 84)	School (n = 44)	Teenage[a] (n = 15)	Older Couple (n = 11)
Town house	32	82	91	67	18
Detached house	0	6	7	7	0
Apartment	28	8	2	0	36
Condominium	40	4	0	27	46

Note: X^2 = 73.19; df = 12; $p < .01$.
[a]Total does not equal 100 percent due to rounding error.

ment opportunities. Over half of the young married women without children and approximately half of the women with teenagers are employed (table 6-2). This is consistent with past national employment trends for women, as noted earlier in this chapter.

The generally lower percentage of women in Twin Rivers who are members of the labor force, compared to the national figure, could lead an observer to conclude erroneously that employment opportunities in Twin Rivers should not have been an important planning priority. However, this would ignore the fact that the majority of women in the young married, preschool, school, and teenage stages of the family life cycle report that they intend to hold a job in the future (table 6-3). In addition, almost one-half of the mothers of teenagers and one-third of the older women also intend to look for paid employment at a later point in time. Furthermore, the great majority of women at all family stages who intend to work in the future

Table 6-2
Women's Paid-Labor-Force Participation according to the Family Life Cycle

	Famile Stage (percent)				
Paid Labor-Force Participation	Young Married (n = 25)	Preschool (n = 82)	School (n = 43)	Teenage (n = 15)	Older Couple (n = 11)
Employed	60	17	23	47	9
Nonemployed	40	83	77	53	91

Note: X^2 = 23.10; df = 4; $p < .01$.

Table 6-3
Women's Intentions to Join the Paid-Labor Force according to the Family Life Cycle

	Family Stage (percent)				
Employment Intentions	Young Married (n = 12)	Preschool (n = 58)	School (n = 36)	Teenage (n = 7)	Older Couple (n = 7)
Intend to take jobs	83	84	92	57	43
Do not intend to take jobs	17	16	8	43	57

Note: X^2 = 13.97; df = 4; $p < .01$.

express the desire to find work in or near the community; a wish not likely to be met there judging from current employment opportunities in the community. How well this future need of the women will be met offers an additional test of the successful planning of the community.

Women's Uses of Community Facilities during the Family-Life Cycle

Women's activities and uses of community facilities during the family-life cycle are examined using a multiple-item scale that measures the number of times women use various community facilities on a weekly basis.[2] Specifically, the scale provides a summary measure of the number of times women went to a drugstore, restaurant, coffee shop, clothing store and recreational facility during the one-week period prior to their participation in the Twin Rivers study. Results of tests of analysis of variance indicate that women at different stages of the family life cycle do use community facilities at different rates; the mean differences are also reported (figure 6–1).

Most noteworthy is the decline in the use of facilities when children are very young and an increase as children get older. Furthermore, there is a decrease once again, as the women advance into late stages of the family-life cycle. In general the facilities are used most often by women with school children and teenagers and least by women in the empty-nest stage. Similar trends are also found when the use of each community facility is examined separately. The most interesting of these findings are shown in figure 6–2. As with the overall scale, the results indicate a "double-dip" effect—women's use of community facilities tends to decline during periods of early family growth and once again in later stages of family development.

The decline in women's use of facilities during the preschool stage does not really come as a surprise, given their traditional lifestyles. As reported by Keller (1976), most of the women in Twin Rivers are part of traditional family arrangements and follow traditional sex roles; husbands are the breadwinners and wives are the homemakers. Indeed family and home life seem to be prime concerns of the women in Twin Rivers and they express their two most important roles as being a good wife and a good mother. During the family stages when children are young, mothers in Twin Rivers are the principal childrearing agents and are thus more likely to spend a good deal of their time at home with their children. It is more perplexing to find that at a time in family development when children are old enough and mature enough to take on responsibilities of their own, there is a concomitant drop in women's use of community facilities. One might actually expect that the empty-nest stage be a time of renewed activities. It is not clear, however, whether this constitutes a voluntary or forced withdrawal

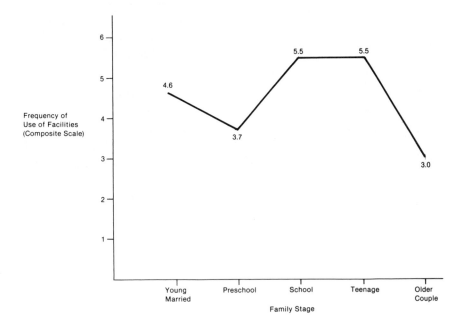

F = 3.65; df = 4,175; p = .007.

Figure 6–1. Women's Weekly Use of Community Facilities according to the Family-Life Cycle (Mean Differences)

from community life during late stages of the family life cycle. Although the Twin Rivers study was not designed to specifically examine this issue, information was collected that provides some insight into this matter, particularly with regard to the social activities of the women in later family stages.

Kaplan (1980) finds that women in Twin Rivers in the later stages of the family life cycle are least likely to be able to meet people who have similar lifestyles and interests. In addition, while approximately half of the women in early and middle stages of the family life cycle (the range is 42 percent to 71 percent) state that their best friends live in Twin Rivers, less than one-fifth of the women in the older-couple stage have best friends in the community. These women are also most likely to feel disappointed with the people in Twin Rivers and the least likely to feel that one of the advantages of living in Twin Rivers is the people in the community. Thus the social life in Twin Rivers favors the women in younger families which in turn, may contribute to the lesser uses of community facilities by women in later family stages.

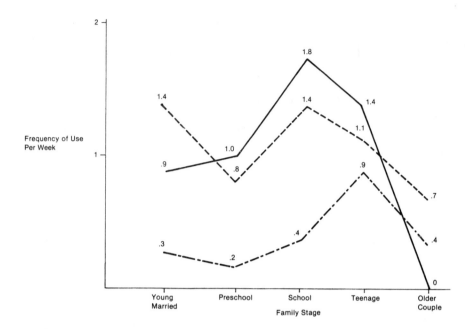

Note: The weekly rates shown in this figure represent the statistically significant differences in rates of going to the coffee shop, department store, and recreational facilities in the five individual facilities examined.

——— Recreation facility: $F = 2.46$; df $= 4,175$; $p = .05$.

------ Clothing store: $F = 2.74$; df $= 4,175$; $p = .03$.

—·—·— Coffee shop: $F = 2.46$; df $= 4,175$; $p = .05$.

Figure 6–2. Women's Weekly Use of Individual Community Facilities According to the Family-Life Cycle (Mean Differences)

Women's Evaluations of Community Facilities during the Family Life Cycle

Although Kaplan (1980) reports an increase in overall feelings of community satisfaction over the family life cycle, she cautions that generalizations about overall patterns of satisfaction are not always accurate indicators of specific types of satisfaction among residents.

In contrast to the findings concerning social life in Twin Rivers, the data indicate that there is a clear, curvilinear relationship between satisfaction with community services such as maintenance and garbage collection and the family life cycle (see figure 6–3).[3] Satisfaction is concentrated in the beginning and later family stages.

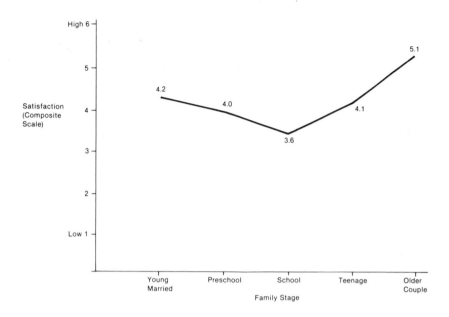

Note: F = 4.02; df = 4,173; p = .004.
Figure 6-3. Women's Evaluations of Community Services according to the Family-Life Cycle (Mean Differences)

A similar pattern is found when women's evaluations of transportation facilities in the community are examined (see figure 6-4). Once again, the most satisfied are women in the young married and older couple stages. These two family stages are at completely opposite ends of the life cycle. Both stages, however, have a common structural characteristic in consisting solely of husbands and wives. Thus at times when families are at their smallest, women report the highest levels of satisfaction. During periods of family expansion, on the other hand, women are the most dissatisfied with community services and transportation facilities.

If periods of family expansion are the times when women become more critical of the community, it would not be unreasonable to expect that women's assessments of the spatial aspects of their homes will also be more negative. In order to determine if this is indeed what happens, a multiple-item scale, consisting of women's satisfactions with the size of different aspects of their homes was constructed, and differences according to the family life cycle are examined using techniques of analysis of variance.[4] A graph of the mean differences indicates that there is a curvilinear relation-

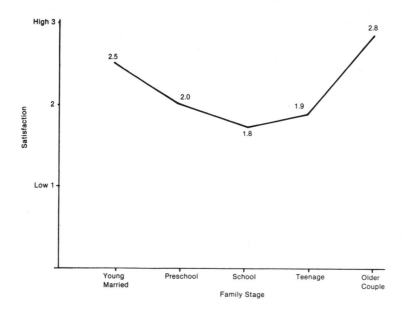

Note: $F = 4.47$; df $= 4,158$; $p = .002$.

Figure 6-4. Women's Evalutions of Transportation Facilities according to the Family Life Cycle (Mean Differences)

ship between family life cycle and satisfaction in a similar direction to those already reported; women in the young-married and older-couple stages of the family life cycle are most satisfied with certain spatial features of their homes and women in expanding family stages are least satisfied (figure 6-5).

All of the findings regarding differences in women's satisfactions suggest that the expanding stage of the family life cycle is a time when conveniences, particularly with regard to community services and space inside the home are critical concerns of the women in Twin Rivers. It is a time when family developmental tasks primarily are home oriented and when women must respond to the demands of their growing families. This is where sensitive planning would seem to be particularly essential.

In sum, this chapter suggests that the family life cycle can be used to help planners assess and anticipate what women's needs are and how these needs change over time. The family life cycle, it has been proposed, can be used as a conceptual tool to provide planners with information needed to make communities more responsive to their residents.

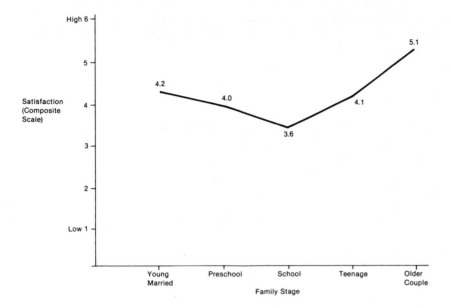

Note: $F = 2.64$; df $= 4,140$; $p = .04$.

Figure 6-5. Women's Evaluations of Spaciousness according to the
Family Life Cycle (Mean Differences)

Notes

1. The 180 married women in the Twin Rivers sample are divided into groups according to stages of the family life cycle. Due to limitations of sample size, the childbearing stage is included with the preschool stage; and the launching, empty-nest, and aging stages are collapsed into an older-couple stage. This results in the creation of a five-stage family life cycle model: (a) young married couple ($n = 26$); (2) preschool family ($n = 84$); (3) school family ($n = 44$); (4) teenage family ($n = 15$); and (5) older couple ($n = 11$).

2. Each item intercorrelated with one another in a positive direction and in a low to moderate range. Multiple-item scales are used because they provide an empirically better measure of an overall concept (that is, use of facilities) than do single-item indicators.

3. The dependent variable (that is, satisfaction with services) is created by summing women's evaluations of maintenance services and garbage collection services in Twin Rivers. Both items intercorrelate in a positive direction and moderate range.

4. The scale consists of women's satisfaction with the size of their living room, kitchen, bathroom, master bedroom, and their yards. The items intercorrelated with each other in a positive direction, in a low to moderate range.

References

Bigelow, H.F. *Marriage and the Family*. Edited by H. Becker and R. Hill, ch. 17. Boston: D.C. Heath and Co., 1942.

Butler, R.M. "Mothers' Attitudes Towards the Social Development of Their Adolescents." *Social Casework* (May-June 1965).

Duvall, Evelyn, *Marriage and Family Development*. Philadelphia: J.B. Lippincott, 1957, rev. 5th ed. 1977.

Foote, Nelson, et al. *Housing Choices and Housing Constraints*. New York: McGraw-Hill, 1960.

Hayes, M., and N. Stinnett. "Life Satisfactions of Middle-aged Husbands and Wives." *Journal of Home Economics* 63 (Dec. 1971):669-674.

Hill, Reuben, et al. *Family Development in Three Generations*. Cambridge, Massachusetts: Shenkman, 1970.

Kaplan, Ilene M. "Family Life Cycle and Women's Satisfaction with their Community." Ph.D. dissertation, Princeton University, 1980.

Keller, Suzanne. "Twin Rivers, Study of a Planned Community." NSF Grant GI41311, report, 1976.

Kirkpatrick, C. "Life Cycle of Family Experience." In *The Family as Process and Institution*, 2nd ed. New York: Ronald Press, 1963.

Kirkpatrick, E., et al. "The Life Cycle of the Farm Family in Relation to its Standard of Living." *Agricultural Experimental Station Research Bulletin* 121 (1934).

Long, L.H., "The Influence of Family Life Cycle and Ages of Children on Residential Mobility." *Demography* 9 (August 1972):371-382.

Lynd, R.S., and H.M. Lynd. *Middletown* New York: Harcourt, Brace and World, 1929.

Michelson, W. *Environmental Choice, Human Behavior, and Residential Satisfaction* New York: Oxford University Press, 1977.

Morris, E.W., and M. Winter. "A Theory of Family Housing Adjustment." *Journal of Marriage and the Family* 37 (February 1975):79-88.

Rapoport, R., and R. Rapoport. *Leisure and the Family Life Cycle*. Boston: Routledge and Kegan Paul, 1975.

Rodgers, Roger H. "Improvements in the Construction and Analysis of Family Life Cycle Categories," Ph.D. dissertation, University of Minnesota, 1962.

Rossi, Alice. "Transition to Parenthood." *Journal of Marriage and the Family* 30 (1968):26-39.

Rossi, Peter. *Why Families Move.* Glencoe, Illinois: Glencoe Free Press, 1955.

Seeley, J.R.; R.A. Sim; and E.W. Loosley. *Crestwood Heights.* New York: Basic Books, 1956.

Sillitoe, K.K. *Planning for Leisure.* London: H.M.S.C., 1969.

Sorokin, P.; C. Zimmerman; and C. Galpin. *A Systematic Source Book in Rural Sociology.* Minneapolis: University of Minnesota Press, 1931.

Speare, T. "Home Ownership, Life Cycle Stage, and Residential Mobility." *Demography* 7 (November 1970):499-458.

Sussman, M. "Activity Patterns of Post-Parental Couples and Their Relationships to Family Continuity." *Marriage and Family Living* 17 (November 1955):338-347.

U.S. Bureau of the Census, "Nursery School and Kindergarten Enrollment, October 1973," *Current Population Reports,* Series p-20, no. 268, August 1974.

U.S. Bureau of Labor Statistics, "Marital and Family Characteristics of Workers, 1970 to 1978," *Special Labor Force Report,* 219, 1979.

Warner, W., et al. *Yankee City.* New Haven: Yale University Press, 1963.

Wirth, Louis. "Housing as a Field of Sociological Research," *American Sociological Review* vol. 12, no. 2 (April 1947):137-143.

Young, M., and P. Willmott, *Family and Kinship in East London.* Illinois: The Free Press, 1957.

7 The Life Space of Children

Sarane Spence Boocock

This chapter examines some issues of community structure and planning from the perspective of children. The relevance of the child's perspective to a volume on women and land use does not require a great deal of justification. Children, at least up to a certain age, cannot live alone. They need at least a minimum amount of attention and care simply to survive, and until now most of this attention and care has been provided by women. Despite the declining birth rate and the disorienting changes in women's roles and family structure that have marked our society in recent years, the majority of American women will at some point in their lives feel constraints as a consequence of the needs of children. Indeed one could argue that children are the major remaining constraint on women's full participation in the larger society outside of the home and that the last battle of the war between the sexes is being waged over the issue of how the responsibilities for raising children are to be divided.

The Status of Children

The care of children has always been problematic, to societies as a whole as well as to individual parents. This is partly because the work is difficult (as anyone who has spent a few hours with preschool children can testify) and partly because of the low status generally accorded to those who work with children, compared with those who work with money, power, or ideas.

However, each time and place has its own unique problems with respect to the care and socialization of the young. The most general conclusion that can be drawn about the childcare system in the United States and developed countries generally is that the status and care of children are undergoing some fundamental and far-reaching changes and that for the moment many children are not receiving the kinds of care consistent with current theories and research findings concerning their developmental needs. These changes in the status and treatment of children reflect changes in the larger society. As the authors of a survey of childcare arrangements in Massachusetts put it, the growing demand for day care and other childrens' services:

is based upon fundamental long-term changes in the functioning of society, the composition of the labor force, the roles of women and men, and changes in family life. Forceful economic and political realities underlie the marked rise in demand for child care services. They will not go away. [Rowe, et al. 1972, p. 11]

The current crisis in connection with the care of children seems to be the result of a combination of social trends unique to modern industrialized societies. They include: (1) changes in sex roles that downgrade parenthood and childrearing; (2) changes in the structure of households and loss of childcare options outside the family; (3) a serious imbalance in the supply and demand for childcare services; and (4) an increase in the costs of raising children relative to the rewards, which is probably reflected in, or related to, the marked recent decline in birth and fertility rates. (For a more detailed discussion of these trends, see Boocock 1975, 1976.)

How a society treats its children depends on its view of what children are like as well as what is perceived as necessary for the smooth functioning of the society itself. To put it another way, children can be seen in many different ways, and the way we look at children affects the social arrangements we make for them including the way we design housing and organize community services. A historical and crosscultural review of the status of children suggests that the following models of childhood have characterized some of the world's societies at some points in time.

Model 1: Children as Miniature or Incomplete Adults. As one historian has put it, "as adults in the process of becoming" (Larrabbee 1960, p. 199). Philippe Ariés' classic study, *Centuries of Childhood* (1962), makes clear that the very notion of childhood as a separate phase of the life cycle did not emerge until well into the seventeenth century; until then children routinely worked by the age of six or seven, either sharing in the regular tasks of their own families or working as servants or apprentices in the households of other persons.

Model 2: Children as Evil Beasts to Be Restrained. John Demos's study of family life in the Plymouth Colony (1970) indicates that all children were perceived as born into sin, which could only be brought under control by strict upbringing in the home, lifelong avoidance of idleness, and the constant vigilance of the church and other community institutions.

Model 3: Children as Empty Vessels or Blank Slates. Children are sometimes considered malleable beings which can be filled or written on as the society desires. In the contemporary world, this model is most fully developed in the thought of Mao Tsetung, who has observed that "the outstanding thing about China's 600 million people is that they are 'poor and blank,' " and this is advantageous because: "On a blank sheet of paper free from any mark, the freshest and most beautiful characters can be written, the freshest and most beautiful pictures can be painted" (Mao 1972, p. 36). Recent Western visitors to the People's Republic of China have been impressed by the insistence of teachers and political leaders that all children have the potential to become good communist citizens and that if they are not succeeding, it is the responsibility of their parents, teachers, and class-mates to "try harder" (Kessen 1975; Sidel 1972).

Model 4: Children as Precious Plants to Be Nurtured. Respect for the spe-cial qualities and needs of each individual child and provision of the enriched environment that will enable each to reach her or his full potential is exemplified in the work of Piaget and other developmental psychologists who posit the human–life cycle as divided into a complex set of develop-mental stages, each with its distinct cognitive, emotional and social modes.

Model 5: Children as Models for Adult Attitudes and Behavior. This view, which urges adults to imitate the childlike spontaneity and openness to new experiences and cautions against restraining children's "natural" develop-ment through any kind of "repressive" socialization had a brief vogue in hippie communes in other experimental communities of the 1960s and early 1970s (see, for example, Zablocki 1978 and 1980; Kanter 1972).

Current American childrearing and educational practices contain ele-ments from several of these models, although model 4 is now probably the most influential standard in this country. Thus the heavy emphasis on disci-pline which still permeates many American schools is a kind of cultural hangover from our Puritan heritage (model 2), while the open classroom structure which is gaining acceptance in many parts of the United States is clearly based on model 4. It has also been found that childrearing ideals and practices differ among social classes and racial or ethnic groups (Kohn 1963 and 1976; Boocock 1980, ch. 3). The general point though is that the design of the physical and social space in which children and their caretakers spend their time reflects in part our models of the life cycle in general and child-hood in particular.

Research on Children and Their Environments

With the possible exception of the elderly, children are the people most affected by and most dependent on their immediate surroundings. The spe-cial impact of neighborhoods on children's daily lives has been described as follows by Elliot Medrich, director of the Childhood and Government Project at the University of California, Berkeley, and one of the few social scientists to express concern for our inattention to the changing patterns of American children's lives:

> Neighborhoods do much more than provide a physical setting in which a child grows up, they effectively define a child's social universe. Who they spend their time with, the things that interest them, the things they do, their habits and values, needs and wants are in part a product of that social setting. Living in one place rather than another means that the schools are different, the things that are easy or hard to get to (and to do) are different, the activities and facilities provided by city agencies are different, the pressures of parents to be "good" at this or *not* do that, are all played out in this social-spatial context. Hence, two children growing up five miles apart may be as different and uncomfortable with one another as two children raised in different countries. [Medrich 1977, pp. 11–12]

Given the importance of what Medrich terms the *social-spatial context* of children's lives, it seems ironic that we know so little about how children perceive their physical and social surroundings. It is also ironic that in planning communities and social programs for children and their families, the children are seldom, if ever, consulted. Community planners are, of course, not alone in this regard. Examination of the research literature on children and childcare indicates that virtually all studies of children have been done by adults. There is no body of research on children in which the data have been gathered or analyzed by children themselves or in which children have had anything to say about the theoretical framework or the research design. Most adults would see nothing peculiar in this state of affairs. Indeed the general view of children in this country seems to be that children are not competent to speak for themselves on matters concerning their own lives and that some adult—mother, teacher, childcare "expert"—can speak for them.

In the past few years, this assumption has been challenged by a few innovative research studies. One is the "Children's Time Study," directed by Elliott Medrich at the University of California School of Law. Interview data from 750 sixth graders in twenty-two Oakland, California, schools was collected on how the children spent their time in an effort to understand the ways in which family and neighborhood life are reflected in the everyday behavior of children.

The second is the National Survey of Children, designed and sponsored by the Foundation for Child Development and conducted by Temple University's Institute for Survey Research. The objective of the National Survey of Children is "to determine the general environment in which children live—their family lives, their friends, schools, health, and neighborhood activities—and to learn their perceptions, feelings, attitudes and values"

(Foundation for Child Development 1977), and it involved interviews with a national sample of over 2,200 children aged seven to eleven and a subsample of their parents.

A third project which investigated the ability of children to speak for themselves about things which concern them is one I conducted for the Russell Sage Foundation. The study focused on the daily lives of children in six different communities in the Northeast, selected for maximum ecological variation.[1] In each of the six communities interviews were conducted with between fifty and sixty children between the ages of four and eight about their daily lives, their contacts with other people in their homes and communities, their competencies, their responsibilities, and the kinds of rules and restrictions which govern their lives. About half of the interviews were conducted by children between the ages of ten and twelve.[2]

The following sections contain some of the results of this research pertaining to how the children studied perceived their own communities or neighborhoods, and how their daily lives were influenced, positively or negatively, by their physical and social surroundings.

The Physical Environment

The activities in which individuals engage and their relationships with other people are affected by many features of their environment, including geographical location; community size, density, design, and resources; and the level of safety versus danger from human and nonhuman causes. In the National Survey on Children, both children and their parents were asked: "How is this neighborhood as a place for kids to grow up in? Do you think it is: very good, pretty good, or not so good?" An unexpected result was that less than one-third of the children described their neighborhoods as a "very good" place to grow up in, while nearly 60 percent of the parents rated their neighborhoods as "very good" or "excellent" places in which to raise children. Children were generally more critical of the neighborhoods in which they lived than were their parents (Zill 1978).

Not surprisingly, children's satisfaction with their own neighborhood varied from one kind of setting to another. In her intensive study of Twin Rivers, New Jersey (which was also one of the six communities studied in the Russell Sage project), Keller (1976) found that the children interviewed tended to be even more positive toward the community than their parents, a finding that suggests that the generally critical attitude of children reported in the National Survey on Children (NSC) may not apply to many specific community situations. The NSC did find that children in low-income areas of large cities were least satisfied with their neighborhoods and children in affluent suburbs were most satisfied overall. Rural areas were also relatively highly rated. But it is important to remember that in no type of American community—city, suburb, town, or country; affluent or poor—did a majority of the seven- to eleven-year-olds interviewed describe their immediate environment as an excellent place to grow up in.

When the children were asked what they would change about their neighborhood to "make it nicer for kids," the two leading changes mentioned were to have more and better places to play and to have less crime and other bad behavior on the part of both children and adults. About one child in six mentioned fighting, crime, vandalism, or meanness as a problem in their neighborhood. Among the specific problems of children suggested by the respondents were: "people steal; people always mean; stop older kids from fighting and picking on little kids; stop kids from breaking bottles and writing on stuff; stop nasty language; get rid of bad kids." More than two-thirds of the children in the survey said they were afraid that "someone might get into your house," and a fourth reported that when they went outside they were afraid that someone might hurt them. Other evidence from the survey suggests that many of them had reason to be fearful. More than 40 percent of the children interviewed said they had been bothered by older kids while playing outside; over 12 percent said they had been bothered by adults. About a third reported that they have been threatened with a beating and about 13 percent said they have actually been beaten up. Over a fourth said they had had something taken from them including money.

As might be expected, children's feelings about their surroundings varied from one neighborhood to another. Anyone spending even a brief period of time in the six communities I studied would sense that the kinds of activities available to a child, the numbers and kinds of people he or she would be likely to encounter during the course of a day, and the opportunities to explore his or her environment would be very different in some settings than in others.

Table 7-1 shows one of the most striking ways in which physical environment can impinge on the life of a child. This table contains responses to the question: "How far away from home are you allowed to go without a grownup?" Thirty-nine percent of the high-income New York children and over half of the low-income New York children were not allowed to go outside of their own building (virtually none have yards), compared to less than one-fifth of the children in Twin Rivers, Columbia, and Brunswick. The percent for Bennington, which contained a number of children who lived in isolated rural households, is lower than for New York but higher than the other three settings. By contrast, the suburban children are likely to be allowed to move about in their immediate neighborhoods, and almost half of the rural and small-town children say they can go outside of their neighborhoods, either to a specific place such as a store or playground or a number of blocks away from their own homes. Only 12 percent of the East Har-

Table 7-1

How Far Away from Home Are You Allowed to go by Yourself, by Setting

Percent of Children Who Are:	New York City High Income	New York City Low Income	Twin Rivers, New Jersey	Columbia, Maryland	Brunswick, Maine	Bennington, Vermont
Not allowed to go outside own building or yard	39	52	16	16	12	27
Allowed to go around the block or across the street	21	25	30	49	25	8
Allowed to go to a specific place[a]	15	10	18	15	25	23
Allowed to go further away than their own block	15	2	14	15	22	27
Total N[b]	(53)	(52)	(56)	(53)	(49)	(60)

[a]E.G., to a playground or swimming pool, to the store, to a relative's home.

[b]D.K., N.A., and vague answers (for example, "pretty far," or "not too far") were not included in this table.

lem children can go further away than their own block. (This is consistent with the finding from the National Survey of Children that more than 15 percent of black inner-city respondents reported that their mother or some other adult had to watch them when they played outside their homes, as compared to only 5 percent of the overall sample.)

Medrich and his colleagues found that the California children studied related to their physical surroundings differently in various neighborhoods. In areas characterized by low-density and predominantly single-family housing (for example, in an affluent Monterey neighborhood), children tended to be tied to their homes and dependent on adults to take them places. "Structured around adult preferences for privacy, individualism and familism, such environments trade children's needs against parental needs" (Berg and Medrich 1977, p. 3). In more densely populated areas, where there is less space and privacy for all family members, children spent more time outside of the home, using it more as a base from which to come and go throughout the day, pausing for food and rest between activities carried on largely outside the home. The researchers' conclusions provide an excellent summary of the impact of differential land-use patterns on children's daily lives.

Children's social relations are an example of the way behavior is affected
by the co-varying relationships among social class, cultural characteristics
and physical aspects of the neighborhood environment. Generally middle
class children have fairly formal friendship patterns. For example, going to
a friend's house may not be a spontaneous activity—parent's permission
may be required or, perhaps, an invitation must be extended. In a way this
fits the formality of the neighborhoods themselves. Land use, especially in
low density, middle and high income neighborhoods suggests a privatized,
not a communal environment. Furthermore middle class children often live
in neighborhoods where there are simply fewer young people around. To
see a friend necessitates some planning—that is, finding a way of getting
there. For children living in higher density areas the concept of friendship
itself is broader, embracing those young and old who live nearby. Their
world is less age segregated, their interpersonal relationships perhaps more
casual. Under any circumstances the spatial setting provides a context facil-
itating certain kinds of social relationships. . . . Within neighborhoods,
topography, geography and land use constrain children's mobility in a variety of ways. Occasionally one finds a neighborhood that is, by chance,
organized so that children can move around safely and quickly. More
often, however, the physical setting inhibits movement and becomes one
more obstacle and constraint affecting their behavior and activities. [Berg
and Medrich 1977, pp. 3–5]

The Social Environment

Medrich points out that neighborhoods are social as well as physical environments and that as social environments they are "manifestations of the
way our society sorts people by social class and ethnicity" (Medrich 1977, p.
33). This means that most children live among children and other people
much like themselves.

I found that children's activity patterns—what they did during a typical
day and who they did it with—varied in certain respects from one community to another, reflecting different patterns of community structure and
resources. All of the children interviewed were asked to tell who lived in
their home, and for each person named were asked: "What kinds of things
do you do with this person?" Table 7–2 tells about the number of activities
they reported doing with their parents. Almost all children in all six communities named at least one activity with their mother (first line of table 7–2),
but there was considerable variation among communities in the proportions
reporting more than one activity. As the second line of table 7–2 shows,
over half the children in Brunswick, Twin Rivers, and Columbia and about
40 percent of the children in the two suburban communities could think of
more than one thing they did with their mothers, compared to only 6 percent of the East Harlem children. The bottom half of the table shows the

Table 7–2
Numbers of Activities with Parents, by Setting

	New York City High Income	New York City Low Income	Twin Rivers, New Jersey	Columbia, Maryland	Brunswick, Maine	Bennington, Vermont
Activities with Mother						
Percent of respondents who name:						
one or more activities	89	86	88	89	86	83
more than one activity	27	6	41	38	53	22
Mean number of activities	1.26	.92	1.50	1.60	1.71	1.08
Activities with Father						
Percent of respondents who name:						
one or more activities	83	67	88	91	92	50
more than one activity	19	8	36	44	45	18
Mean number of activities	1.06	.75	1.45	1.70	1.65	.68
Parental involvement mean score	4.51	2.96	4.75	5.28	5.02	3.32
Total N	(53)	(52)	(56)	(53)	(49)	(60)

results of a parallel analysis for interaction with fathers. Again the most interaction with fathers is reported by the children in Brunswick, Columbia, and Twin Rivers. However, while nearly all children named at least one activity with mother, only half of the Bennington children and two-thirds of the East Harlem children could think of anything they did with their fathers. These are the two settings with high proportions of single-parent households, and in many cases the father's absence from the home also severs the child's contact with him. (By comparison, over 70 percent of Columbia children in father-absent homes reported some activity with their fathers.) Of course, it is possible that when a child has little or no shared activity with one parent, the gap is filled by "extra" interaction with the other parent. Our analysis indicated that this did not happen for the children in our study; on the contrary, the children who did not do anything with their fathers were the ones least likely to do a lot of things with their mothers.

The bottom line of table 7–2 shows for each community the mean score on a scale created to measure the level of parents' involvement in their children's lives. The total score for each individual child is based on the number of activities with both parents, plus responses to questions about eating meals, attending church, and going places with one or both parents. As the table indicates, the mean scores ranged from a low of 2.96 for the East Harlem subsample to a high of 5.28 for the Columbia subsample. In sum, the table as a whole indicates that on all of our indicators of parent-child interaction, the greatest amount and variety of shared activity occurred in the suburban and small town settings, the least in the two settings with high proportions of children from low-income and single-parent families, although the ecology of these two settings differed considerably.

Tables 7–3 and 7–4 show data on the *substance* of reported activities with mothers and fathers. In four of the six communities, the activity most often reported with mothers is work or help in the home, with the highest percentages in the two rural and small-town settings. New York high-income and Twin Rivers children were more likely to participate in games with their mothers, and games and play were the other activities mentioned by relatively high percentages of children (games were more characteristic of the relatively affluent subsamples, play more characteristic of the lower income settings). Very few of the high-income New York children reported working in the home with their mothers; in this subsample the most named activities were games, shopping, and recreational and cultural activities (the latter options which are more readily available in a large city and which their affluent families can afford).

By comparison with table 7–3, table 7–4 shows that relatively few children said they engaged in work and helping activities with their fathers, though they were more likely to cite yard work and other outdoor activities with fathers than with mothers. Fathers were more likely to be called on for sports and games or, in some settings, for informal socializing—accompanying or visiting activities or simply talking and laughing together or entertaining each other (that is, the activities classified as prosocial in table 7–4).

Not many children in any setting mentioned schoolwork or learning activities, though there was slightly more interaction with mothers than fathers on academic activities. This result is consistent with crosscultural time studies indicating that American parents spend less time than parents in other countries supervising their children's homework (Szalai et al. 1972).

In addition to asking children about their family activities, they were

Table 7–3
Types of Activities with Mother, by Setting

Activity	New York City High Income	New York City Low Income	Twin Rivers, New Jersey	Columbia, Maryland	Brunswick, Maine	Bennington, Vermont
Organized sports	0	0	4	0	0	0
Unorganized sports	6	0	2	4	2	2
Games	19	0	30	19	8	2
Playing[a]	9	19	11	9	6	12
Crafts, making things	6	2	16	4	4	2
School work or learning activities	11	4	11	15	2	4
Working or helping at home						
indoors	4	23	20	25	57	40
outdoors	0	2	0	2	2	2
Shopping	19	8	5	17	4	15
Recreation[b]	17	8	2	0	2	5
Accompanying or visiting activities	9	8	7	2	2	3
Watching TV	0	0	5	2	4	7
Eating	2	2	4	6	4	0
Prosocial[c]	6	10	11	11	8	8
Antisocial[d]	0	4	2	4	0	3
Other	6	0	2	4	10	7
Total N	(53)	(52)	(56)	(53)	(49)	(60)

[a]Includes general "playing" and play with specified toys.
[b]Going to movies, sports events, and cultural activities (for example, museums).
[c]Talking or laughing together, sharing, entertaining each other.
[d]Teasing, fighting, hitting.

asked also whom they did things with in their neighborhoods, schools, and elsewhere. The most distinctive finding of this analysis was the large number of social contacts reported by the East Harlem children, who also named by far the largest number of contacts with kin or relatives in or outside of the household. The high-income New York City children named relatively few total social contacts and contacts with other children, though their contacts with teenagers and adults were relatively high. The fewest contacts with all kinds of people except kin were reported in the Bennington

Table 7-4
Types of Activities with Father, by Setting

Activity	New York City High Income	New York City Low Income	Twin Rivers, New Jersey	Columbia, Maryland	Brunswick, Maine	Bennington, Vermont
Organized sports	0	0	8	2	0	0
Unorganized sports	17	2	13	17	28	2
Games	19	0	18	21	12	5
Playing	13	13	18	11	8	12
Crafts, making things	6	2	9	2	4	0
School work or learning activities	6	0	4	9	0	3
Work or helping at home						
indoors	2	8	9	13	14	8
outdoors	0	0	0	9	12	8
Shopping	0	2	4	8	4	3
Recreation	9	6	5	0	10	8
Accompanying or visiting[a]	17[a]	13	9	11	16[a]	3
Watching TV	6	2	5	4	4	5
Eating	4	0	5	8	0	0
Prosocial	2	19	16	8	8	5
Antisocial	0	2	2	4	2	2
Other	0	2	0	4	6	3
Total N	(53)	(52)	(56)	(53)	(49)	(60)

[a]Includes visits to father's place of employment.

subsample, suggesting that many of these children were socially as well as geographically isolated.

In all of the communities we studied, and regardless of the way in which questions were asked, the majority of the persons named by children as persons they did things with were children and not related to the respondent.

Rules and Responsibilities

The findings considered so far indicate that the nature of children's environments affects the kinds of people and experiences to which they are exposed, their physical mobility and autonomy, and their personal safety (perceived and actual). Another source of information on differences in behavioral opportunities and restrictions in different settings came from a set of questions in the Russell Sage Foundation study pertaining to family rules and modes of punishment. Responses to these questions in four of the six communities are shown in tables 7-5 and 7-6. Unfortunately, most of the questions pertaining to rules were not asked in the two rural and small-town settings.

Table 7-5 shows responses to the questions: "Does your family have rules—things that you must do or must not do? What are they?" The mean number of rules (shown in the first line of table 7-5) ranged from about one in the high-income New York setting to almost two in Columbia. Among the figures that stand out in the table are the high proportion of East Harlem children who reported rules against destructive behavior (31 percent) and play activities in the home (44 percent). These two items included running or making noise in the house, breaking windows or furniture, and jumping on the beds and sofas. By contrast almost none of the affluent New York City children mentioned rules about nondestructive behavior but about a third reported rules about time, in particular about bedtime or not staying up too late, a type of rule mentioned by only two East Harlem respondents. These differences in percentages probably reflect the different ecology within homes in these two neighborhoods. While only 21 percent of the East Harlem children said they had their own bedrooms and 12 percent shared a bedroom with two or more other persons, 68 percent of the high-income New York children had their own room and none shared with more than one other person. Thus the restrictions on active play mentioned by so many of the former are understandable, and it is also understandable that so few of these children reported rules about bedtime, since few of them had a private quiet place to go to bed before the older persons in their households. Likewise, the relatively small number of rules reported by the more affluent urban children may reflect the spaciousness and lack of density in their homes as well as a parental philosophy of relatively loose supervision of their children's activities.

Very few of the suburban children reported having no family rules, and they were more likely than the urban children to mention rules requiring helpful behavior, including the kinds of home responsibilities discussed earlier, and general "good" behavior. Columbia children mentioned a number of rules concerning personal health and safety, ranging from brushing their teeth to not eating between meals to not playing with matches. The project field director, who was a resident of Twin Rivers, attributed the high proportion of space restrictions in that setting to the lack of clear spatial demarcations and the traffic patterns in the community. Because the boundaries between the property of different families and between play areas and other areas are not very clear and because there is quite a bit of automo-

Table 7–5
Family Rules, by Setting

	New York City High Income	New York City Low Income	Twin Rivers, New Jersey	Columbia, Maryland
Mean number of family rules per child	1.06	1.58	1.52	1.85
Percent of children who say their family has rules about:				
Appropriate behavior				
respectful	8	12	9	13
helpful	11	13	21	21
nonviolent	6	4	14	6
nondestructive	4	31	13	17
unspecified "good" behavior	2	0	14	9
Play	21	44	18	9
Work	2	8	9	11
Time	32	4	11	21
Space	6	10	20	8
Health or safety (including food)	14	6	12	29
Other	2	6	4	27
Nothing	28	31	7	4
Percent of children who say they can:				
Watch as much TV as they want	59	77	57	59
Eat as much candy as they want	42	52	30	23
Total N	(53)	(52)	(56)	(53)

bile traffic throughout the day,[3] parents often construct rather elaborate rules about where their children are and are not allowed to go in their neighborhoods.

One kind of behavioral opportunity or freedom that is enjoyed by most American children, regardless of where they live and how their lives differ in other respects, is relatively unlimited access to the television set. Both in the Russell Sage study and in the National Survey of Children, the majority of children reported no restrictions on their television viewing, although children from low-income and single-parent families were more likely than

Table 7-6
What Happens If You Break a Rule? by Setting

Percent of Children who report:	New York City High Income	New York City Low Income	Twin Rivers, New Jersey	Columbia, Maryland
Physical punishment	11	52	18	20
Verbal punishment	28	4	9	8
Physical restrictions[a]	6	0	21	25
Allowance or TV withheld	0	2	0	2
Other specified punishment	4	0	7	8
Unspecified punishment	9	6	18	9
No punishment	13	8	4	13
Total *N*	(53)	(52)	(56)	(53)

[a]For example, have to stay in room, indoors.

other children to say they could watch what and as much as they wanted (see bottom section of table 7-5). A similar pattern was found with respect to restrictions on eating snacks and candy; relatively fewer children in communities with high proportions of high-income and intact families said they could eat as much candy or other snacks as they wanted. In each setting, however, children reported more restrictions on snacking than television viewing. (Apparently American parents are more concerned about rotting teeth than rotting brains.)

Table 7-6 suggests that like the rules themselves, the punishments for infringement of rules reflect the environments in which the children live. The high-income New York children were more likely than other children to get scolded or "talked to," and the second highest form of punishment in this setting was no punishment at all. A majority of the East Harlem children reported that they were hit, spanked, or beaten when they broke a rule. The suburban children, most of whom had rooms of their own, were more likely to be restricted to their room or some other isolated part of the house, a form of punishment that was not really feasible in many East Harlem families. It has been pointed out by students of family dynamics that violence is a cheap form of punishment or social control, and it is understandably most often used in families that lack other resources (Collins 1975, p. 268; Goode 1971). Anthropologists studying household types across cultures have also reported associations between community and household arrangements (including size, density, and the presence in households of relatives other than parents and their children) and both the emphasis on controlling aggressive behavior and the severity of the sanctions imposed for infractions (Whiting 1961). It is too bad that there is no data on these questions from the Bennington subsample, so that we could see whether families which also lacked monetary resources but whose household and community density were lower than in East Harlem used different modes of controlling their children's behavior.

In recent years, a number of observers in this country and elsewhere have expressed concern over developments in modern industrialized societies that have tended to work against the integration of the young into the larger society. It has been pointed out that for the first time in history, most children are not expected to make any real contributions to the productive life of the community. As Robinson et al. comment in an analysis of American childrearing manuals:

> . . . the focus is on the individual child, his "self-realization" through "self-discovery" and "self-motivated behavior." While other people are to assist him in this process, they are not to get in his way. As for the question of the child's obligations to others—especially to those not his own age—the training manuals are strangely silent. [Robinson et al. 1974, p. 381]

A similar conclusion was drawn by an anthropologist who studied the "culture of childhood" in a number of different societies:

> In the matter of minimal expectations, modern American middle-class people have probably no peers in all the world. They may expect developmental precocity, or at least rejoice in it—clear speaking, walking, evidence of talent, or intelligence, for example—but this is quite unlike an expectation of work and assumption of real responsibilities. [Goodman 1970, p. 66]

The separation of children from the workaday life of the larger society is a quality American children share with children in developed countries generally, but it distinguishes them from not only the majority of children in the smaller and less industrialized societies of the past but also from children in such contemporary societies as Israel and mainland China. In Israel kibbutz children tend gardens and animals from a very early age, and elementary-school children in Jerusalem took on such community responsibilities as mail delivery and garbage collection during the Six Day War (de Shalit 1970); in mainland China elementary-school workshops turn out machine components for buses and other heavy equipment, and school children routinely spend a month or more a year in some form of productive labor (Kessen 1975). The anthropological literature indicates that the age period from about four to seven—that is, the age which was studied in the Russell Sage project—is the period when children in preindustrial societies assume serious obligations and responsibilities in their homes and communities. For example, a study of data from fifty cultures in the Human Relations Area File,[4] in which children's roles were scored according to twenty-seven different categories, concluded that during this age period:

> . . . parents relegate (and children assume) responsibility for care of younger children, for tending animals, for carrying out household chores, and gathering materials for the upkeep of the family. The children also become responsible for their own social behavior and the method of punishment for transgression changes. Along with new responsibility, there is the expectation that children between five and seven begin to be teachable. Adults give practical training expecting children to be able to imitate their example; children are taught social manners and inculcated in cultural traditions. Underlying these changes in teachability is the fact that at five to seven children are considered to attain common sense or rationality. . . . All of these variables indicate that at five to seven the child is broadly categorized differently than before this age, as he becomes a more integral part of his social structure. [Rogoff et al. 1976, p. 266]

One of the major substantive objectives of my study was to examine the kinds of expectations that children in different American subcultures perceive as applying to themselves and the extent to which they acquire new role expectations during this period (that is, whether the seven-year-olds perceive their rights and obligations differently than the four-year-olds). The children were asked: "Are there jobs you have to do at home to help out? What are they?" Table 7-7 shows that the home resonsibilities most frequently named in all communities are cleaning up their own room, helping with the general housework, and helping with meals, although with one exception (Columbia, where 52 percent of the children said they helped clean or straighten up the house), fewer than half of the children in any setting claim to do any of these tasks. Even smaller numbers of children mention helping with the laundry, looking after younger siblings, helping outdoors, or helping with the shopping, and between 15 and 37 percent of the respondents in a given setting said they had no regular household responsibilities. The mean number of home responsibilities (bottom line of table 7-7) ranged from less than one job per child to about 1.3 jobs per child; the lowest mean was in the low-income New York City setting, the highest in Twin Rivers.

Our prediction was that small towns and rural communities would be the last strongholds of childhood chores or home responsibilities in this country, but contrary to our expectations, the highest proportions of children listing no household responsibilities were in Brunswick and Bennington. However, the mean number of home jobs was higher in these two communities than in the two urban ones. Indeed the mean figure for Brunswick was about the same as for Columbia; apparently Brunswick children who did have household responsibilities were likely to have multiple ones.

Table 7-7

Reported Home Responsibilities, by Setting (Open-Ended Question)

Percent of Children Who Say They:	New York City High Income	New York City Low Income	Twin Rivers, New Jersey	Columbia, Maryland	Brunswick, Maine	Bennington, Vermont
Clean their room or make their bed	36	12	16	26	8	20
Help clean or straighten up the house	12	35	25	52	37	35
Help with meals (cook, set the table, wash dishes)	8	14	27	12	18	19
Help with laundry	2	0	4	0	6	2
Look after siblings	4	2	5	2	4	0
Do yard work or other outdoor work	0	0	4	6	6	5
Help with shopping	2	0	2	2	4	0
Other	15	0	30	11	16	15
None	23	23	23	15	37	35
Total N[a]	(53)	(52)	(56)	(53)	(49)	(60)
Mean number of home responsibilities per child	.91	.77	1.29	1.15	1.14	.95

[a]Column percentages do not add up to 100 percent because respondents could give more than one home responsibility.

The New York City high-income children, who nearly all had their own bedrooms, were most likely to be expected to clean their rooms or make their beds, and less likely to help out with the general housekeeping or with meals. Twin Rivers children were less likely to help with cleaning their rooms or the house but more likely to help with cooking, setting the table, and dishwashing.

Because the care of younger children is one of the major responsibilities of children in many societies, the respondents were asked: "Do you ever take care of children younger than you?" (For purposes of comparison, we also asked whether there were persons other than their parents who took care of them.) The data indicated that most children, even by the age of seven, were still more likely to receive care than to give it. A substantial majority of the children in all settings said they were cared for by persons other than their parents, and most children named multiple caretakers. On the other hand, over a third of the respondents (about half in some settings) said they engaged in some kinds of caregiving activities, although few did it regularly, few considered themselves capable of assuming a regular babysitting role, and even fewer identified caregiving as one of their major areas of competence.

Conclusion

In what kinds of physical and social environments are children better off? The results of the limited research on this question, including the still-rare studies in which children themselves are asked how they feel about their neighborhoods and communities, indicate: (1) that there is no obvious or simple answer to this question; and (2) that no setting seems to maximize all desirable outcomes for children. The research reviewed here does indicate, however, that children's daily lives are shaped by their surroundings and supports Medrich's claim that while children often display extraordinary initiative and imagination in coping with their surroundings, still "neighborhoods do reflect substantially different opportunity sets which invariably affect what children do and can do" (Medrich 1977, p. 34).

Research on children's daily lives has identified some direct consequences of neighborhood location and safety. For example, urban children are more restricted in their exploration of their physical surroundings, although the greater external constraints imposed by urban life in the case of affluent families may be partially offset by fewer adult-imposed controls within the home (for example, fewer rules governing behavior or fewer restrictions on the use of tools and appliances). By contrast, poor children in large cities are not only prevented from going far from their own homes, but their freedom of action within the home may be limited by rules against unruly or aggressive behavior, with relatively harsh punishments for infractions of home rules.

Children's autonomy is not simply explained by socioeconomic status. The activities of even affluent suburban children may be limited when low residential density and geographical and topographical constraints (for example, hilly terrain, no sidewalks, or widely dispersed houses) make it difficult for children to get to other people. While they focused on different geographical areas of the United States, both the Children's Time Study and the Russell Sage project found that children in low-income but densely settled neighborhoods were the richest in social contacts. Although their interaction with their parents was relatively limited (partly because many of these homes did not contain the child's father), the lesser parental involvement seemed to be balanced by more frequent contacts with other adults, especially relatives other than parents and siblings. The suburban children studied claimed more interaction with their parents than other children, but their relatively high total contact scores were explained mainly by contacts with nonkin. The most socially isolated of all children appear to be from poor rural families, who had the lowest interaction with both kin and non-kin.

Most observers agree that middle-class residential suburbs, like Columbia and Twin Rivers in the Russell Sage study or Monterey in the Children's Time Study, are the most child-oriented communities in our society (they have on the average higher proportions of children than do the urban and rural sectors), and many people move to such suburbs specifically for the sake of their children (Devereux 1977; Alexander 1973; Gans 1968). Children in Columbia and Twin Rivers did more things with their parents, possibly because more of the mothers in these subsamples were not employed outside the home; they also claimed to have more home responsibilities, possibly because their parents had more time and inclination to create and supervise such tasks.

The affluent suburb has long been criticized for failing to meet the needs of persons in some phases of the family or life cycle (in particular teenagers, mothers of young children, single parents, and retired persons), but it is only recently that its suitability for young children has been questioned. For example, Christopher Alexander, professor of Architecture at the University of California, argues in an article entitled "The City as a Mechanism of Sustaining Human Contact" (1973), that the low density of suburban areas and the privacy of suburban homes and yards, combined with lack of common land where children can find each other, severely limits the development of children's play groups; by contrast, children in crowded urban areas have greater opportunity to meet greater numbers of children and adults and develop skill in social relations.

Similarly, sociologist Alice Rossi argues that while much has been made of the isolation of young mothers in suburban homes, "such a household is an isolating hot-house for young children, too, cutting them off from easy access to other children of their own age" (Rossi 1977, p. 23). Moreover, the small family size and relatively close spacing of children in such homes may stimulate greater sibling rivalry than in families with more children and wider spacing and may prevent older children from assuming the role of assistant in home and childcare that characterized simpler societies. Rossi proposes the creation of "child growth centers" to compensate for the isolation of children resulting from the residential and work patterns of their homes and communities, although she does not provide details on the organization and program of such centers.[5]

The present level of understanding about the ecology of childhood does not allow us to draw very firm conclusions about the effects of many specific aspects of children's physical and social environments. What we do know raises some troubling possibilities, for example: that our current land-use patterns may inhibit the behavior and activities of many children in rather major ways; that the interests of adults and the interests of children may not always be congruent, may indeed be in conflict with respect to many aspects of lifestyle; that the childcare system lacks the flexibility and diversity that the great majority of parents in all industrialized countries say they want. The limited evidence we have obtained from children themselves rather than from older persons speaking for children suggests that the environment affects children at least partly as a consequence of the way it affects the other significant persons in their lives. While children's desires and interests may be not identical with those of their mothers, fathers, and other adults, I would still conclude that children's lives are enhanced in communities that are good places for their "significant others" to live and work; that is, in communities that provide not only the kind of child growth centers recommended by Rossi but also such amenities for busy parents as nearby jobs with flexible working hours, shopping facilities located to reduce dependence on the automobile, and a variety of childcare possibilities. Moving beyond the realm of evidence to the realm of speculation (if not wishful thinking), it seems that one useful function of a book such as this is to think together about the way we would like to live and use our fantasies as yardsticks for measuring the quality of life in our real-life communities.

Notes

1. The six settings were: (1) Brunswick, Maine, a small town with rural surroundings and a fairly heterogeneous population; (2) Bennington, Vermont, a rural municipality, with a sample designed to overrepresent low-income and single-parent families; (3) an upper-income neighborhood in New York City, where many of the children attended elite private schools; (4) a low-income neighborhood in East Harlem, New York City, whose residents are mainly Black and Puerto Rican; (5) Columbia, Maryland, one of the most widely publicized new towns in this country, in which special efforts were made to design a city that would be racially and socioeconomically heterogeneous, and where there was a serious attempt to innovate not only with respect to land use, but also with respect to social services in support of families and family life; and (6) Twin Rivers, New Jersey, a planned community in suburban New Jersey, with a disproportionate number of stay-at-home mothers and a disproportionate number of husbands and fathers in technical, professional, or business occupations which require them to commute more than two hours a day to New York, Philadelphia, and other parts of New Jersey.

2. Space precludes a full discussion of this unique aspect of the project, but I would like to note that the quality of these children's work was extremely high—only one interview out of all those done by children had to be discarded because of incompleteness—and in my opinion children of this age constitute one of the greatest unused resources in society.

3. Although Twin Rivers advertises itself as a "pedestrian community," the lack of many basic services within the community and the distance of most dwelling units from what shops and services there are, mean that, as Keller found out in her detailed study of this community, the car is "a staple if not an absolute necessity." Keller (1976) found that 44 percent of the residents of Twin Rivers had two or more cars, and 34 percent of the children in our sample said that they rode in the car every day.

4. The Human Relations Area File (HRAF) is a collection of data on a large number of societies, consisting of exerpts from scholarly works, classified, coded, and evaluated by specialists. The materials are organized by society and are further broken down into a number of categories (such as language, ideas about nature and man, socialization, and kin groups) and by subtopics with categories. Started at Yale, the HRAF is now housed at several additional universities where it is available to researchers and students.

5. Rossi's proposal was echoed in the comments of one of the Lincoln Institute conference participants, Moshe Safdie, who described the Youth Palaces in the People's Republic of China and suggested that the United States may also need an additional institution for the young, where they can learn skills and gain social experiences not currently available in the home or school.

References

Alexander, C. "The city as a mechanism for sustaining human contact." In *Urbanism: The Psychology of Urban Survival,* edited by J. Helmer and N.A. Eddington. New York: Free Press, 1973.

Aries, Philippe. *Centuries of Childhood.* New York: Vintage, 1962.

Berg, Mary, and Elliott A. Medrich. "Children in Five Neighborhoods." Report of Children's Time Study, School of Law, University of California, Berkeley, 1977.

Boocock, Sarane Spence. "The Social Context of Childhood." *Proceedings of American Philosophical Society* 119 (1975):419–428.

Boocock, Sarane Spence. "Children in Contemporary Society." In *Rethinking Childhood,* edited by A. Skolnick, pp. 414–436. Boston: Little, Brown and Co., 1976.

Boocock, Sarane Spence. *Sociology of Education: An Introduction.* Rev. ed. Boston: Houghton Mifflin, 1980.

Collins, Randall. *Conflict Sociology: Toward An Explanatory Science.* New York: Academic Press, 1975.

Demos, John. *A Little Commonwealth: Family Life in Plymouth Colony.* London: Oxford University Press, 1970.

de Shalit, N. "Children in war." In *Children and Families in Israel,* edited by A Jarus. New York: Gordon and Breach, 1970.

Devereux, E.C. "Psychological Ecology: A Critical Analysis and Appraisal." Paper prepared for Conference on Ecology of Human Development, Cornell University, Ithica, New York, 1977.

Gans, Herbert J. *People and Plans: Essays on Urban Problems and Solutions.* New York: Basic Books, 1968.

Goode, W.J. "Force and Violence in the Family." *Journal of Marriage and Family* 33 (1971):624–636.

Goodman, M.E. *The Culture of Childhood.* New York: Teachers College Press, 1970.

Kanter, R.M. *Commitment and Community: Communes and Utopias in Sociological Perspective.* Cambridge, Massachusetts: Harvard University Press, 1972.

Keller, Suzanne. "Twin Rivers, Study of a Planned Community." Princeton University, School of Architecture. Report to National Science Foundation, 1976.

Kessen, William, ed. *Childhoods in China.* New Haven: Yale University Press, 1975.

Kohn, M.L. "Social class and parent-child relationships: an interpretation." *American Journal of Sociology* 68 (1963):471–480.

Kohn, M.L. "Social class and parental values: Another confirmation of the relationship." *American Sociological Review* 41 (1976):538–545.

Larrabbee, E. "Childhood in twentieth-century America." In *The Nation's Children,* edited by E. Ginsberg, vol. 3, pp. 199–216. New York: Columbia University Press, 1960.

Mao Tsetung. *Quotations from Chairman Mao Tsetung.* Peking, China: Foreign Languages Press, 1972.

Medrich, Elliott A. "The Serious Business of Growing Up: A Study of Children's Lives Outside of School." Report of Childhood and Government Project, School of Law, University of California, Berkeley, 1977.

Robinson, H.B. "Early Child Care in the United States of America." International Monographs on Early Child Care, no. 3; *Early Child Development and Development* vol. 2, no. 4 (1974).

Rogoff, B., et al. "Age of Assignment of Roles and Responsibilities to Children: A Cross Cultural Survey." In *Rethinking Childhood,* edited by A. Skolnick, pp. 249–268. Boston: Little, Brown and Co., 1976.

Rossi, A.S. "A Biosocial Perspective on Parenting." *Daedalus* 106 (1977):1–31.

Rowe, R.R., et al. "Child Care in Massachusetts: The Public Responsibility." A Study for The Massachusetts Advisory Council on Education, 1972.

Sidel, Ruth. *Women and Child Care and China.* New York: Hill and Wang, 1972.

Szalai, Alexander. ed. *The Use of Time: Daily Activities of Urban and Suburban Populations in Twelve Countries.* Atlantic Highlands, New Jersey: Humanities Press, 1972.

Whiting, J.W.M. "Socialization process and personality." In *Psychological Anthropology: Approaches to Culture and Personality,* edited by F.L.K. Hsu, pp. 355–380. Homewood, Illinois: Dorsey Press, 1961.

Zablocki, Benjamin. *Other Choices: A Sociologist Explores Alternatives to the Contemporary American Family,* Report no. 3. Philadelphia: Smith Kline and French Laboratories, 1978.

Zablocki, Benjamin. *Alienation and Charisma: American Communitarian Experiments.* New York: Free Press, 1980.

Zill, Nicholas. *Summary of Preliminary Findings: National Survey of Children.* New York: Foundation for Child Development, 1978.

Part III
Open Space

Iris Miller discusses the emotional and cultural qualities of space and territories with reference to the design of gardens in chapter 8, "Space and Values: Urbanism and Gardens." Her review of European landscape history reveals the important role of women, particularly those of the aristocracy, as shapers of taste and canons of beauty, consultants, patrons, and users but rarely as professional designers.

A similar theme is sounded by Galen Cranz in "Women and Urban Parks: Their Roles as Users and Suppliers of Park Services." Cranz's case studies of urban parks in New York, Chicago, and San Francisco at four periods of American history, show women as important users of parks but not as policy makers. She recommends a new perspective on parks as a vehicle to meet the needs for health, recreation, play, and leisure of contemporary women.

8

Space and Values: Urbanism and Gardens

Iris Miller

"People dream of ideal places." Can we fully know these places of the mind by looking at the environments in which humankind actually dwells?[1]

The range of urban-design forces at play in recent Western history includes an interrelationship between the principles applied to the design of cities and gardens of the same period. In Europe between the sixteenth and eighteenth centuries the medieval conception of the vertical cosmos slowly yielded to a new secular dimension—the horizontal landscape. The vertical dimension had been charged with meaning, signifying transcendence and affinity with time. The gradual progression from the medieval inward-looking spatial attitude toward a more flexible outgoing means of embracing space is manifest in cultural attitudes. The dignity of man was established together with the celebration of human intelligence. This concept was emphasized in the horizontal component of motion.

Space, a concept lacking in precision and objectivity, is the universal foundation of human experience. A person's notion of space may be conscious or not, interpreted by a range of nonstatic impressions of the urban landscape. The spatial field is charged with meaning that varies from individual to individual. Perceptions of spatial axes and orientations are built on an accumulation of actions and sociocultural influences. Spatial linguistics and notation systems contribute to the articulation of one's identity with environment.[2] Space, as a representation of a mental image, becomes a setting symbolizing an "occasion" answering to the specialized associative concept of "place."[3] In this sense, interchangable meanings, memories, and perceptions relating to a space accrue to the individual.

The essence of space is volume, infinite or finite, defining an object or becoming an object, a self-contained entity or containing objects, the focus of attention or receding background related to another space or a force.[4] The structure of space in the urban landscape is generated by and responds to the configuration of vertical wall planes juxtaposed against horizontal linear and curving extensions. Exterior spaces are dependent on transition spaces and adjacent interior spaces which stimulate their own perceptual presence. An increase in spatial size tends to decrease spatial definition unless accompanied by a strong sense of containment.

We look to the past for insights in creating exterior city space, that is, to those traditions which suggest positive alternatives socially, operationally and aesthetically. This reasoning is the basis for review of European landscape history—to deduce relationships between garden building and city building. If we accept the notion of the garden as a high art form, we are obliged to acknowledge the rigorous standards of design composition applied thereto. It follows that the transformation of these principles to the urban landscape offers the possibility for a highly refined expression of beauty and order. To the extent that this goal is attained, Alberti's corollary, the creation of an "atmosphere of welcome,"[5] will undoubtedly follow.

The gardens of the Renaissance, and thereafter, are a product of leisure, representing an idealized view of the world. They are rooted in the concomitant interplay between the physical opportunities of the site, the prevailing philosophy of the master designer's imaginative approach to design, and the spiritual needs of people. Until recently gardens were considered one of the highest, albeit most ephemeral, art forms reflecting the luxurious extension of an individual's private life.

Ancient Garden Prototypes

Garden art of the Italian Renaissance, pattern on the Roman prototype, had to be relearned. Preoccupation with survival after the disintegration of Rome virtually caused the disappearance of even the memory of great gardens in the Western world. The gardens of the ancient world were linked to these newly created masterpieces of the Italian Renaissance through several threads. The first link was the physical proximity of overlapping sites; people actually lived amidst the Roman ruins. The second connection came through the study of literary descriptions, particularly the letters of the Younger Pliny. And the third common thread was through the influence of Byzantium and remnants of Moorish Spain.[6]

Ancient gardens of the Middle East and eastern Mediterranean generally had no privileged dimension. The roughly square space was subdivided for orchards, tree groves, and ponds. Irrigation and drainage channels were provided similar to those presently existing in the Spanish gardens of the Alhambra at Granada and the courtyard of the Mosque in Cordoba. Other ancient models include the public parks created by the Greeks for social gatherings and games and the legendary hanging gardens of Babylon (ca. 605 B.C.). The latter encompassed the terraced hillside and symbolic ziggurat gardens which ascended steplike through a series of cool tree and trellis covered promenades or rooms planted with shrubs and flowers.[7]

The preserved gardens at Pompeii were essentially open-air courtyards, peristyles, contained by colonnades with shady passages somewhat patterned after the Greek town houses. To compensate for the relative absence of ground plants (due to necessity, not choice) and to simulate the extension of space, walls were painted with trompe l'oeil of garden scenes. Potted plants and flowers were abundantly used. The raised flower bed with topiary, statuary and water basins were the most consistent feature of the Roman gardens.[8] A wall or fence separated an informal planting area which had lattice-work arches, open pergolas, and ornamented pitchers and vases.

The Roman villa of the wealthy patrician families was an enormously large unit, often looking more like a village than an English mansion or Renaissance villa. Hadrian's Villa is frequently discussed in literature for its large-scale site planning and its compositional method for interlocking geometric forms and shifting axes of circulation.

The less affluent people dwelling in multi-unit buildings along the narrow, congested city streets, unable to afford the ambience of a beautiful "cortile," built their gardens on balconies and roof tops making use of available light and air.

Medieval Gardens

Although the monastic and secular medieval gardens were primarily functional rather than ornamental, they were also enjoyed. These gardens included herbs for cooking and healing, vegetable gardens and fruit orchards, flowers for culinary and medicinal uses as well as for table or church decoration. The more elaborate types featured an ornamental central water fountain or wellhead, orderly repetition of elements, fence or shrub borders to keep off poultry and dogs, trellis and balustrading covered with vines for shade and privacy. Gardens were most frequently symmetrical and squared off. Size was the distinguishing factor between those of humble people and those of noblemen. Gradually gardening grew from a craft to an art form.

The medieval garden was introspective and protected, preserving itself physically, spiritually, and socially behind walls. The towns of the Middle Ages reflected this fortress-like quality of private life existing behind walls. Defense was the most significant factor. Consequently space was seldom spared for elaborate gardens. The pointed arches and soaring towers of the Gothic cathedral and noble warring families were, dramatic structures symbolic of a finite universe, centered in the vertical dimension of the cosmos and exalted by the spiritual relationship of the human soul to heaven.[9]

New Axial Forces in Italy

The subsequent axial shift in European spheres of culture and learning, of commercial economic development, accompanied by the rise of a new affluent merchant class, extended to the representation of three-dimensional spatial depth in painting. Greater understanding of scale, color, light, and shade led to new attempts to depict perspective. The history of European landscape painting affords most persuasive evidence of a shift toward horizontal vision.

The trend toward emphasis on the horizontal axial extension of space and vistas was reflected in the grandeur of the gardens of the Renaissance villas. Use of perspective and the illusion of distance was produced through manmade vistas at station points on the tiered hillsides of Tuscana, the region in Italy in the vicinity of Florence and Siena. The fortress slowly was replaced by the villa; the wall, was lowered to pursue the outward-looking rather than inward-looking view. The garden's disposition on an incline permitted free vista into the outer world. An elaborate rectangular pattern of beds and paths organized around a central axis with parallel service paths grew increasingly complex.[10]

The Italian climate provided the impetus for the wealthy class to build their great villas on the beautiful inclined slopes of the campagna. The justification, in part, was to escape the unpleasant summer heat of the cities for the cooling breezes of the nearby hills. In addition, there were those who wished to be near to their vineyards and farms. Topography in large measure was interrelated to the formal development of the villa garden. Villa Vicobello near Siena by Peruzzi typifies the features of the Italian villa. Its sequence of terraced garden rooms consists of an orchard of potted orange trees and a well near the main house. There are also pools and fountains, formally arranged plantings in geometric patterns beside long parterres, topiary, and extended outward-looking framed vistas.

Italian Gardens of the Renaissance and Baroque Periods

Italian villa gardens might be divided loosely into three periods of design development. The first period, between 1450 and 1503, began with Alberti's literary dialogue of the joys of villas and gardens and his theories of site planning. The principles that he set forth greatly influenced the other architects of the day. The second period, 1503 to 1600, had two major thrusts: the gardens of Rome and Frascati, commencing with Bramante's immensely successful terracing of the Belvedere at the Vatican; and the work of Vignola, which inventively incorporated the use of water. The last period, from

1600 to 1775, can be seen as one of elaborate embellishment and gradual decline.

Influence of Alberti

The sites for the villas outside of Florence were chosen not solely for security but for the prospect. While small enclosures, arbours and grottoes were still possible, their purpose within the garden was to increase the emotional intensity of the experience when contrasted with vistas down long garden paths and over the Tuscana countryside. Pergolas became avenues open to the sky. The basic square lost favor as a result of the imposition of new forms. Paths in search of views tended to lengthen; those which were only internal grew shorter. The garden was an integral part of the building, reinforcing the singularity of composition. The ideation of these early Renaissance gardens lay in thought.

In his work *De Re Aedificatoria*, Leon Battista Alberti referred to the gardens of Pliny with the conscious intention of knitting together the spirit of Florence with "the glorious past of his people."[11] Alberti reduced his descriptions of *garden principles* "after the fashion of the ancients" to the following: unified harmony of the whole, well-mannered proportion fostering an aura of good-humored welcome, effortless gently inclined planes, the absence of self-conscious poetic melancholy.[12] His prescriptive considerations of site planning are still valid: choice of site on well-drained solid ground, relation of site to prevailing and seasonal winds, orientation to horizontal and vertical sun angles, use of local contextual materials, adequacy of the water supply fashioned into enchanting water elements. Alberti's philosophical attention to proportion and site planning details was equally as important for the countryside villa as for the urban landscape, palazzo, church, interior court, and public building.

The Medici family rivals all others for its significant contribution to the course of Renaissance history. The Medici women are among the few listed in the annals of history for their influence upon architecture and landscape of both an urban and private sort. For it was not just what they had proposed and set out personally, but also, their enormous impact upon the schemes of others across the continent and abroad. The cultural, economic, and political influence of the Medicis, and consequently, of Italy, upon other countries was solidified through the marriages of its children to monarchs and nobles from all parts of Europe. The Medicis produced popes, princes, and queens. As a family of continuous prosperity, engaging in commerce and patronizing the arts, its great houses and villas were handed down from generation to generation, having been altered according to the varying taste of the times.[13] Located in Rome, Florence, and the Tuscana hillside, these villas were works of beauty, intellectually conceived. The Medici contributions to urban design merit equal praise, especially Piazza Signoria, one of the primary public spaces in Florence. The rule of this great house lasted until the late eighteenth century, suffering from a succession of destructive influences from without and misfortunes from within.

Villa Medici at Fiesole (1450), designed by Michelozzi according to the principles of Pliny, was modest in scale and design. It established a pattern of unification of house and grounds, treating gardening as a fine art.

Francesco de Medici, having retired from the adventures of his youth, wished to create a paradise for his bride, Bianca Cappello . . . a secluded place in the mountains suited to "all the joys of summer."[14] Pratolino, begun in 1568, lays claim for its statuary (Apennino, in particular), its grottoes and watercourse, its hedges and artificial mounds, and its recreational attractions.

Yet another Medici residence was the imposing Florentine home, Palazzo Pitti near Porta Romana. Its huge Boboli Gardens were begun by Spanish Princess Eleonora de Toledo, wife of Cosimo I, in 1549, with the help of Tribolo and others. She brought with her some of the paradigmatic themes of the great gardens of Iberia. A hint of the might of the family might be ascertained by the realization that a large Florentine palazzo could actually stand in one of its grandest garden courts. Adjacent to the large court is an amphitheatre, or prato, "for games of the nobler sort."[15] The gardens themselves were divided into two quite separated parts, laden with waterworks, grottoes, statuary, pillars, niches, alcoves, terraces, and long criss-crossing hedge-lined avenues. Its elevated location enabled an especially fine view of the architecture of Florence. The Boboli Gardens were monumental in size. With all their prototypical formal architectural unity, however, one finds a substantial disparity here as a purveyor of taste and charm.

In addition to the Medici villas scattered about the Tuscana hills outside of Florence, Medici villas also existed in the environs of Rome. Two of enviable splendor were Villa Madama and Villa Medici. Each was built in stages; the former was never completed as originally designed. Each claimed privileged views of Rome and had unique geometric architectural expressions, which have been the subject of praise, imitation, and transformation by architects of succeeding generations up to the present time.

The vivid images of these lovely Medici gardens were to serve as inspiration for several great gardens of Paris. Two Medici daughters, Catherine and Marie, were united in political marriages to French kings, Henri II and Henri IV. Each of these women consulted with prominent garden designers of Italy and France commissioning them to construct gardens in France fashioned after the Italian style. Catherine de Medici instructed the development of the Tuilleries. Marie de Medici was responsible for the Jardin Luxembourg. Each has been applauded for her imaginative design and unusual plantings.

Gardens of Rome and Environs

Italian gardens from 1503 to 1600 emphasized the architectural features found in the villas in and near Rome. The Belvedere (1503) on the Vatican grounds in Rome was a major accomplishment in site planning. It was a small villa standing 330 yards higher than the Vatican Palace.[16] The garden terrace was 80 yards in width. The significant design feature was the use of flanking sweeping horizontal stairs to terrace the top portion of the slope and link the upper level court to the lower level palace. At the base of the hillside one encountered a wide straight set of stairs. Bramante devised a magnificent arrangement of staircases, balustrading, and terraces to provide access from one level to another and to balance and enhance the visual weight of these buildings of dissimilar moods. The grand use of stairs as an architectural link was a new feature of western design. Bramante had uncovered the secret of horizontal emphasis in combination with the technique necessary to control steep slopes. The garden also became a museum for sculpture, heightening the pleasure of passage and prescribing a pace. The white carved marble figures linked the trees and hedges with the villa, gave visual emphasis, and softened the transition from stone to leaf. This wonderful scheme effectively produced a gradual transition of space and mood. It set a new precedent for the future in urban and private garden design.

During the period that the Medici family was at the peak of its glory, Florence was preeminent in the development of villa and garden. However, as the greatness of the Medici house began to wane, Florence gradually relinquished this fragile position to Rome. The predominance of the church from the middle of the sixteenth century fostered a favorable situation in Rome for the continuing visionary development of the garden. The vanished glories of several decades can be glimpsed by the stamp of beauty preserved in the town villa of Rome. Having been previously confined to the valley of the Tiber for the lack of an abundance of water, Pope Sixtus V succeeded in satisfying an overwhelming demand for the hillside villa. He installed a second conduit, Acqua Felico (the first conduit, Acqua Vergine, was built by Pope Sixtus IV). The Romans were then able to introduce a quasi-ideal villa prototype of aesthetic perfection for a utopian aristocratic society—the ennobled hillside villa—possessing charming vistas, acquiring larger parcels of land for long stretches of parterres displaying intricate bedding patterns, as well as enthusiastically satisfying their great love for water play.

High on Monte Pincio, the garden mountain of the ancients, overlooking the City of Rome between the old town wall and the Field of Mars lies the narrow garden and villa of the Medici. When Cardinal Francesco bought it, it was unfinished, having changed hands a number of times. He acquired a piece of ground on the northeast from a lady of his own house, Catherine de Medici, in order to enlarge and complete the garden. The flat somber entry facade of the villa borders the street of splendid vista, while the garden, accessible by a grand stair from this lower entry level, lavishly spreads out along the enclosed upper terrace with controlled perfection. The top story of the decorative garden facade steps back between two terrets. A pillared hall or loggia, in the Palladian style, extends into a garden becoming a low semicircular balcony. From here at either side stairs descent into the garden. The main garden composed of formal square beds enfolds at right angles to the axis of the house terminating at the high town wall. It would seem that Ferdinand di Medici bought the villa in 1584 with the intention of converting it into a great garden museum, and he produced one of the finest in Rome.[17]

On the slopes of the Monte Mario in 1516, Villa Madama was begun for Cardinal Guilio di Medici, also of the great house of Medici. Caught in the midst of political strife, the house and gardens were sacked, eventually rebuilt, but never completed. However, this villa is considered one of the loveliest jewels of the Italian Renaissance. Even in its unfinished state, traces of its ineffaceable beauty remain.

The original intention was an interlocking of house and garden creating a wholly unified composition: both inside to outside and terracing down the slope.[18] The elephant grotto just beyond the formal gardens is woven naturally into the depths of a woodland cleft. A playful shift of axial symmetry in the plan and elevation of the villa and in the garden captures the delight and imagination of its viewers.

Water Play in Gardens

The role of water in gardens began to change from the functional to the playful: garden water play, the water stairway, the cascade, the fountain spilling into a pool, the grottoes. A positive delight at water in the garden was learned indirectly from Islam and the Spaniards. Full use of water was long delayed, however, because of short supply at Rome and Frascati. Subsequently, the strong desire for fountains and water tricks led the Romans to install great water conduits to carry enough water throughout the city for its many public fountains and private gardens.

Two of the finest gardens outside of Rome have been attributed to Vignola: Villa Farnese, Caprarola, and Villa Lante, Bagnaia near Viterbo. Although quite different in configuration, these inconspicuously spacious gardens have some similar characteristics. Positioned above their respective towns, together they form a powerful, wholly unified composition. The lessons of the Belvedere of integrating house and garden into a terraced hillside are herein expressed. Although inward looking, there is no strong feeling of enclosure. Both have casinos at the highest elevation from which a water course extends in visionary splendor. Both communicate a dynamic partnership with their objects. Caprarola is larger than Lante; its primary shape is pentagonal, while at the Villa Lante it is rectangular. The carvings and statues at Caprarola make it one of the chief sculture gardens of its type. Lante with its pools, fountains, diagonal crisscrossing paths, terraces, and symmetrical axes is applauded for its unifying idea and perfect moderation. Two separate buildings on each perimeter of the crossaxis retain all the character of dwelling houses. The scheme is a simple form of extraordinary arrangement.

In marked contrast to the villas of Rome, Lante and Caprarola boast a natural woods and an abundance of water. In addition to the visual effect, water also fulfilled a social role, incorporating itself into the party play of the guests. At Lante the water course followed the symmetrical axis from the top of the slope through the center of the formal "house-garden" site to the trough adjacent to the outer wall just below the garden. This nutrient rich water (from human regurgitation and discarded food products) became a source of feed for the horses of the neighboring peasants.

Horizontal and Vertical Spatial Layering

An imaginative and technically exacting approach to the articulation of interrelated levels and the creation of an introspective center from which all energy radiates was accomplished by Vignola at Villa Guilia (1550) in Rome. Architecturally this masterful work assimilates design concepts of simplicity of form and ornamentation, unity through repetition, and scale manipulation of complex shapes. Vertical movement is brilliantly achieved through the hollowing out of the central garden terrace to create a remarkable three-level space composed of balconies, curving staircases, and elaborate decorative elements. An increasing changing degree of complexity characterizes each level. Climaxed by a semi-cylindrical canal, a nymphaeum grotto with caryatids supporting the balcony above is tucked into the lowest terrace. The dominant central axis of Villa Guilia preserves a view from the entrance through a series of arches to the figural terminus at the far wall. The arch motif is a dominant motif. The exquisite conceptual idea is quite contemporary.

Villa D'Este (1550) at Tivoli is the antithesis of the moderation employed at Lante. An extravagant combination of complex parts of natural and artificial arrangements, of steep terraces joined to one another by diagonal paths and side steps and lapses in taste ingeniously merge into a unified whole. All the traditional garden elements are found here, grottoes, trellises, mazes, long paths and allies with distant views, shady boscos and twin casinos. The extremely steep incline of the hill required gigantic retaining walls. The design is emphatically organized around a strong major axis with minor parallel and crossaxes to accommodate a controlled sense of containment pierced by selected vistas into the Campagna.

This is an instance of an exaggerated aesthetic magnificence inspired by the water. A branch of the River Anio was diverted to descend and weave through the natural and man-made landscape with visionary beauty. The drama of the water reigns supreme. It leaps, gurgles, and cascades down a series of terraces and fountains coming to rest in a large basin below. The lavish excesses of such a garden lack the peaceful tranquility of other Italian villas.

Relationship of Urban Landscape to Gardens

The configuration of the great gardens of the Renaissance and Baroque periods had been subject to many of the same influences affecting the urban landscape. Expression of design relationships were equally applicable to the large formal spatial order and to the small scale "place." The same designers frequently were responsible for setting out both physical environments. The influences consisted not only of site considerations but also of the philosophical tenants of humanism and the political and economic values of the newly emerging merchant class. In evolutionary periods of great intellectual and commercial activity, a pervasive excitement carries over from one discipline to another. Thus, at such times there might be a correlation between the underlying principles of garden design and urban design.

The concepts of urban design in Italy support this thesis. These same notions hold true for other European countries, and, to some extent, for the United States during certain periods of city building. One of the organizational design patterns common to the Renaissance and Baroque periods was a sense of spatial grandeur within a contained unified whole, achieved through the adaptation to lineaments of the natural setting with a strong axial system of order. There was also a sense of centricity at the focal point of a space; a hierarchical network of movement radiated away from each central place, or node, in a diminishing relationship of dominance. Spatial planes, literal or transparent, reinforced the sequential order. There was a unity and coherence of building to landscape, inside to outside. The total energy of the composition was dependent upon terminus and depth perception, as revealed through the intrinsic reciprocity of the terracing of levels of space horizontally and vertically, and, through a multiplicity of such elements as paving, sculpture, and water. Obelisks were introduced as unifying design features and focal points, particularly at nodal points. This suggests the importance of connecting networks and transition spaces. The compositional device of the figural void—piazzetta or piazza—enforces an impressionable ordered identity. Plant material was less frequently used in urban design at this time. The new play with geometries in garden art was also to be found as fragments in urban design and in architecture, aesthetically transformed into various manipulations and imagery of curving forms.

France: Rationalism and Landscape

The influence of the Italian garden and urban design made its way across Europe. Intellectual and cultural development came later to France than to its neighbor to the south. Because of its involvement in military conflict combined with only a gradual evolution in maritime commerce, feudalism continued in France after it was no longer practiced in Italy. Land development also differed in France due to its political system of monarchy and its hierarchy of noblemen. France was far more conservative in its pursuit of change, as evidenced by the persistence of castles and moats, and dictated by its geography and climate.[19]

The initial influences of the Italian garden form gave way to allow the pragmatic evolution of a decidedly French style relating to its own topography and culture. The emerging rationalism of Descartes encouraged a horizontal extension of space and vista in both garden and urban design. Instead of cascades of water flowing down terraces, the preference was for large flat sheets of water and colorful floral displays. These gardens allowed the visitor to lose his ego, while the stations (at which new vistas emerged) boosted it.[20] Elevated walks, *parterres,* as they came to be known, subdivided the garden and contributed to the notion of horizontality. Knot gardens, consisting of elaborate flower beds, were woven in intricate patterns. Mazes provided mystery and physical obstacles, designed to be penetrated and conquered. The gardens of France reached their most sophisticated form at the end of the seventeenth century, a duality of expression combining intellectual empirical reasoning with an aesthetic art form. Garden avenues became models for the design of cities.

Other principles of French garden art, as expounded in a seventeeth-century book by Boyceau, were the need for proportion and symmetry harmoniously composed around a strong central axis. The height of trees and hedges demanded careful relationship to the length and width of paths.[21] Embodied in the garden concept was the idea of a nobel retreat providing solitude for a gentleman of affairs—a place of pleasure, peace, and spiritual refreshment. Also contained in the ideology of the French garden were the notions of love and courtship expressed in the allegorical tale, *Roman de la Rose,* which describes the elaborate protocol of ritual, music, poetry and "manly" trials to replace rudeness.

Influence of Italy

The earliest landscape influences from Italy occurred at the beginning of the sixteenth century centering around the Loire. Heavily fortified chateaus were picturesquely set on the crest of steep hills with the town below. Their overriding concern for seclusion resul d in small formal gardens within protective walls.

New prosperity, peace, and stability in the seventeenth century allowed French kings to move beyond the fortified moated castles into the more extravagant countryside chateaux with great gardens. Italian gardeners and hydraulic engineers were recruited to complement the work of the French designers.

Quintessence of Rational Order

The most extravagant expression of garden design was at Versailles (1664) by the celebrated André le Nôtre. Versailles remains an astonishing example of the imposition of aesthetic taste on nature and the glorification of man. All of the elements of human conception and ambition were to be found here: radiating avenues focusing on the palace, decorative objects and an enviable assortment of botanic specimens, long vistas and paths on major axes, secluded secret gardens among the groves on the wings of the cross-axes, forest and park, water play, paving texture, color, intricate patterns, careful attention to scale, sequential movement, the sudden opening of vistas as a series of set pieces, and reflections in the flat sheets of still water.[22]

In *Collage City,* Rowe and Koetter present the following description of Versailles. Versailles is a total design . . . an organism entire and complete . . . organized about a single controlling idea. It anticipates a state of mind esconsed in rational order and scientific society.[23] Rowe and Koetter suggest that Versailles is a radical criticism of the Paris of that period.[24]

Ultimately, a strong cohesion of plan remains the most salient asset. "Versailles was an instance of stiff magnificence in the formal style."[25] The spectacular park was a triumph that had significant influence not only in garden design, but in the design of cities. Peter the Great of Russia departed France following a stay at Versailles with a French gardner, Le Blond. So impressed and overwhelmed was he, that he wished to capture the grandeur and splendor for Peterhof, "a Versailles on the Neva." Another reminiscence of France were boskets containing water devices and some weeping trees similar to the boscage at Marly-Le-Roi and Les Marais at Versailles designed by the mistress of Louis XIV, Madame de Montespan.[26]

It seems to have been a French tradition that the design and use of gardens and great country manors was often closely related to the romantic involvements of kings and nobles, a new garden or new dwelling was built for the most recent mistress or wife. Changes in preference for residence at one chateau or another was the norm. Royalty and those of the privileged society frequently had several homes. The development and changes in Versailles' gardens and edifices reflect the social relationships and love affairs of an epoque in French history. The gardens served not only as a place of beauty and repose but also as a stage for grand fetes.

As patrons and consultants to supremely capable landscape designers, women of French aristocracy were intimately involved with the composition of great gardens. Such families as the Le Notre and Mollets included several generations of talented gardeners and designers. Freer rein existed in France than in Italy, largely the result of uncertainties regarding political fortune, impatience with nature's slow growth, and the concept of the garden as a temporary stage set. Thus the designer was permitted to express his imagination and ordered vision on great expanses of land. The seventeenth century saw the creation of the great French gardens at accelerated speed.[27]

At Versailles the women who were associated with King Louis XIV and Louis XV, and Napoleon during the seventeenth and eighteenth centuries included Madame La Valliere; Madame de Montespan; Madame de Maintenon; Madame Pompadour; Madame de Sevigne; Henrietta, wife of the Duc d'Orleans; Marie-Antoinette; Empress Josephine Bonaparte, and Marie-Louise. Many of these same women could be listed among those associated with other great gardens of the French countryside and what was formerly suburban Paris.

The opulent St. Cloud, set with animated extravagance on a hillside overlooking Paris and the Seine, is now threatened by suburbia.[28] Famous for its imposing cascade and jet d'eau which spouts water ninety feet high, it continues to be a favorite of Sunday strollers and nobility. Its history is filled with romance and scandal. The King's (Louis XIV) brother, Vita Sackville-West fought with his wife over who would wear the family jewels to a ball; the night he died there was only a brief pause in the activities of the "pleasure-palace."[29] St. Cloud was the setting for Henry III's assassination in 1589. It is said that Madame de Sevingne, en route to Paris, would stop here to bathe in the ornamental waters surrounded by sculpture. Marie Antoinette, seeking fresh dry air and tiring of the forced country life of Versailles, moved there with her ailing son, the Dauphin, in 1785. For an interim just before her divorce Josephine, now l'imperatrice, lived at St. Cloud. It was here that Napolean III staged his extravagant welcome for Queen Victoria and Prince Albert. In 1871, after the departure of the Emperor and his Spanish Empress, it was burned, leaving only the cascades and unequaled views.

The ample water supply of St. Cloud was the source for fountains and pools of the Tuilleries. It has been conveyed by aqueduct since 1564 when Catherine de Medici began her formal garden plan. The wealthy Italian Gondi family, members of the entourage of Marie de Medici, were responsible for the first cascade and ornate design of St. Cloud reminiscent of favored Italian gardens and long unsurpassed in France.[30] They had acquired the estate in 1564, selling it to Philippe d'Orleans in 1658. Antoine Répautre was hired to build a new cascade and elaborate hydraulic system.

The garden at Chateau Anet was a product of tight unity and formality created by Jacques Môllet in the sixteenth century for the mistress of Henri II, Diane de Poitier. At a young age Henri II was forced into a political marriage to Catherine de Medici of Florence causing him great unhappiness. His relationship with Diane de Poitier was a result of his rebellion against this situation. The king's formal entertaining, great fetes and firework displays, took place at Anet, where Diane de Poitier served as hostess.

Several other gardens deserving mention are Sceaux, Arcueil, and Malmaison. Chateau de Sceaux was built southeast of Paris in 1673 by Colbert, the grand manipulator of French national policy. He was careful to exercise enough restraint in the design of the estate to avoid the fate of Fouquet at Vaux-le-Vicomte, where extravagance brought about the latter's demise. Sceaux represented the clashing of elements in opposition and tension at the boundary between city and countryside. A long avenue stretching from the hillside chateau to an octagonal basin below was the chief feature of the park. In 1700 the crippled bastard son (eventually legitimized) of Louis XIV and Marquise de Montespan the Duc de Maine, purchased the estate. His wife, Louise Benedicte de Bourbon, of the House of Condé, herself a dwarf, set up her isolated pastoral paradise as a "perpetual source of amusement for Parisian Society"[31] containing lotteries, gambling, feasts, masquerades, theatricals, ballets, madrigals, and fireworks. She hosted such companions as Voltaire, Madame de Stael, the Spanish ambassador, and the king. "Filled with great ambition, the treasonable overtures of the Duchesse du Maine led to her temporary imprisonment, after which she returned to her retreat to continue her parties and performing in her comedies. The site of these productions, the Pavillon de l'Aurore and the Orangerie, became popular restaurants during the Second Empire. The park itself was so large and too neglected to be maintained.

Also to the south of Paris is Arcueil, where an aqueduct, designed in 1613 in the style of the Roman ruins, carried water to Paris for the Luxembourg gardens of Marie de Medici. The classical Roman motif was typical of the steep hillside gardens.

Empress Josephine's years with Napolean are rich in human interest. Her devotion to the gardens of her favorite home at Malmaison are equally fascinating. She bought the estate in 1799 during the Egyptian campaign.

Here she constructed a fantasy world of rare botanical specimens, a Temple de l'Amour ablaze with rhododendrons, a menagerie and zoological park with gazelles and kangaroos and Swiss cows among other animals, a mineral and shell collection, a museum, an impressive rose collection, and greenhouses where pineapples were introduced. Josephine was responsible for introducing many new exotic varieties of seeds and plants to France which are now commonplace.[32] She was not only a great patron of several important gardeners, scientists, botanical gardens and museums, but she was a collector of specimens becoming continually more knowledgeable about horticulture and design. Her interest in gardens and her enlightened tastes extended to landscape painting, botanical illustrations, and sculpture.

Urban Landscape and Parks in Paris

The correlation between the high art of garden design and urban design can be seen in the development of Paris. In medieval times the Tuilleries was the site where feudatories of the crown assembled to renew their allegiance. The ground just west of the Louvre was purchased in 1519 by Francois Premier as a retreat for his mother, Louise of Savoy. Nine years later a new palace at the Louvre was begun.

In 1560, Italian-born Queen Catherine de Medici, wife of Henri II, acquired more land to begin her palace and gardens which were derivations of Italian concepts. The gardens were almost too stiff, of near-perfect symmetry, surrounded by an imposing wall, and little use of water. Visitors, who were only welcome on limited occasions, seemed to enjoy a semicircular region that produced echoes. They were also entertained by an elaborate menagerie and a labyrinth. Catherine, of superstitious nature, abruptly abandoned work on the grounds after consultation with an astrologer. She did, however, engage Bernard Palissy, a potter and grottoiste, to build the Queen's grotto.[33] Water was brought from St. Cloud, as previously noted.

Extensive damage was caused by fighting in the gardens following the St. Bartholomew's Day massacre of 1572. Order was restored; and following her custom, Catherine, now Queen Mother, periodically staged a "magnificence" in the garden to placate and divert warring factions around the court. One such took place to celebrate the marriage of her daughter to Henri of Navarre, signaling the night of the murder of enormous numbers of Huguenots.[34]

Later during the reign of Henri IV and Marie de Medici, the parterres, planted with great avenues of mulberries, received particular attention. The great lace embroidered flower beds received much admiration. Catherine's palace and gardens were rebuilt, maintaining their spine to link with what is now Place de la Concorde.

Louis VIII was responsible for further improvements to the Tuilleries. Besides his great lacy embroidered flower beds, used in arabesque patterns with astonishing effect, he contributed to the ordered enhancement of the Tuilleries in urban axial context of Paris.

However, a major impact on urban and garden design, which significantly changed the face of Paris, took place under Louis XIV at the direction of Le Notre. What had become a family cynosure was totally redesigned forming the *grandes lignes*. A superb outdoor theatre was created in the northwest corner. Parisians maintained the tradition of frequenting their parks. Therefore, public outrage at the attempt to make the gardens accessible for the exclusive use of the court during the seventeenth century was to be expected.

Fate has not always been kind to the Jardin de Luxembourg. Little remains of Marie de Medici's original fifty acres except the outline. Wishing to transpose a concept of her native Italy and the Boboli Gardens at Palazzo Pitti, she commissioned Boyceau and Salomon de Brosse to plan the castle and gardens. Here the grounds were relatively flat, like those of the Tuilleries, requiring great ingenuity to achieve a cohesive effect with the appearance of variation in levels. A depression was constructed around the parterre adjacent to round terraces of complicated patterns. The unified design preserves a geometric symmetry of sequentially separated components, compartments de broderie. A great crossway avenue at right angles to the main axis was employed by Marie de Medici to resemble the Boboli. She had water brought in from the aqueduct at Arcueil to supply the many fountains. She was spurred to strive to constantly improve her gardens, first, because of her rivalry with Cardinal Richelieu and, second, to impress the entourage of wealthy Italians who followed her to the picturesque Paris.[35]

The special quality which Marie de Medici envisioned for Jardin de Luxembourg remains: the privacy, variety and intimacy of experience of garden life within an enormous space. Le Nôtre skillfully created pools and fountains using water to hide the monotony of vast acres and distract the eye. Here, too, the suggestion that the gardens might be closed following provocative descriptions of the parties of the Duchesse de Berri brought shouts of public outrage.[36]

The explosive energy of axial extension, tree-lined boulevards, formal public gardens with enchanting floral patterns and shrubbery as embodied in the gardens of Versailles and the French countryside, emerged in Paris. This was followed by urban-design developments that strengthened and unified the structure of Paris through a network of interconnected boulevards, avenues, parks, and impressive open spaces and plazas and through a strong dominant axis, interfaced with diagonal and crossaxes as in garden design.

Industrialization and the evolving industrial town came to France about half a century after its development in England. In 1793 the Plan de la Commission des Artistes was prepared for the improvement of the city of Paris, thus becoming the basis for future development and restoration. Paris, still a late-baroque city whose growth patterns since medieval times had been largely by accretion, was transformed by Baron Georges-Eugene Haussman, Prefet de la Seines, into a unified form and a lovely setting for the display of historic monuments and the provision of new amenities. The goals set forth by Napoleon III in 1853 emphasized improvement of circulation throughout the city, particularly allowing for access from palaces and barracks in time of emergency. There were to be new and wider streets creating a pattern of grand focal rond-points at intersecting crossings that formed links with the railway stations. The public-health improvements were to be accomplished by clearing narrow alleys and introducing light, air and sanitation. A comprehensive pattern of parks and gardens—some new, others redesigned—were to be connected by heavily planted boulevards, creating the first European urban park system. The Bois de Boulogne, upon which work had previously begun, was to be a "place of recreation for the elegant world"[37] a rival to the royal parks of London. The Bois was laced with curving drives and paths, lakes, cascades, formal gardens, a zoological garden, and a race course. Wild flowers flourished unharmed in the woods. The French style of clipped trees was abandoned here. In addition, there were numerous structures of many architectural styles and materials, restaurants, brasseries, bandstands, rotundas, and gates.

Jean-Alphonse Alphand, jardinier-ingenieur (who collaborated with Haussman and with Barillet-Deschamps on the landscape design of the Paris parks, squares and boulevards), believed that trees or shrubs from all countries should be placed in harmonious relation to the eye, grouped on silky green lawns recalling a meadow. They were to be accented by narrow bands of flower collars and brilliantly colored flower baskets. Barillet-Deschamps is credited with the introduction of much of this exotic vegetation into the gardens of Paris.

To balance the recreational opportunities offered to the bourgeois quarter to the west of Paris by the Bois de Boulogne, in 1858 Haussman transformed the Bois de Vincennes for the working class on the eastern part of the city. Here he employed complementary notions of design and recreational devices. On a smaller scale, to fulfill more local needs three "parcs-interieures" were provided: Parc de Monceau, Parc de Montsouris, and Parc des Buttes-Chaumont. Parc de Monceau had originally been laid out as a landscape park following the designs of the poet, Carmontel, in 1778 by the Duc de Chartres. In 1852 it returned to the state, following several changes in ownership during and after the Revolution. The original size had been diminished to accommodate new construction and two new roads. Les Buttes-Chaumont, according to the English author, William Robinson, is "the most distinct and interesting garden in Paris."[38] These parks were arranged to convey the harmonious imagery of a miniaturized natural landscape combined with elements of a formal garden. There were winding paths presenting ever-changing scenery, sloped hillsides and long stretches of lawn, serpentine lakes and streams emanating from grottoes, colonnades, ruins, and formally landscaped terraces. The French were quite serious about their daily custom to gather in their neighborhood parks, a practice that continues to this day. Benches lining the walks are never empty. One encounters people of all ages establishing a parcel of territory for one person or for a social group.

Influenced by the emperor's experiences in London and his enthusiasm regarding the English character of small parks and squares, Haussman's urban-design scheme attempted to reproduce the essence of this concept. Twenty smaller open spaces which were laid out by Alphand, were incorporated into his plan for Paris. Some of these squares, completed between 1855 and 1868,[39] were detailed with great care, providing a lingering source of delight, while others were less successful than the parks. However, each contributed to the urban vocabulary of Paris: a system of small open spaces providing light, air, color, and repose. During this period gardens were remodelled along the Champs-Elysees, Jardin du Luxembourg, the Tuileries, and along the boulevards. Axes were strengthened and accented with the introduction of garden strips and avenues of trees in single or double rows. Haussman's major achievement as an organizer, more than as a technician, changed the face of Paris within fifteen years and established a communication system, a park system, and a new sense of unity for this elegant city. The quintessential characteristics of French civilization unfolds in the visual images and impressions of its great public spaces.

Across the Channel in England

The gradual loosening in the formality of garden art was carried across the channel into the natural landscape gardens of England. English taste had moved toward an aesthetic acceptance of the principle of irregularity in nature and in art. The picturesque garden represented a change in kind to some extent, however, it retained features of its continental predecessors. The aesthetic experience was controlled through a series of formal gardens with a definite visual focus close to the mansion. In addition, greater emphasis was placed on the kitchen garden. Beyond the formal gardens, the carefully engineered natural landscape attempted to draw on the graces of the surrounding landscape and distant views.

The Picturesque landscape garden or park is typified by the work of Lancelot "Capability" Brown during the early eighteenth century. Among the garden commissions of this designer were those at Blenheim, Castle Howard, and Chiswick. Brown may be credited with changing the course of

English garden history and establishing a new conceptual heritage. The justification for the natural garden blindly encouraged the removal of all traces of the former formal gardens of Renaissance England. Thus it was Brown who initiated the creation of the picturesque and the understated but in the process destroyed some of the lovely remnants of a former era.

The natural garden contained such features as rolling hills, pastures with grazing cows, ponds or small rivers with architectural bridges, an orangerie, a temple, obelisk, clumps of trees, shrubs and flowers, woodland, and meandering paths. The *ha-ha* embankment wall was purely an English invention for the modern landscape, introduced to give the allusion of a contiguous landscape . . . a foss that sets free the garden lawn "from its prim regularity, that it might assort with the wilder country outside."[42] An ancient device, the ha-ha served the purpose of a sunken fence that allowed the destruction of walls for boundaries. It was an invisible barrier; an instrument used to hold back livestock and deer.

Great country houses in England are an important aspect of the cultural heritage. For the painfully class-conscious English society these mansions became symbols of status. Even before the popularity of the "natural" garden, these privileged dwellings dotted the countryside. Hampton Court, Penshurst, and Knole, among the earliest of the country houses, bore great resemblance to the villas and chateaux of the Continent. The later natural gardens reflected a desire for a greater harmony with nature. Even as economic wealth and aristocratic privileged declined, eliminating the viability of great mansions, the form of the modified country homes embraced by the emerging capitalistic class, addressed the same principles of site design: visual manipulation of receding perspective and multi-directional views.

Renaissance England

Generally, little opportunity remains to learn much about the development of the English garden at the time of the Renaissance. Gardens today seem to combine a modern fancy with an inherited art that lacks historically sound tracings to this early period. Not until the latter quarter of the seventeenth century were there copperplate engravings and pictures. However, lovely descriptions of the English garden found in literary works of the period allow these gardens to live again.

Henry VIII inherited a series of royal gardens in 1509. But it was his powerful minister Cardinal Wolsey, who embraced the new garden art which was favored across the channel on the Continent. Wolsey consulted learned men of London and Padua to aid in the design of his new residence and garden at Hampton Court. After extensive research and thoughtful study, the site was specially selected for its fine situation. By 1516 the castle was ready to receive guests and soon became the center of gay festivities and masquerades. Henry VIII was fond of visiting the gardens in disguise to enjoy the music and revelry, later revealing himself to statemen with whom he took long walks discoursing an affairs of state. In an expedient political gesture the flamboyant Wolsey subsequently presented his castle to Henry VIII.

The interdependence between the English social and political milieux is typified by legislation resulting in the modification of environment, the establishment of a new garden prototype, and the intensification of social class disparity. In 1541 the growing popularity of tennis, a sport imported from France, resulted in the diminishing skill in archery. Concern relating to military strategic needs caused tennis to be prohibited in public places. The wealthy class began to acquire tennis licenses and lay down courts as a part of their private gardens.

Henry VIII was succeeded by two of his daughters, who only indirectly influenced the formality of garden design and use. It is said that Queen Mary loved flowers. Upon visits to Hampton Court as a princess, she received bunches of flowers from the gardener. Although her gardens were lovely, she was not a builder of new gardens. Nor was Queen Elizabeth, who did not share her father's need to surpass all others in matters of gardens and buildings. Instead, she encouraged nobles to take pride in creating their own more splendid surroundings. She reinforced this aspect of flattering them with her visits. However, at Hatfield the cult of mulberry trees was well known. It is said that Queen Elizabeth personally set out four prize specimens.

Sociopolitical Implications

The configuration of the English garden was a response to the equivocal sociopolitical nature of English society; the rigid ideas of social class, of pomposity and propriety; English climate and terrain; and to a greater acceptance of the influence of the natural environment. Changing attitudes stemming from the opening up of the Orient greatly influenced the latter point.

Urban Landscape

The concept of the term *square,* or open area for public use and gathering, has existed throughout the history of civilization. Public gardens had been laid out in ancient cultures; for example, the Porticus Livia in Rome. However, the public park, as it is known today, essentially has evolved since the beginning of the nineteenth century. Prior to that time the park was an area of land or a garden adjacent to a grand home, developed according to axial and spatial principles employed in garden art and urban design.[43] Occasionally these private parks were open for public use on certain days. A number of estates were subsequently acquired by the towns, most notably the Royal Parks of London to which the people of London have long enjoyed access. As early as 1635 Charles I opened Hyde Park to the public. It was here that numerous great occasions were celebrated.

The Landscape Movement, as it was first expressed in the urban environment, established the creation of new urban parks exclusively for private use and enjoyment requiring membership to enter. Systems reflecting the ingenuity of the British class system allowed the high-placed gentleman and his lady and children to mingle with select company, even in such public places as the private city park. In Bath in the 1760s the Circus and Royal Crescent, and subsequently Landsdowne Crescent and the Queen's Square, were designed for private purposes. Similarly, the wholly fashionable squares in London were solely for the use of persons living in surrounding dwellings. Access into these squares, which were enclosed with wrought iron fences and gates, was gained with a key. However, visual penetration could not be prevented thereby adding to the charm and open space of the town. The quality of spatial ambience provided enjoyment for everybody in that even from the outside looking inward one experiences visual delight.

The urban city *square,* a symbolic interpretation of the transformed country house, was typically a neighborhood park bounded by low-scaled townhouse-type dwellings. The townhouses themselves were designed to relate more symbolically to the park than to each other. These urban squares succeeded in providing a void of space in the tight urban fabric. The green plants also created a pleasant microclimate.

Incorporating recreational landscapes within the town for public use and enjoyment is essentially Victorian. A zealous desire for reform stemmed from abhorrent conditions brought about by the rapidly growing industrial town. People began to realize during the late 1830s that they were "living on a dung heap."[44] There were those who sought means of changing this condition. The public park was undoubtedly one device to influence a refinement of the public domain. It was to have "high moral value as well as more prosaic ones"[45] and would reinforce the aspirations of polite society.

English urban landscape and park design displayed the same combinations found in garden art: formality, stage set, and informality; deviation from rigid symmetry and rectilinear geometric forms. There were fashionable pleasure gardens as well as public walks to bring advantages to humbler classes, the redesign of the Crown Parks and the creation of the Queen Victoria Parks. One should not fail to mention the urban designs and dwellings of John Nash and the Crystal Palace and park plans of John Paxton, both among the significant contributors to English design.

Garden as an art form was the concern of the prolific writing and work of John C. Loudon, an advocate of the Gardenesque style. Following his death in 1843, his wife, Jane, published books on landscape in her own name. Jane Loudon's *Gardening for Ladies* was also published in the United States in 1852 at the direction of noted landscape architect, Andrew Jackson Downing.[46] Although women are infrequently mentioned in English literature of the period except as users, the title of the book suggests that women were indeed actively involved in land use and garden art, particularly on the private level. Certainly participation in horticultural societies (such as the Royal Horticultural Society, the rose and chrysanthemum societies) was a common activity of the elite leading eventually to more professionally trained women.

Challenge to Existing Taste

The history of the English garden and urban landscape was periodically the subject of fierce verbal battle and challenge to existing taste. The Picturesque of the "Capability" Brown school of the eighteenth century was criticized by the evolving Repton Victorian school of the nineteenth century which in turn became the scene of controversy for the Loudon Gardenesque. The Formalist school of thought of the 1890s repeated the same verbose ammunition in stating its philosophy. Among the foremost protagonists of this warfare were John Sedding, William Robinson, and Gertrude Jekyll.

Architect John Sedding was primarily concerned with the formal character of the garden near the house . . . order, geometry, and an awareness of plant material and its decorative capabilities. William Robinson registered scathing criticism against all formal garden design. He propounded the view that the purpose of the garden was to capture on a small scale the precious loveliness of vegetation as found in its natural habitat. This was not the romantic concept of wilderness attributed to the Picturesque; it was the botanical or cultural idea expressed in exquisite natural visual effects. It chided the Gardenesque for its almost constant need of maintenance. Curiously enough, Robinson's wild gardens seldom achieved the unity possessed by the formal garden.

Brilliant balance between formal and informal garden design was successfully perfected by Gertrude Jekyll. Miss Jekyll skillfully adapted the system advocated by Robinson into a garden setting of natural beauty and order. As an accomplished painter who possessed great knowledge of plants and practical expertise as a gardener, she was able to combine her interests to great advantage. She had a profound admiration for the French Impressionists who generated a metaphorical influence over her compositions.[47] Many of the prominent artists and philosophers of her day were personal acquaintances.

Gertrude Jekyll was a prolific writer on themes of nature, gardens, and land use.[48] Her books, like her garden designs, stressed the intrinsic reciprocity between garden art and its meaning for the individual. Her work represents the conscious intention of combining architectural form with plantings—illusion of the mind harboring images of the landscapes. Her remarkable powers of visualization were elaborated upon in a prodigious 350 gardens which she designed.[49] The unified assemblage of ideas, fundamental to her garden plans, found expression in the wide variety of plant materials, construction devices, and intepretive effects.

Miss Jekyll's rewarding association with Sir Edwin Lutyens resulted in an extended collaboration on some of the finest country houses and gardens. The source of their earliest commissions was family and friends. This soon broadened to the growing class of highly successful, self-made merchants, industrialists and intelligencia rather than the old aristocracy. Lutyens first become intimately acquainted with her early work at Munstead Wood, Jekyll's own home, where she was able to experiment. This garden became the catalyst for the emphasis on the alliance between house and gardens; or architecture and landscape, as a means to increase the total level of richness. By example and precept, Lutyens and Jekyll demonstrated just how much beauty might exist. While based upon traditional imagery, their treasured landscapes drew on a modern expression.

The qualities found in the primitive simplicity of vernacular farmhouses and buildings of the seventeenth and eighteenth century prompted study and visits by Lutyens and Jekyll. Compositional attitudes concerning detailing and massing were derived from these antecedents. Infused with romantic references and symbolic notions, the physical presence of the landscape was an abundant storehouse of ideas. The geometric structure of the house is extended into the whole site or into garden elements. Although always subordinate to the entrance of the building, the garden retains its place as an intrinsic perceptual piece of the composition.

Design on a Grand Scale—Delhi

The twentieth century baroque planning of the Viceroy's residence and capital at Imperial Delhi in India by Lutyens with consultation of Jekyll successfully blends the elements of the Mughal Garden tradition with a series of complex geometric forms. The effect is a highly original design on the grand scale of a public garden. Parks occur incidentally between great formal avenues. The conceptual intent respects the complex set of axes, the proximity of the existing site to Delhi, the grandeur appropriate to a great capital with its own local situations. Lutyens's soaring imagination, together with the results of the immeasurable achievements of his collaboration with Jekyll, enabled Lutyens to produce a work to delight fantasy and function.

An Emerging Design Force—The Influence of Women

The developing interest of women in both the public and private realm of landscape design emerged as a dominant force at this time. From the social and botanic involvement in horticultural societies, women now receive formal training and education in the field: at first primarily in landscape architecture, and more recently in architecture and urban design as well. Although generally less well known as designers than their male counterparts, women have gained a position of prominence and respect for their research and documentation.

Continuing the thrust of the work of Gertrude Jekyll, women now affirm their own identity. Among the prominent authors and authorities on the historical and philosophical ideologies of great gardens and landscape are Georgina Masson, Eugenia Sheppard, Edith Wharton, Elizabeth McDougal, and Marie Louise Gotheim.

The Garden City: An Extension of an Idea

The growth of the public park was extended and transformed into a larger conceptual image—the garden city. This was to be a setting for private dwellings and public buildings interwoven into the green tapestry of winding pedestrian paths and recreational facilities. The stimulus for the creation of the garden city was the increasingly dreadful condition of the industrial city. Ebeneezer Howard is credited for the garden city movement. The conceptual framework and ideology of the garden city has been explored in schematic transformations in search of the ideal reality in new communities across the European continent and in the Americas.

A New Landscape: The United States

Urban streets, public parks, and even private gardens of the United States have felt the influence of European gardens and urban-design concepts. The dominant relationship is with the natural English gardens and urban landscape attitudes stemming from the strong Anglo-Saxon heritage. Some cities in the United States, such as Savannah, were planned on a tight orthagonal grid that incorporated public squares as the prime unifying and structural symbols. Conversely, many other cities are devoid of strong form-giving elements which promote urban order and image making.

An indigenous influence on urban landscape concepts of this nation is typified by the Jefferson's and Thoreau's notions of the glorification of the countryside, the attitudes of rugged individualism, and an expansive amount of available rural land. These interrelated influences are reflected in the city-park systems of many of the cities. The parks combine small formal squares and large natural preserves of woodland and green open space. Frederick Law Olmstead took great care to adapt the English landscape concepts to the new circumstances of Central Park in New York City in 1856. Central Park was of integral importance to the life of that city, and significant to the development of our urban parks. In addressing urban-design issues in Washington, D.C., however, Olmstead respected the existing plans by L'Enfant and Ellicott, based upon Versailles. His work for the gardens and terraces of the Capitol and environs of the Mall, therefore, focused on the formality of the Italian villa and French chateau.

The United States does not have an accumulated tradition of design principles for the making of cohesive urban spaces.

Following the custom of many European gardens, there are a number of great estates in the United States which are now open to the public. One such is Biltmore, the Vanderbilt mansion by Robert Morris Hunt in North Carolina. Another is Dumbarton Oaks, known not so much for the architecture of the house as for its collection of Byzantine and Pre-Columbian art and wonderful garden. The garden was designed by Beatrix Farrand (the Gertrude Jekyll of the United States) for the Robert Woods Bliss family of Washington, D.C. [50] It is noted for its unusually fine specimens of plantings; its careful attention to detail and ornamentation of such features as stairs, gates, benches, pools, stonework and fences. Its picturesque attitude combines the formal with the informal. The transition from one "garden room" to another is so skillfully accomplished that one is greeted with visual delight and surprise at each new space.

Transformations in Ideal and Identity

The scenes of the urban landscape present physical images which suggest ideal images of a liveable environment. The formal properties of the present-day Western city are derived from two roots: the structure of its spaces (streets and open space), and the structure of its solids (a more or less contiguous arrangement of buildings). The volumetric characteristics and inter-

dependent combination of elements (ornament) function literally and meta-
phorically to assume the attributes of urban room or urban landscape.

A precondition to the making of a place is the articulation of a high
degree of order. In the antilandscape situation in many urban areas, no specific hierarchical unifying order exists. Ambiguity is manifested in the spatial reading of form, use, and contextual continuity. The concept of sequential spatial progression or promenade, inherently necessary to make a
"landscape," often has been neglected in the contemporary American city.

Historically certain dominant devices have served to characterize form.
The contemporary city has been dominated by abstract forms of industrial
and scientific production which serve as a composite mode of representation of the city. From the Renaissance through the beginning of nineteenth
century, the vision of the garden with its controlled unifying vistas and horizontal spatial paths and networks were drawn on for presentation and
transformation in the urban landscape. Thus the picturesque and its aesthetic sensation and attendant rules of composition, claimed expression and
imitation.

Communication rests on tradition and structure in the environment.[51]
Fundamental to this notion are the relationships between anticipation and
retrospection and between fantasy and memory. The notion of the utopian
ideal of what the city might be should recognize the limitations of evaluation based on immediate visual and practical criteria "for its rationale is
cosmic and metphysical; and here, of course, lies its peculiar ability to
impose itself on the mind."[52] Realizing the dynamic nature of society, "so
there are no criteria which cannot be faulted, which are not in continuous
fluctuation with their opposites."[53]

In the cities of the past the garden outside the city "discloses what the
city ought to be. The garden, as a criticism of the city, a criticism which the
city abundantly acknowledged,"[54] represented a prophetic vision of an
energetic affirmative theme. The controlling idea is essentially one of unity,
that is a unity of inclusion. This implies an acceptance of the richness of
complexity and duality and of the complete organism (the garden or the
urban landscape) as an accumulation of fragments and set pieces. Implicit is
a hierarchal system of spatial order, of solids and voids, expressed in the
city as in the garden.

The city as an emotive place promotes infinite levels of meaning. The
idea of continuity does not seek solutions of mere reproduction but the
amplification of respect. The conditions for assertive identity in urban
design envisage an understanding and sensitivity to its physical and social
aspects. Wit and imagination must find a place among the multiplicity of
design experiences.

The ideality of the modern movement in architecture frequently
neglected to consider some of these fundamental perceptual sensitivities of

the human being. Increasingly it would seem that the idea of freedom from clutter, of ultimate simplicity has left many of us with a growing feeling of sterility. Dissatisfaction with the directional mode of our recently constructed environment has fostered a state of discomfort. Architecture as object in itself has denied the relevance of context in the immediate sense. It therefore has separated architecture from landscape, building from street. We have been seduced into adopting illusive spatial images without understanding the consequences.

The repertory of accessories of the urban landscape are manifestations of a particular response to a particular culture, need, idea, and time. The idea of transformation of fragments is a condition of contradiction, a dialectic of past and future, which seeks to subvert the old in the creation of the new. As we aspire to the imperfect image of the built environment, we seek the ideas that affirm meaning and identity. The ephemeral components of our symbol systems and perceptual formulations need metaphoric expression in easily identifiable architectual and garden fragments which create ambience in urban landscape.

As the historical development of garden and park is traced as a philosophical and conceptual idea that has been projected as an ideal model into the urban environment, there is a decided absence of women among the names of those who have been instrumental in shaping the reality of the world in which we live. Investigation of existing descriptive literature leads to the assumption that the influence of women on gardens and land use during the Italian Renaissance was practically nil. If women filled the role of consultant in such matters, it is not noted in historical texts which expressly link Italian villas and palazzos to their male owners or designers. There are accounts of women serving as inspiration (both positive and negative) for gardens. Edmund Wilson writes of the brutally distorted sculptural figures at Bomarzo, so disfigured to reflect the host's pain stemming from his wife's romantic involvement with another member of his family.

One notices, therefore, the emergence of several new roles for women in the hitherto male-dominated realm of the environment, as revealed in various sources dealing with France and England where women have had considerable impact. Those women of wealth and advantaged social class had more leisure with which to delve into the utopian world of the garden. It is not surprising that the convergence of the formal aspects of design with the enlightened interest in botanic specimens became the focus of orientation for both men and women. This paralleled changes in philosophical and economical development and scientific experimentation.

Initially, women have played several roles: patron-consultants or user-participants but never professional designers. The Industrial Revolution brought about great changes. Women were needed to work in production. The resultant liberalization in societal mores allowed women the opportun-

ity to make new choices. One choice was the traditional role as expressed by
John Kenneth Galbraith in *Annals of an Abiding Liberal:*

> The decisive economic contribution of women (apart from the economic
> disadvantaged) in the developed industrial society is rather simple—or at
> least it so becomes once the disguising myth is dissolved. It is, overwhelm-
> ingly, to make possible a continuing and more or less unlimited increase in
> the sale and use of consumer goods . . . for economic growth.[55]

This requires increased production and, it follows, increased consumption.
The role of the woman, the wife, becomes that of administrator and man-
ager. With greater family income the greater the complexity of the function,
as well as the social competition for excellence among the exhibitors. This
includes excellence in the quality, taste, and imagination of house and garden. Therefore, many women of superior education and intelligence performed the social rites and in so doing became quite expert in the area of
garden and land use design. Some chose the avenue of the garden club
and the horticulture societies. Some developed proficiency to the extent that
their services were solicited for financial remuneration. There is a growing
number who have made the choice to seek education and work in professions concerned with land use.

    We cannot precisely establish whether the involvement of women as
writers or designers of the environment has made a contribution that differs
in attitude from that of men. It does appear that the perceptual response to
those formative situations which women have influenced have had the
effect of creating a humanizing, spatially ordered landscape.

    Our cities, in a metaphoric sense, have been ultimately the evocation of
the vocabulary of the realm of urban garden; our streets, the celebrated
grande allées. The elements of the dwelling-garden have been fragmented
into our streets and plazas to accommodate the context of urbanity. The
simultaneous perception of unity between artifice and environment has
been the domain of our cultural urban heritage. It is toward that harmonious end, the reconciliation of the aesthetic, social and functional mode, that
is the promise of the urban landscape: relationships to transform the ideal,
delight the senses, and inspire the mind.

Notes

1. Tuan, Yi-Fu. *Topophilia: a Study of Environmental Perception,
Attitudes, and Values* (Englewood Cliffs, New Jersey: Prentice-Hall, Inc.,
1974). p. 113

2. Beck, Robert, "Spatial Meaning," from *Environmental Perception and Behavior,* Lowenthal, David, editor, p. 19. (Chicago, Illinois: University of Chicago Press, 1967).

3. Harbison, Robert, *Eccentric Spaces* (New York: Alfred A. Knopf, 1977), p. 3–4.

4. Arnheim, Rudolf, *The Dynamics of Architectural Form* (Berkeley: University of California Press, 1976), p. 9–12.

5. Gotheim, Marie Luise, *A History of Garden Art,* Vol. I (New York, London: E.P. Dutton and Company Ltd., 1928), p. 207–208.

6. Clifford, Derek, *A History of Garden Design* (New York: Frederick A. Praeger, 1963), p. 18.

7. Ibid., p. 21.

8. Tuan, Topophilia, p. 139.

9. Ibid., p. 137.

10. Clifford, *A History of Garden Design,* p. 20.

11. Gotheim, *A History of Garden Art,* p. 207.

12. Ibid., p. 207.

13. Ibid., p. 280.

14. Ibid., p. 281.

15. Ibid., p. 288.

16. Clifford, *A History of Garden Design,* p. 36.

17. Gotheim, *A History of Garden Art,* p. 299.

18. Ibid., p. 232.

19. Tuan, Topophilia, p. 139.

20. Clarke, David, "Notes on 'Epistle to Richard Boyle, Earl of Burlington,' " *Journal of Architectural Education,* vol. 32, no. 3 (Feb. 1979), p. 8.

21. Clifford, *A History of Garden Design,* p. 68.

22. Tuan, *Topophilia,* p. 140.

23. Rowe, Colin, and Koetter, Fred, *Collage City, Architectural Review* (April 1975):80.

24. Ibid., p. 81–82.

25. Clarke, "Notes on 'Epistle to Richard Boyle, " p. 8.

26. Gotheim, *A History of Garden Art,* p. 204, (Vol. II).

27. Adams, William Howard, *Atget's Garden* (New York: Doubleday and Company, 1979), p. 20.

28. Ibid., p. 24.

29. Ibid., p. 25.

30. Gotheim, *A History of Garden Art,* p. 104 (Vol. II).

31. Adams, *Atget's Garden,* p. 28.

32. Jouanin, Christian, "Josephine and the Natural Sciences," in *Apollo, The Empress Josephine and the Arts,* Denys Sutton, editor (London, July 1977):p. 52–55.

33. Adams, *Atget's Garden,* p. 33.

34. Ibid., p. 33.

35. Gotheim, *A History of Garden Art,* p. 428–430 (Vol. I).

36. Adams, *Atget's Garden,* p. 36.

37. Chadwick, George F., *The Park and the Town: Public Landscape in the Nineteenth and Twentieth Centuries* (New York: Frederick A. Praeger, 1966), p. 154.

38. Ibid., p. 158.

39. Ibid., p. 159.

40. Jarrett, David, *The English Landscape Garden* (London: Academy Editions, 1978), p. 10.

41. Ibid., p. 11–12.

42. Ibid., p. 12.

43. Chadwick, *The Park and the Town,* p. 19.

44. Ibid., p. 112.

45. Ibid., p. 181.

46. Ibid., p. 164.

47. Ibid., p. 247.

48. Dutton, Ralph, *The English Garden* (London: B.T. Batsford, 1937), p. 99.

49. Chadwick, *The Park and the Town,* p. 247.

50. Hatfield, Miles, *Gardens* (New York: G.P. Putnam's Sons, 1962), p. 107.

51. Schumacher, Thomas "Buildings and Streets: Notes on Configuration and Use," in *On Streets,* Anderson, Stanford, editor (Cambridge, Massachusetts: MIT Press, 1978), p. 139–141.

52. Rowe, Colin, *The Mathematics of the Ideal Villa and Other Essays* (Cambridge, Massachusetts: MIT Press, 1976), p. 206.

53. Ibid., p. 216.

54. Rowe, Colin and Koetter, Fred, *Collage City,* p. 78.

55. Galbraith, John Kenneth, *Annals of an Abiding Liberal* (Boston: Houghton Mifflin, 1979), p. 38.

References

Acton, Harold. *Tuscan Villas.* (Italy: Thames and Hudson, 1973).

Anderson, Stanford, editor. *On Streets.* selected articles by Vidler, Anthony; Ellis, William C.; Schumacher, Thomas; Wolf, Peter, Cambridge, Massachusetts: MIT Press, 1978.

Bacon, Edmund N. *Design of Cities.* New York: Penguin Books, 1967.

Coffin, David, editor. *The Italian Garden,* Dumbarton Oaks, Harvard University: Washington, D.C., 1972.

Collins, George R. and Collins, Christiane C. *Camillo Sitte and the Birth of Modern City Planning*. London: Phaidon Press, 1965.

Elgood, George S., RI, and Jekyll, Gertrude. London: Longmans, Green and Company, 1905.

Fawcett, Jane, editor. *Seven Victorian Architects*. London: Thames and Hudson, 1976.

Franck, Carl L. *The Villas of Frascati*. London: Alec Tiranti, 1966.

Girourard, Mark. *Life in the English Country House*. New York: Penguin Books, 1978.

Greenwood, W.E. *Villa Madama, Rome*. New York: William Helburn, Inc.

Hatfield, Miles. *The Art of the Garden*. New York: Dutton Vista, 1965.

Howard, Ebenezer. *Garden Cities of Tomorrow*. London: Faber and Faber, 1946.

Jekyll, Gertrude and Weaver, Lawrence. *Gardens for Small Country Houses*. London: Country Life, 1912.

Lansdale, Maria H. *The Chateaux of Touraine*. New York: The Century Company, 1905.

Lavedan, Pierre. *Histoire de L' Urbanisme*. Paris: Henri Laurens, 1959.

———. *French Architecture*. London: Penguin Books, 1956.

Masson, Georgina. *Italian Villas and Palaces*. London: Thames and Hudson, 1959.

———. *Italian Gardens*. London: Thames and Hudson, 1961.

Miltoun, Francis. *Royal Palaces and Parks of France*. Boston: L.C. Page and Company, 1916.

Shepherd, J.C. and Jellicoe, G.A. *Italian Gardens of the Renaissance*. London: Alec Tiranti, 1953.

Venturi, Robert. *Complexity and Contradiction*. New York: Museum of Modern Art, 1966.

Vidler, Anthony, editor. "Oppositions," selected articles by Vidler, Anthony; Grumbach, Antoine; Brooks, Peter. Cambridge, Massachusetts: MIT Press, Spring, 1977:8.

Weaver, Lawrence. *Houses and Gardens by Sir Edwin Lutyens*. London: Country Life, 1913.

Wharton, Edith. *Italian Villas and Their Gardens*. New York: The Century Company, 1908.

Wilson, Edmund. *The Devils and Canon Barham*. New York: Farrar, Straus, and Giroux, 1968.

9 Women and Urban Parks: Their Roles as Users and Suppliers of Park Services

Galen Cranz

This chapter reviews the status of women in urban parks both as users and suppliers of recreational services from a historical perspective. Based on case studies of New York, Chicago, and San Francisco, the paper looks at the role of women as actors and pawns in the history of efforts to solve urban problems (1850 to 1979).

Women have had different statuses in each of the four periods of American urban-park history. In the pleasure-garden era (1850 to 1900) women's role as users was largely restricted to a family role; as suppliers they worked through the channels of philanthropy. In the reform-park era (1900 to 1930) age differentiation dictated different offerings for mothers, children, and workers. As suppliers they worked primarily through social-work agencies or the recreation division, rather than the park division, of municipal departments. In the era of the recreation facility (1930 to 1965) women were hired to do men's jobs during the war and for the first time were appointed to the boards of park commissioners. In the era of the open-space system (1965 to the present) females were less important than riot-prone youths, but as middle-class shoppers they were the focus of attention and consequently influenced the form of the vest-pocket park. As suppliers of recreational service they brought the arts into the parks and continued to serve, albeit as a token minority, as commissioners.

The chapter analyzes the demographic characteristics of male versus female commissioners, the different kinds of problems that interested male versus female commissioners, the pattern of staff positions held by women and men. Finally, the chapter concludes with some suggestions for how women might claim parks as a means to serve their needs and their societal goals.

Presented at the Symposium on Leisure Research, New Orleans, 28 to 29 October 1979. The theme of women as park users is fully elaborated in "Women and Urban Parks," *Signs* (Spring 1980). The theme of women as park–policy makers is in "Women and Urban Parks: Their Roles as Users and Policy Makers," *Lincoln Institute of Land Use Policy*, Cambridge, Massachusetts, 8 November 1979. For an intermediate draft write the Institute of Urban and Regional Development, University of California, Berkeley, California, 94720.

Introduction

American urban parks were a nineteenth-century creation, designed to right the imbalances of industrialization and urbanization. Parks were one of the first welfare institutions—right after sewer systems and before all but the most rudimentary housing, welfare, and school regulation—that municipalities adopted as an appropriate government function. Mid-nineteenth-century policy makers were cautious about deliberate intervention in the theoretically free market economy; at that time parks were a big first step toward state spending. Their justification was that a judicious land-use policy could be a mechanism of urban reform. City leaders hoped to ameliorate class conflict, family disintegration, the commercialization of culture, density, pollution, disease, and psychological stress.

Over time political and cultural leaders perceived different sets of urban problems, each, in turn, corresponding to an underlying concept about the nature of the city. They adjusted their notions about what kind of parks would best solve these problems accordingly. Four different ideal types have emerged since the 1850s as the most suitable ways to redress urban problems. They are the pleasure garden (1850 to 1900), the reform park (1900 to 1930), the recreation facility (1930 to 1965), and the open-space system (1965 to the present).[1]

The significance of parks for urban–land use lies as much in their history as in their present life. Parks have had a physical impact on the city in that their sites often shaped patterns of urban development, especially the location of wealthy residential areas and transit lines. Present patterns of open space and built areas are a product of past site selection. The pattern of institutional development is also largely the product of the parks movement. It was one of the first urban-reform movements, enveloping to a greater or lesser extent the issues of public health, class conflict, mental health, delinquency, alcoholism, prostitution, child welfare, family welfare, traffic congestion, and slum clearance. Many of these other urban-reform movements have since distinguished themselves from the park movement, but the origin of urban-reform institutions often lies imbedded within the same groups who agitated for public parks.

Women have been involved with these issues primarily as users and secondarily as policy makers. Each model had distinctive assumptions about how women should use each park type and about what ends would be served as a consequence; the ways in which park leadership has tried to deploy females have varied with the historical perceptions of what was wrong with society and the city. But leadership has consistently used women to solve other problems rather than treating them as a users' group in their own right.

Assumptions about female use of public parks partially limited women's range of possible behaviors. The link between parks and public life meant that assumptions about female behavior in parks potentially influenced women's general civic involvement, not only their activities within parks themselves.

Women played a minor role in the formulation of park policy, relative to that of men. Yet some served as commissioners, employees, or volunteers. Up to now, those few women have usually shared the male diagnoses of contemporaneous problems. The records do not reveal differences of opinion between male- and female-policy makers; nor do they show distinctive ideas coming from women. Official records are unlikely to report any conflict whatsoever and probably not likely to credit female employees, commissioners, volunteers, or philanthropists with introducing an idea. Nevertheless, if women ever appropriate parks to meet their own needs and solve their own problems, we can anticipate a new park type, different from the preceding four.

Women as Users

Women in the Pleasure Garden (1850 to 1900)

Nineteenth-century reformers believed that the family could cushion the individual from many urban stresses, yet they feared that the family itself was being undermined. Women's central role in the family meant that urban reform and women were often linked explicitly. The park commissioners, not wanting to compete with the home as the proper mechanism of moral reform, insisted that the park would help reinforce the family unit. Park advocates thought that a respectable setting where a woman could appear in public with her husband would contribute to a family's sense of itself. Additionally, "A large use of the Park by families, by good women and dutiful children," would set a tone that would demand high standards for public behavior from everyone.[2]

For a public setting to function in these ways, it had to be a respectable setting for middle-class women, and accordingly an endless theme was that the park must be made a safe resort for unprotected ladies, women, mothers, wives, and children. Since the park was to be a respectable setting for women alone or in the company of men, refreshments were ideally nonalcoholic, although municipalities experimented with wine and beer in order to broaden the appeal of park restaurants. Since the park was for respectable women, prostitutes were automatically excluded from park life.

Women's ideal role was not as a user of facilities for games and sports but as a stabilizing presence. Nevertheless, women, especially young women, were responsible for much of the burgeoning interest in athletics. They began to play lawn tennis, croquet, and basketball, and to ride bicycles in the 1890s. When girls, wives, and mothers diverted from their passive function—as they did almost immediately—newspapers responded with disbelief and disdain. Despite psychological ambivalence and denial on the part of reporters, they noted in the same breath that women used park facilities more than did men.[3]

The artistic images of women's role in public parks were slow to acknowledge the reality of their active sports life. Artists, like park planners, confirmed the ideal that women would be tied to the family and their men, while extending a calming presence on the public scene. In photographs, however, the ideal is betrayed by reality: women are seen in pairs teaching each other how to skate or fixing their own bicycles and equipment without help from men.[4]

Women in the Reform Park (1900 to 1930)

Settlement house workers wanted to bring wholesome recreational opportunities to the working class, especially the "children and women of the wage-earning families," who had neither the time nor the money to travel to the outlying pleasure grounds.[5] At the same time playground advocates wanted to ensure that urban children got enough physical exercise in a safe setting. At the turn of the century park and playground advocates successfully pressured for legislation to create the small park in the heart of the dense tenements. Because this new park was a part of the larger progressive era, its purposes are succinctly summarized by the term *reform park*.

In order to counteract the commercialization of culture and at the same time organize the working person's unprecedented increase in leisure time, reformers hoped to replace movies, dance halls, and saloons with wholesome sports. However, they decided they had better accept the popularity of social dances by sponsoring and chaperoning them closely rather than pretend they did not exist.

Park promoters wanted to use the park to assimilate immigrants, reduce nervousness, and fight delinquency. Park departments all around the country took special pride in the potential of the park movement to reduce juvenile delinquency. Since this problem was defined by and large as a male problem, park administrators did not even collect statistics for girl offenders.

Both women and girls began to use the parks for active sports in the pleasure-garden era. Thus their increasing participation after 1900 was not the dramatic reversal claimed by reform-park theorists, but an acceleration and rationalization of a previously established behavior. The reform-park philosophy began to catch up with this reality by treating women as users in their own right and not primarily as instruments through which to influence men's behavior.

The relationship between the sexes changed dramatically. The pleasure garden emphasis on the family unit entailed both age and sex integration; in contrast, the reform model turned age and sex segregation into virtues. The theoretical justification was grounded in developmental theory:

> The psychological, sociological, and physiological factors involved in the play interests of a group of sixteen-year-old boys differ from the interests of a group of seven-year-old boys, and the interests of a group of fourteen-year-old girls differ from both. Separate and distinct gymnasiums, therefore, with apparatus of the character, sizes, and heights adapted to these groups' interests were planned and installed.[6]

The family would no longer use the park, but its individual members would use it as their own time schedules permitted, set by the rhythms of their own schooling or work. Park organizers divided the day into sections and offered programming appropriate to the school children who would come before and after class, the mothers who would bring toddlers in the late morning, the working men who might take lunch breaks there, working boys and girls who could visit in the evening after work and dinner. Idealists no longer used the park as a setting for trying to counter the fragmented, scheduled rhythms of urban industrial life but rather attempted to integrate it temporally as well as physically with the surrounding industrialism.

Designers divided parks into separate spaces for each age and sex. If males and females or different age groups happened to use the park at the same time of day, staff expected them to use the part designed for them. The outdoor gymnastic equipment for men and women was located at opposite ends of the park, with a building or trees, shrubbery, and lawns in between. Furthermore, a fence enclosed the women's area, in turn concealed by shrubbery. (In accordance with today's preoccupation with safety, rather than propriety, this screen of shrubbery would have been eliminated and the area prominently lit in order to increase surveillance of the area.) A recurrent specification in park reports and other literature throughout this entire era was that areas of a park, and especially benches, should be reserved exclusively for the "use of women and their children."[7] Boys and girls were also segregated. The spaces, the equipment, the games, and the rules of the game all reflected sex-role differentiation. Park planners thought that segregation promoted safety (although today urban planners believe that only mixed use peoples places enough to make them safe).

The reform park also contained public baths, originally introduced as a sanitation measure, but immediately popular as a form of recreation. Soon "provision was also made for their use by women during certain restricted periods."[8] Generally, women had two days and nights each week, whereas boys and men got three days and nights.[9] In the 1920s, when mixed bathing was finally allowed in pools, attendance increased.[10]

Sexual segregation, sex-role stereotyping, and unequal treatment to the point of discrimination are closely linked. The theoretical rationale for separating boys and girls assumed that they were different and at the same time guaranteed that treatment of the sexes would not be equal. For example, boys often had a larger playground than girls, or other resources were allocated unevenly.

The park programming reinforced stereotypes on the one hand but threatened them on the other. The sheer fact of accommodating females, separate or not, suggested that women's needs for recreation were similar to males'. Furthermore, the vigor with which females pursued activities must have laid many ideals about female passivity to rest. The varied reactions to female sport left a zigzag trail of pronouncements throughout park records. The prevailing cultural attitudes toward women's ultimate goals as wives and mothers meant that athletic activity for women and girls had to be justified in terms of motherhood. Even when the public record acknowledged that girls have a competitive spirit and might like to join in athletic contests, their tournaments still had to be held under special conditions because of the widespread opinion that respectable girls could not appear in public without supervision. This was the case even after World War I, when park planners began to recognize that girls needed more freedom to engage in a wider range of sports.

Women in the Recreation Facility (1930 to 1965)

Sex-role segregation, although still practiced, began to wane in the era of the recreation facility. The practice of designing special sections of the park, playground, or beach for females dwindled.[11] Planners included more types of females in more types of activities.

Special classes for women's activities continued into the mid-thirties, but segregation reached its limits. Park departments concluded that "co-recreation parties had greater appeal than when segregation of the sexes is enforced."[12] The pragmatic impetus toward sex-role integration was that park departments wanted to increase their attendance figures, but ideology was soon hot on its trail. The emphasis in the 1950s was on family togetherness, and the idea that "Mom, Pop, and the kids must do things as a group," returning full circle via new sources to pleasure-garden attitudes toward the family.[13] In direct opposition to reform-park ideology, the recreation theorists said that a recreation program should be directed at "keeping the family together instead of separating it into skill and age groups."[14]

As females came to be perceived as less distinctive and less in need of protection, the literature no longer insisted that women should not go out alone in public. But apparently objective conditions did not change, for complaints regarding "offenses against women" became more frequent.[15]

Despite the decrease in sexual segregation, sex-role stereotyping did not decline.[16] By the end of World War II, public-relations stunts had reached a peak and programming a nadir, epitomized by Chicago's "Easter hat parade."[17] In order to combat the image of women as workers as they had been during the war, park publicity introduced photographs of women in sexually alluring poses. Sex-role stereotyping was also perpetuated through children's activities.

Women in the Open-Space System (1965 to Present)

The central goal of the open space system was to help revitalize the inner city visually, economically, and socially. The new attitude toward open space was that it was valuable wherever found. Planners abandoned previous standards regarding size, shape, topography, and location. Consequently, park departments picked sites as small as a lot for both the adult vest-pocket park and the children's totlot and adventure playground.[18] Designers believed that the value of all unbuilt spaces—streets, sidewalks, plazas, parks, and playgrounds—would be enhanced if linked together into a network. Accordingly, street–tree planting, street furniture, and attention to surfaces would help make streets and other open spaces seem continuous. Programming reinforced the idea by organizing events (*happenings*) in the streets or from one place to another through the streets.

Implicitly, the goal of central-city revitalization focused on middle-class users—the businessmen and businesswomen on their lunch breaks from downtown offices—and the upper-middle-class suburban shoppers being courted back to the central business district. Thus the needs of middle-class women for a safe and attractive urban environment have directed park planning for adults. Paley Park in New York City is an example of an environment designed for the relief of the shopper and white-collar worker: tucked between two buildings, its sheet of falling water at the back muffles traffic noise.[19]

The concern for riot control in the late 1960s meant that ghetto youth were also a target population for the park department. Cultural programming was updated to include elements of popular and hip culture: rock concerts, be-ins, experiential celebrations, dancemobiles. Keeping swimming pools open at night was credited with having directly helped keep New York City "cool" while other cities erupted in riot. Planners seldom needed to explain that "ghetto youth" were black adolescent males; girls' recreational needs have not been enunciated clearly in this era. Women's athletic needs have been acknowledged by maintaining separate programs in volleyball, basketball, and softball, while adding belly-dancing and yoga classes. Nevertheless, park programming has remained predominantly male oriented.

Women as Policy Makers and Employees

Most of the ideas about how women should behave in parks, and what good this would accomplish for the rest of society, were espoused by men. Men made the decisions and the plans for women and carried out the programs that they designed. Over time, women started to take a greater role in the organization of park affairs, but they have not yet gained enough control to enable one to assess whether or not they will bring a new vision of park service with them. The force of female influence has remained weak, despite the large numbers of women supervisors at the beginning of the reform park era.

Women participated in designing park activities as volunteers—including philanthropists, commissioners, and the civic-minded—or as paid employees. In the twentieth century the professional recreation worker has tended to replace the volunteer, in keeping with the decline of amateurism in so many spheres of life. The consequence of the rise of paid professionalism for women, whose major contribution has been through voluntary work, is a reduced arena for decision making; unless they reverse this historical trend by seeking paid positions.

Volunteers

When nineteenth-century park–fund raisers were looking for support from philanthropists, they looked to wealthy gentlemen not to women. Similarly, no women served as commissioners during the pleasure-garden era, the period of large-scale capital construction. But women philanthropists did support the neighborhood reform parks in the early twentieth century,[20] and thereafter women supported major projects in pleasure gardens as well as reform and recreation-style parks. Moreover, since the emphasis on socialization of children and direct moral tutelage made the association of women with the reform movement acceptable—childcare was perceived as in keeping with their primary roles as mothers and socializers of children—women began to serve as commissioners. In San Francisco, where the Recreation and Park Commissions remained separate for nearly fifty years, the Recreation Commission always had two female members by charter requirement. Because of this division, San Francisco's Park Commission was able to avoid women members until the two Commissions joined in 1950.[21]

After 1920 and equal suffrage, mayors began to appoint females to park commissions, in token numbers. Whether a contributory cause or one of the many effects, the rise of female appointees coincided with the decline in the occupational and social status of male commissioners.[22] In either case, both corresponded to the decline of parks in the public mind as a viable mechanism of urban reform.

Men and women have been represented equally in the passionate one-person crusades to rally support for parks.[23] In recent years, the presidents of the Friends of Central Park, the Greensward Foundation, and so forth, have been women. And women's organizations, civic clubs and charities have always been active promoters of park projects.[24] Sometimes women's organizations have even been vocally critical of park actions. Thus, after the merger of the Recreation and Park Commissions in San Francisco, women's organizations circulated a resolution claiming that the merger had hurt parks and demanding that they be separated again.[25] In the nineteenth century such groups were influential. Newspapers claimed that the support of women's groups could make or break a reform movement. In particular, when the playground movement was first getting under way in New York City in the 1900s, its failure was attributed to several factors, among them the fact that the women in the community were ignored. During the reform era, the Annual Reports and the minutes of the cities of San Francisco, Chicago, and New York report numerous letters and delegations from groups of women advocating a policy, requesting the establishment of a park, or offering some recreation-related service.

After women were granted the vote, *Park International* ran a special article on women in park work.[26] Women's influence was thought to be different from men's; for example, women voted four and one-half to one in favor of parks, whereas men voted only two to one in their favor. The editors argued that women had a particularly strong interest in civic welfare, so that they, more than men, campaigned to turn unused land into successful parks. Then, as now, women took a special interest in both natural and architectural preservation. Restoration, rather than construction, was one of their cultural bailiwicks.

The recreation movement heralded the switch from volunteer to professional labor as "one of the most significant developments since 1900," but volunteerism did not disappear entirely. Most of the volunteers were women who offered their help during Depression unemployment, brought food to servicemen's centers during the war, worked through the numerous women's organizations which cosponsored many special events, such as the victory gardens of the wars, and the garden for the blind in the 1950s.[27]

Women's clubs were one of the major categories which a park department took into account in mounting a park campaign.[28] The League of Women Voters supported park operations, for example, by paying for a study to see how a park plan would fit into the overall master plan for a town.[29] Through community development associations women had an influence on park activities; these groups often appear in park minutes as supplicants, and women often played a substantial role in these neighborhood groups.

Park commissioners and administrators like women's support to come through voluntary organizations. Their description of this kind of help is effusive:

> Democracy brought with it . . . women's emancipation from serfdom. But more than relief from domestic drudgery and release from lives lived out behind the four walls of the home, it lent emphasis to the feminist democracy of the women's club movement. The ideals of the mothers of men are becoming articulate as this mobilization of the women of the city moves forward.[30]

They did not have to be beholden to them as they would to a big-name philanthropist; they did not have to worry about women professionals taking jobs away from men, nor volunteers inadvertently doing the same. Finally, through women's clubs, men could vicariously express their own idealism:

> Enrichment of the cultural life of their community is not their only aim . . . they are also introducing new forces of united determination that the problems of living closely associated with one another shall find happier practical solutions than a male society has yet evolved, with the brief attention men can spare from business to devote to social well-being.[31]

Through women's greater idealism, safely parceled and isolated, men could acknowledge their own altruistic side without having to change their behavior.

Employees

The landscape profession let women into its ranks only at the very end of the pleasure-garden era. At the turn of the century, the landscape gardeners, represented in San Francisco by the Pacific Coast Horticultural Society, considered whether or not ladies in the trade should be admitted into membership.[32] The American Park and Outdoor Art Association organized a Women's Auxiliary with a membership of 8, which jumped to 221 in two years.[33] When the first president of the Women's Auxiliary retired in 1903 addressed the association, one wonders just how much tongue in cheek: "My only excuse, being a woman, in speaking to park makers is that I have visited nearly all the important parks of Europe and America and know something about them, and that it may be a new experience to hear a woman's ideas about parks."[34]

In contrast to this slow acceptance of female employees in the pleasure garden, reform-park commissioners hired women professionals as readily, if not more so, than in any other profession, including education. At first women were in all ranks of employment, including the top. The most prestigious women in this field entered through their involvement with settlement-house work (for example, Mary E. McDowell in Chicago), and by the end of the era were represented by social scientists (for example, Professor Jessica Peixotto, Department of Economics at Berkeley, 1922). Suddenly, female attendants and "competent women" were hired to supervise playgrounds and public toilets.[35] During the first quarter of the century, a majority of the paid leaders were women.[36] The 1932 Yearbook of the National Recreation Association reported nearly 26,000 play leaders employed at the beginning of the recreation era. Slightly over half of them were men, which means that women were still unusually well represented in this profession.[37] However, fieldhouse directors were almost always men "of refinement, education, initiative, and social training. . . ."[38] Implicitly, only a man could be "head, guide, and promoter."[39]

Despite their equality in numbers, educational requirements and pay for men and women were always unequal. Females were more educated for the job but paid less than male instructors; the reasons were so self-evident and so just that no explanation had to be offered in either the official public records or the newspapers.[40] The New York Annual Report for 1912 stated explicitly that women's duties on the girl's side were more complicated than on the boys' side, and called for a wider diversity of talents, partly because girls' work and play required more individual instruction, but nevertheless women were paid one-half to three-quarters as much as men; the inequity was built into civil-service regulations.[41]

On the whole, women–policy makers showed no more sensitivity to women's needs than men had. In 1931 a women superintendent of the Playground Commission recommended that the commission set up a demonstration playground where mothers visiting the San Francisco Annual Food Show could leave their children. Similarly, in San Francisco in 1926, a representative of the Golden Gate Kindergarten Association, most likely female, was turned down when she asked the Playground Commission to consider the purchase of property near Mission Playground so that their group could use it for a nursery kindergarten.[42] But there is little record of pressure of this kind, and despite the influx of female administration and staff, no changes in policy occurred. This suggests that the differences

between the "pure-park" adherents and the "recreationists" were not
really male-female differences and that women were no more interested in
direct service than in an indirect impact through landscaping. Indeed the
men themselves argued the difference between a policy of maintenance and
construction and one of service. But whether or not women were more
sensitive to the needs of women and girls than men had been, they were
operating in a structure controlled if not staffed by men, so not many differences surfaced.[43]

In both World Wars park commissions had to remove restrictions
against women in order to fill certain jobs. During World War I,
women–staff members provided continuity in the face of male turnover.
Women took over men's jobs during the first World War, with the clear
understanding that this was a temporary measure. Despite female help, the
park stewards could easily overlook them: one landscape architect wrote,
"As much if not more than anyone else has the *park man* a mission to fulfill
in these days of strife and in the days of readjustment that will follow"
[emphasis added].[44]

During World War II, park bureaucrats established a new grade of
employment to allow women to assist at traffic crossings, automobile parking lots, band concerts, and special events. Females were an adjunct to the
police department, uniformed, but without the authority to make arrests.
By 1942 Chicago administration also recruited women as florists and
laborers,[45] and a year later it decided to accept female applicants for the
position of lifeguard.[46] Of the ninety women so employed, they "performed
their duties splendidly despite the fact that they were all 'rookies.' They . . .
were, for the most part, conscientious and punctual. The public accepted
the women lifeguards with very little comment and much respect."[47] Golf
course personnel also became female, but

> . . . to combat the prejudices of the public in the innovation of women
> ticket-sellers, unusual care was taken in the selection of the employees and
> a continuous program of instruction was maintained with reference to rules
> and regulations of registration, ticket sales, operation of case registers, and
> compiling of daily reports. As a result, the turnover rate was reduced and
> complaints of unsatisfactory service were rare.[48]

Eventually age limits were cut in order to recruit boys.[49] The Park Departments had to rely increasingly on boys, since women were not always available since they, too, could get higher wages in war industries.[50]

Men came to view female dominance of the new playground work as a
weakness of the recreation profession which they wanted to reverse. They
were successful during the depression, when relief spending was used primarily to hire male workers, on the grounds that their income was what

kept a family going. The practice of hiring women to fill men's jobs while they were at war was anxiety producing to those who had higher ambitions for the recreation professions. Four-fifths of the women employed throughout the nation in all fields wanted to stay in their jobs after the war (according to Chafe), but they were replaced by men.[51] Thus women lifeguards were still judged "punctual, conscientious, and obedient, and generally their work was indeed commendable" in 1946.[52] By 1951, however, the same reports did not mention women lifeguards, giving the impression that the report writers are holding their breaths in hopes that no one would remember that women had once been commendable.[53] And by 1956, after the effects of the war had evaporated, the Yearbook of the National Recreation Associated boasted that men outnumbered women in both part-time and full-time categories. The association viewed the rising percentage of men as an indicator of the increasing prestige of the profession: "This striking increase indicates a growing recognition of recreation as a worthy field for service. . . ."[54]

Still, though men silently edged women out of their leadership responsibilities in this movement, women could not be ousted entirely.[55] They were valuable because "generally girls do not come as readily to a center when there is only a male director present."[56] Another reason for keeping both male and female instructors was that they had worked out an unspoken division of labor. The men taught classes in gymnastics, square-dance calling, archery, construction, and shotting, clubwork; whereas the women taught advanced tap dancing, ballroom dancing, and millinery.[57]

Park departments created public-relations divisions during the recreation-facility era. This new kind of bureaucratic self-promotion had strange consequences for the role of women. Photographs of beautiful women were used to promote parks, but women themselves did not invent these campaigns, so in this capacity they were neither park users nor policy makers. Immediately after the war, presumably in order to help reestablish women's proper place, park reports, newspapers, and other park publications for the first time, began to show women in sexually alluring poses. For example, a "Hollywood starlet" posed as sexily and appealingly as possible with a bow and arrow to promote archery in San Francisco's parks.[58] In Chicago, the park reports show women in closeups with flowers. An upper torso and head shot of a beautiful young woman surrounded by azaleas ostensibly promoted the annual azalea and camellia show, but subliminally it promoted the idea that women are like beautiful flowers—passive, pickable, and otherwise controlled and appreciated at the will of others. Beautiful flowers, of course, should not be lifeguards and garage attendants. The pageants of the reform era became blossom-time festivals at which a woman was crowned "Blossomtime Queen."[59] If this equation of women with flowers were not enough, it was reinforced linguistically in another bizarre

way. Immediately after the war, new chrysanthemums were created by
hybridization and were named after women: Peggy Welch was a dark pink
pompom, Doris Dowling was a dark bronze, Mrs. Maree Silence an amber,
Shirley Head a pink, Flowertec a light bronze single, Miss Rita Fitzpatrick a
pink pompom anemone, and Jeanio Winters a white pompom anemone.[60]
This trivialization of women's imagery for public-relations purposes corresponded with the move to the suburbs and the removal of women from
public life.

If the goal were to honor women symbolically, other ways of doing it
were available. For example, a representative of the Illinois Federation of
Women's Clubs asked that a roadway leading to the Adler Planetarium in
Chicago be named for the first woman born in the state or for some woman
who had achieved prominence because of her outstanding work.[61] This was
rare. In 1926 the San Francisco Chinese community requested that their
local playground be named after a woman recreationist, Mildred Pollack,
but the commissioners named it after a man instead, citing their policy
against naming a park or playground for a living commissioner. In this simple act, two basic patterns are exposed: the white Anglo-Saxon commissioners, chose, rather than the Chinese community, and a male was com-
memorated rather than a female.[62]

In the open-space era, feminism surged a second time, stimulating a
number of firsts regarding female employment. The first female zookeeper
in San Francisco was appointed in 1975 at age 35, and one-third of the
applicants for the job had been women.[63] Women became park rangers in
the county, state, and federal park systems.[64] In 1976 women organized a
class-action suit against the San Francisco Park Commission for an "illegal
and discriminatory" requirement that they lift a 140-pound sack to qualify
for employment.[65] Women professionals were recruited to participate in the
new programming of the open-space model. For example, in the late 1960s
when park departments were trying to embrace the fine arts, a woman
sculptor was hired to install an exhibit of large female figures in Central
Park's Conservatory Garden. These "bountiful, full-bodied nanas" were,
according to feminist artist Niki de Saint-Phalle, "messages of joy from the
matriarchal society, which is what," she hoped, "will bring us back to
warmth and peace."[66] A feminist organizer used a park to stage a rally in
favor of the Equal Rights Amendment and to spur implementation of a
childcare initiative passed by San Francisco voters in 1973.[67] These women
were not agitating for the appropriation of Golden Gate Park itself to serve
their special needs, but they did use the park as a stage for pressing for general societal needs.

Female members of the city-planning staffs and open-space activists
have been major actors in the creation of and lobbying for open-space legislation.[68] Since the mid-1970s, schools of architecture and urban planning

have experienced an enormous increase in the proportion of women students, jumping from less than 10 percent to approximately 40 percent in major schools around the country. As these graduates begin to filter into the city-planning agencies, design firms, and environmental protection agencies perhaps parks will receive fresh attention.

Prospects

If women begin to advocate the kind of park service they want for themselves in their own interests, some specific programs are likely to surface. For example, nothing in the definition or practice of park service suggests that the women's movement could not turn around the old image of women as unathletic and make full use of the athletic facilities that now lie partially dormant during fiscal crises. Existing facilities are currently overcrowded by women of all ages who increasingly understand the value of exercise for their appearance, physical health, and mental well-being, especially since most of their jobs are sedentary. They should organize to demand better and more extensive hours for swimming pools and gymnasiums, for example. Parks could be turned to the purposes of the human-potential movement, since so many women are struggling with self-actualization and fulfillment. Compatible with this direction, parks could become holistic-health centers and sense centers with saunas and whirlpools.

As another example, community gardens, so popular with both sexes during both World Wars, should be reestablished. Vegetable and flower gardening offers activities which all ages, from children to elderly, have enjoyed. It is educational for children and relaxing for many adults: it involves exercise and yields a useful product. When park departments have issued permits for allotment gardens, the demand has always been greater than the spaces allocated.

Finally, because one of the most pressing needs of this society is for a rational process for raising children, parks could become a setting for private and governmental experimentation with different types and styles of day-care centers. Parks are an ideal site for this activity because they are near neighborhoods but not within them, so that their noise would not disturb local residents. The architecture is there, and the landscape is there; what is needed is money for staffing and the attitude that childrearing is a social, not only individual and family, function.

More generally, a fresh consideration of women's usage of parks is needed, one which puts it in the larger context of their distinctive urban needs and opportunities. Because women have not constituted a "social problem," few people, including women themselves, have realized that their use of the city might have a distinctive character. Yet F.L. Olmstead, the nation's first professional park designer (beginning with Central Park in 1853), said women benefitted from cities because of their cultural advantages; schools, music, and fine arts: ". . . the greatest wealth can hardly command as much of these in the country as the poorest work-girl is offered . . . in Boston at the mere cost of a walk for a short distance over a good, firm, clean pathway, lighted at night and made interesting to her by shop fronts and a variety of people passing."[69] More recently, in *The City Is the Frontier,* Charles Abrams has emphasized the potential advantages of urban life for single females looking for mates, as well as for mothers needing childcare support.[70] His recommendations fly in the face of the patriarchal controls regarding sexuality.[71] Most recently, feminists have begun to write and convene about the issue of women's need of cities and how women must come to see urban-planning issues as women's issues.[72]

For women to identify themselves with urban issues will throw them headlong into the divisive issues—social, political, and economic—which park departments have traditionally skirted. Abolition, women's suffrage, temperance, the civil liberties, and the new feminism have received virtually not one word in 125 years of park reports; and partly as a result the role of women in public places is as problematic as it was in the nineteenth century. We must address these problems with an awareness of the power of planned physical environments to reinforce social structure. This awareness elevates the significance of parks as a vehicle for social reform which women can and should appropriate to serve their own needs.

Notes

1. This typology is currently available in Galen Cranz, "The Changing Roles of Urban Parks: From Pleasure Garden to Open Space System," *Landscape* vol. 22, no. 3 (Summer 1978):9–18.

2. The source is quoted in Thomas E. Will, "Public Parks and Playgrounds," *The Arena* vol. X, no. LVI (July 1894):277; and the City Council, *Documents for the City of Boston for the Year 1890* Document 15: 15th Annual Report of the Board of Commissioners of the Department of Parks, (Boston: 1890), p. 30.

3. For example, "San Francisco Belles Gain Health and Muscle on Stowe Lake," San Francisco *Call* vol. 15, no. 1 (11 October 1896).

4. Museum of the City of New York, photos and lithos pre-1900, Central Park File.

5. F.L. Olmsted, Jr., *Pittsburgh* (Pittsburgh: Commission of City Planning, 1911).

6. Gym Director's report in Chicago South Park, *Annual Report for 1905* (Chicago: 1905), p. 46.

7. A small park might be divided by a fence, within which women and girls and little children would be allowed, while boys and men would be seated outside. (New York Park Commission, *Annual Report for 1913,* p. 7.) As late as 1922, the San Francisco Park Commission received a request for more benches in Huntington Square with signs to read, "These Benches and This Part of This Square is Hereby Reserved for Ladies and Children." The motion passed. (San Francisco Park Commission Minutes, April 1922, p. 620, in McLaren Lodge, Golden Gate Park.) And in August 1926, the Department of Health similarly requested that a portion of Columbia Square be fenced or roped off for the use of women and children, and again the park commission complied. Only in the 1930s did this kind of protective segregation wane.

8. New York Park Commission, *Annual Report for 1904,* p. 19.

9. Chicago South Park Commission, *Annual Report for 1904,* p. 34; and Chicago South Park Commission, *Annual Report for 1908,* p. 119.

10. P. Horace, "Park Architecture: Bathing Establishments," *The Park International* (July 1920):25–34.

11. The last example of a special area for women and children on a San Francisco beach was mentioned in May 1934 in the minutes of the San Francisco Park Commission.

12. Chicago Park Commission, *Annual Report for 1939,* p. 150.

13. Charles A. Boucher, "Family Recreation: Foe of Juvenile Delinquency," *Recreation* (February 1957):46.

14. Ben Solomon, "Preventive Recreation," *Recreation* (March 1951):566.

15. San Francisco Park Commission, Minutes for 6–7 November 1941, in McLaren Lodge, Golden Gate Park.

16. Of the few new activities developed just for women, all were sexually stereotyped. Toward the end of the Depression they decorated the lounge rooms in the local Chicago field houses. They hung wall hangings, draperies at the windows, brought in furniture and rugs. (Chicago Park Commission, *Annual Report for 1939,* p. 153.) Recreation programming during the war was oriented exclusively to servicemen, since only men were drafted into military service, so one female activity was to prepare entertainments for the men.

17. Chicago Park Commission, *Annual Report for 1947,* p. 18.

18. John Lindsay, *Urban Parks* (New York: Fusion Candidate for Mayor, 1965). Also, see the New York Park Commission's *Annual Park Report for 1967.* Park designers who expressed these new ideas included Paul Friedburg and Richard Dattner. (Personal interviews with administrators Thomas Hoving, Doris Freedman, Karin Bacon, Phyllis Robinson, and August Hecksher.)

19. See, for example, Whitney North Seymour, ed., *Small Urban Spaces* (New York: New York University Press, 1969).

20. For example, Betsey Head gave money to the New York park system (New York Annual Report, 1915). In San Francisco, Helene Strybing willed money to Golden Gate Park to build an arboretum modeled on Harvard's arboretum and named in honor of herself and her husband (Elizabeth McClintock, "History of Strybing Arboretum," vol. 31, no. 2 *California Horticultural Journal* (April 1970):60–64. Mrs. Sigmund Stern (Rosalie) was a patron of the arts in San Francisco, a member of the Recreation Commission since 1929, and the donor of the Stern Grove Park and its music concerts. For a review of her service to the City of San Francisco, see San Francisco *Call-Bulletin,* 31 January 1956. Most of the San Francisco newspaper clippings can be found in a scrapbook series called the *San Francisco Clipping File* in McLaren Lodge in Golden Gate Park. Otherwise they can be looked up individually by the page and date in any library which carries those papers on microfilm. Mrs. Stern funded a women's dormitory at the University of California and contributed to scholarships for girls and youths (boys) (*ibid.*). In 1933 Dr. Emma L. Merritt, Sutro's daughter, told the president of the Parks Commission that because of the Depression she would be unable to maintain the grounds at Sutro Heights any further (Minutes of the San Francisco Park Commission for April 1933, in McLaren Lodge, Golden Gate Park). When she died in 1938, she left the grounds of the Sutro Mansion to become a public park (Works Progress Administration Writer's Project, *San Francisco,* p. 318). The city never did anything with this donation and allowed the mansion to deteriorate so that it had to be pulled down once it was beyond repair. In 1933 Mrs. Ghirardelli donated a game shelter to a park (Minutes of the San Francisco Park Commission, March 1933, p. 14, in McLaren Lodge, Golden Gate Park).

21. *Supervised Recreation* (San Francisco Recreation Commission, 1939).

22. Galen Cranz, "Models of Park Usage: Ideology and the Development of Chicago's Park System," Ph.D. dissertation, 1971.

23. For San Francisco's Raymond Clary there is Eleanor Rossie; for New York's Henry Hope Reed there is the daughter of Samuel Parsons.

24. For example, the California Club, a women's organization, was established in support of the first playground in San Francisco at Bush and Hyde Streets as early as 1898.

25. Park administrators answered that they had run the new department at the peak of efficiency and the women's petition got nowhere. *San Francisco Examiner,* 15 April 1954, and *San Francisco News,* 20 April 1954.

26. "Park Chronicle: Women Active in Park Work," *Park International* (November 1920).

27. For a short time in the 1950s, men volunteers outnumbered women, which especially tickled the profession. *Park and Recreation Yearbook for 1951* (National Park and Recreation Association, 1951), p. 7.

28. Fred G. Heuschling, "Progress with 'Park and Recreation Week' ", *Parks and Recreation* vol. 32, no. 1 (January 1949):4.

29. For example, Robert W. Ruhe, "Skokie, Illinois: A Village of 24,000 Approves a $1,755,000 Master Plan for Parks," *Parks and Recreation* (July 1955):8.

30. Chicago Park Commission, *Annual Report for 1937,* p. 161.

31. Ibid.

32. San Francisco *Post,* 18 July 1901.

33. M.K. Christensen, "Condensed Report of the Secretary of the Women's Auxiliary," American Park and Outdoor Association (Rochester, 1902), p. 51.

34. Mrs. Herman J. Hall, "Park Inconsistencies," 7 *American Park and Outdoor Art Association,* (July 1903):19.

35. Women had been attendants at toilets for women and children even in pleasure-garden days (F.L. Olmsted, Jr., "To Those Having the Care of Young Children," in *Forty Years of Landscape Architecture,* ed. T. Kimball, p. 418). The greater frequency of female employees started in the *San Francisco Annual Report of 1903,* p. 413, the *New York Annual Report for 1904,* p. 74, 76. In 1910 and thereafter, the San Francisco Park Commission hired "numerous" women Directors of Play (not the same as director of the field house) (San Francisco Park Commission, Minutes 1910 to 1914).

36. *Recreation and Park Yearbook,* 1956 (National Recreational Association). When the National Recreation Association had a school at Washington, D.C., most of the students were women; this is inferred from the students' being referred to as "girls" (Clarence F. Rainwater, *The Playground in the United States* [Chicago: University of Chicago Press, 1927], p. 189 fne 146).

37. Quoted in Jay B. Nash, "Playgrounds," *Encyclopedia of Social Sciences,* vol. 12 (1932):163.

38. Chicago South Park Commission, *Annual Report for 1909,* p. 10.

39. Ibid., p. 37.

40. By 1905 Chicago had ten women instructors, eight graduates of normal schools of physical education, two college graduates, and four graduates of county or state normal schools. Of the ten men instructors, their educational qualifications were on the average slightly lower than those of the women. Chicago South Park Commission, *Annual Report for 1905,* p. 47.

41. Report of the Bureau of Recreation, New York Parks Commission, *Annual Report for 1912,* p. 44, and *Annual Report for 1913,* p. 112, describe the same rates.

42. In 1943 the Recreation Commission requested funds from the Lanham Act for day care after school hours from three to seven in the evening. The service lasted only a year. In the 1950s the idea was implicitly rejected through the emphasis on family togetherness.

43. Some hints at conflict between the commissioners and women play directors occurred when several were fired preemptorily, despite their protests, on various charges in the reform era.

44. S.R. DeBoer, "The War and Park Work," *Parks and Recreation* (July 1918):3.

45. Chicago Park Commission, *Annual Report for 1942*, pp. 23, 24, 26.

46. Chicago Park Commission, *Annual Report for 1943*, p. 173.

47. Ibid., p. 174.

48. Ibid., p. 220.

49. Ibid., p. 30.

50. Chicago Park Commission, Annual Report for 1944, p. 34, and *Annual Report for 1945*.

51. Chafe, *The American Women: Her Changing Social, Economic, and Political Roles, 1920–1970* (Oxford: Oxford University Press, 1972).

52. Chicago Park Commission, *Annual Report for 1946*, p. 48.

53. Chicago Park Commission, *Annual Report for 1951*, p. 68.

54. *Recreation and Park Yearbook*, p. 25.

55. Subliminal use of gender in the language of the park reports aided in the process of replacing women with men. While images of women in saccharine and banal moods could be used to promote park activities, commercial advertisers also used the image of women in parks to promote their own products. For example, a five-by-five photograph of a women showed her setting off for a picnic in Golden Gate Park. The text explained that Golden Gate Park was a playland full of natural and manmade wonders to explore, even though in the heart of the city. Because the park was so full of things to do, the "picnic-minded woman dresses for carefree comfort and variety of activity. Here she's wearing her Pooh-Bah Fake Fur Sweatshirt of washable orlon pile. It's light and cozy and soft, it handles like chiffon. Cuffs and the softly rolled boatneck àre in a matching cablestitched knit. Available in beige or moss green. . . ." *San Francisco News,* 6 August 1959. This was an advertisement of the Emporium Collegian Active Sportswear Department.

56. *The Story of San Francisco's Teenage Centers* (San Francisco: Recreation Department, 1947).

57. Chicago Park Commission, *Sixth Annual Report* (Chicago: 1939), p. 236.

58. Or possibly these photos served to persuade men to patronize park services. *San Francisco News,* 16 February 1946.

59. Chicago Park Commission, *Annual Report for 1948*, p. 53.

60. Chicago Park Commission, *Annual Report for 1951*, p. 55.

61. Chicago Park Commission, Biennial Report for 1932 to 1933, pp. 25, 177. The road was named Achsah Bond Drive in honor of Mrs. Shadrach Bond, wife of the first governor of Illinois.

62. San Francisco Playground Commission, minutes for 21 July 1926, and 5 October 1927, in McLaren Lodge.

63. *San Francisco Examiner,* 14 July 1975.

64. Karen R. Quist, "Women in the Parks," *Parks and Recreation* (January 1972):91–108.

65. This classification suit was filed by Elsie Davis, aged 34, of San Francisco, and was reported in the *San Francisco Examiner,* 29 January 1976.

66. Gail Sheehy, "Nanas in the Park," *New York Magazine,* 3 June 1968, pp. 18–21.

67. "A Day in the Park for Women's Rights," *San Francisco Examiner,* 8 March 1976. The organizer was Linda Nordquist.

68. Allan Jacobs, *Making City Planning Work* (Chicago: American Society of Planning Officials, 1978), p. 286.

69. Frederick L. Olmsted, "Public Parks and the Enlargement of Towns," *Journal of Social Science: Containing the Transactions of the American Association* (1871):1–36.

70. Charles Abrams, *The City is the Frontier* (1965).

71. The obsession with proper clothing—dress length, bathing suits, slacks, bikinis—expresses an anxiety about sexuality getting out of hand. Patriarchal controls established strong prohibitions against prostitution, unchaperoned trysting places, and dances.

72. For example, UCLA Conference of Planning for a Non-Sexist Society, Spring 1979; Gerda Wekerle, Rebecca Paterson, David Morely, eds., *New Space for Women* (Boulder, Colorado: Westview, 1980); Gerda Wekerle and David Popenoe, chairpersons, "Spatial Inequality in American Life: Consequences for Women," American Sociological Association, paper session, August 1978, San Francisco; Gerda Wekerle, "Women in the Urban Environment," *Signs* vol. 5, no. 3 (1965):5188–5214.

Part IV
Changing Laws
and Trends

Nadine Taub and Geraldine O'Kane review recent changes in legislative, common law, and constitutional developments that affect women's status in and out of marriage in "Women, the Family and Housing: Legal Trends." Specifically, the authors consider marriage contracts, nontraditional living arrangements, and operational definitions of the family as well as new rights in housing and credit. The general trend is toward a growing recognition of women as individuals in the eyes of the law, responsible for themselves, hence full participants in the economic, social, and political life of their communities.

Mildred Schmertz and the other participants in a roundtable on the architectural and planning implications of current social trends present their views on designing for change in "Housing and Community Design for Changing Family Needs." Their proposals range from transforming storage, cleaning, cooking, and maintenance facilities in modern kitchens to designing for a sense of community in large-scale housing developments. All the issues discussed—energy, housing, poverty, and social isolation—focus on a need to integrate social policies with architectural innovations, so as to achieve more viable, productive, and satisfying communities for all.

10 Women, the Family, and Housing: Legal Trends

Nadine Taub and
Geraldine E. O'Kane

Constitutional and Common-Law Decisions Regarding Women and the Family

Marriage and Women's Individual Identity

Traditionally the Anglo-American legal order has placed women in the home under the authority and protection of their husbands with whom their identity was merged under the doctrine of coverture.[1,2] In Blackstone's classic formulation, coverture meant that

> the husband and wife are one person in law; that is, the very being or legal existence of the woman is suspended during the marriage, or at least is incorporated and consolidated into that of the husband, under whose wing, protection and cover she performs everything.[3]

A series of legislative, common-law, and finally constitutional developments, however, have eroded the doctrine of coverture and the disabilities it engendered. Increasingly the law embodies both the perception that women possess an identity and role independent of their husbands' and an altered view of marriage itself.

The Married Women's Property Acts, enacted in England and the United States in the latter part of the nineteenth century, allowed women to contract, to sue and be sued, and to manage and control their separate estates and earnings. More recent legislation aims at eliminating all male prerogatives over jointly held property as well, and securing, on behalf of the homemaking spouse, an equitable interest in the accumulated property of a wage-earning spouse upon dissolution of marriage. The cases are likewise clear that coverture no longer confers on a husband the right to deny his wife necessary medical treatment. Similarly, contemporary developments have begun to recognize the right of a wife to choose her surname and domicile.[4]

Developments in tort law also reveal that marriage is no longer seen as a unfair relationship in which the woman's identity is submerged. Most jurisdictions have abolished, at least in part, the doctrine of interspousal immunity,[5] which bars personal tort actions between spouses. In so doing they have abandoned the fiction that husband and wife are one as well as the notion that allowing personal tort actions will disrupt the peace and harmony of the home. Just as most courts no longer refuse legal redress for the torts of one partner against the other, they also affirmatively protect each partner's interest in the marital relation. Thus the common-law action for loss of consortium, although originally limited to a husband's action for loss of the wife's services, is now generally available to both partners to compensate for deprivation of society, companionship, and affectionate relations.[6] The spousal interest in harmonious conjugal relations is likewise protected against direct interference by third parties. Here, too, the husband's interest in his wife as chattel or servant has been transformed into a general, gender-neutral interest in the relationship shared by both spouses.[7]

In short, the common law is beginning to consider marriage a union of two equal individuals with rights enforceable against each other and the outside world. This view is, of course, strengthened by legal changes, such as no fault-divorce, which facilitate the dissolution of marriage.[8]

A similar progression is evident in the constitutional sphere. Up until 1971, when the Supreme Court first applied the equal-protection clause so as to invalidate sex-based discrimination,[9] the differential treatment of women was repeatedly upheld on the assumption that women's natural role as childbearer and childrearer precluded her full participation outside the home. Since that time, the Court has repeatedly identified such stereotypic assumptions in state and federal laws and found them inadequate to justify sex-based distinctions. Thus social-welfare programs have been invalidated when based on the sex stereotypes that men are family breadwinners and women are not.[10] Fringe-benefit programs connected with military service have been invalidated as embodying similar stereotypes.[11] And domestic-relations legislation, which is justified only by the notion that women will remain in the home, has been struck down also.[12] The Court has, moreover, acknowledged that as a result of "an attitude of romantic paternalism, which, in practical effect, put women not on a pedestal, but in a cage . . . our statute books [have become] laden with gross, stereotypical distinctions between the sexes,"[13] whose validity appear to be in jeopardy.

Just as constitutional notions of equal-protection doctrine have come to reflect an altered view of the roles available to women, constitutional notions of the right to privacy have come to reflect an altered view of marriage. Initially, the right to privacy was derived from the special protection afforded the marital unit. Thus in *Griswold* v. *Connecticut*, invalidating Connecticut's ban on the use of contraceptives, the Court emphasized the state's intrusion into the realm of marital decisions, saying:

We deal with a right of privacy older than the Bill of Rights—older than our political parties, older than our school system. Marriage is a coming together for better or for worse, hopefully enduring, and intimate to the degree of being sacred. It is an association that promotes a way of life, not causes; a harmony in living, not political faiths; a bilateral loyalty, not commercial or social projects. Yet it is an association for as noble a purpose as any involved in our prior decisions.[14]

But increasingly the rights of the marital unit to be free from state intervention "emerge as rights of individuals only."[15] So, for example, the state is limited in its ability to restrict the choice of partners,[16] and, further, its ability to prevent the termination of marriage.[17] Moreover, even during marriage, it is now recognized that

the marital couple is not an independent entity with a mind and heart of its own, but an association of two individual and emotional makeup. If the right of privacy means anything, it is the right of the *individual,* married or single, to be free from unwarranted governmental intrusion into matters so fundamentally affecting a person as the decision whether to bear or beget a child.[18]

Even more to the point, the Supreme Court has acknowledged both the existence of cases of conflict between the two partners and, at times, the privacy of the woman's right. In cases of conflict, since there is no way the state can strengthen the marital relationship by remaining neutral, the state inevitably aligns itself with one side or the other. So, for example, when the state requires spousal consent to abortion, it does not in fact promote "the mutuality of decisions vital to the marriage relationship"; rather it assures the husband's power to exercise an absolute veto over the wife's choice.[19] This, the Supreme Court has said, it cannot do without violating the woman's right to privacy.

In sum, the institution of marriage is no longer a simple concept, denying the woman's independent identity and foreclosing state intervention in all circumstances. Unlike the days of coverture, marriage is now recognized as composed of two individuals, each of whom has an equal right to participate in the outside world and generally is entitled to press legal interests, both with respect to the marriage itself and against the marital partner. Moreover, as partners are able to move more easily in and out of marriages, it is easier to recognize their "emergence [as] self-determining, separate individual[s] from the network of family and group ties."[20]

In keeping with these changes in the law's view of marriage and women's role in it, there are legal developments governing the relations of unmarried couples. Until relatively recently courts regularly refused to enforce even express agreements between cohabiting couples concerning their property and income on the ground that the agreements, resting in part on an illegal consideration, were tainted by the "meretricious" association.[21] This approach was initially undercut by decisions, starting as early as the 1930s, which upheld and enforced express agreements where the agreement concerning property or household services could be severed from the agreement regarding sexual relations.[22] In the early seventies, courts began to make available a number of theories traditionally employed in other contexts where parties have not made an express agreement.[23] The most widely publicized of these decisions is *Marvin* v. *Marvin,*[24] in which the California Supreme Court suggested that an unmarried cohabitant might recover on theories of implied contract, implied partnership or joint venture, constructive trust, resulting trust or quantum meruit,[25] in addition to the express contract remedy. Developments such as the *Marvin* case reflect a judicial recognition of changing social attitudes and provide a judicial sanction for greater flexibility and thus independence in living arrangements. However, as feminist commentators[26] and others[27] have cautioned, to the extent that such developments imply that a woman's right to recover for her services is based simply on a long period of economic dependency on a man, they may depart from the expectations of the parties and established legal principles, and in essence create a uniform quasi-marital status with fixed consequences.[28] As such, they may represent a step backward into protectionism rather than a forward movement in keeping with the modern role accorded women in the marketplace.

Land-Use Decisions and the Definition of Family

Two key cases define the parameters of the federal constitutional protection to be afforded variations in living arrangements. In *Village of Belle Terre* v. *Borass,*[29] the Supreme Court upheld a Long Island community ordinance that prohibited groups of three or more persons unrelated by blood or marriage from sharing the same household. The court summarily dismissed the argument that the ordinance impinged on freedom of association on the ground that the "ordinance places no ban on . . . association . . . for a family may, so far as the ordinance is concerned, entertain whomever it likes."[30] But only a few years later, in *Moore* v. *City of East Cleveland,*[31] the Supreme Court struck down a municipal ordinance that restricted occupancy of a dwelling unit to members of a single family where *family* was defined to exclude many categories of related individuals.

In attempting to reconcile these seemingly inconsistent decisions, the plurality in *Moore* focused on the privacy right to live with one's family rather than the right of association. However, in tracing the roots and values underlying of this privacy right, the Court revealed its limits.

Our decisions establish that the Constitution protects the sanctity of the family precisely because the institution of the family is deeply rooted in this Nation's history and tradition. It is through the family that we inculcate and pass down many of our most cherished values, moral and cultural. . . .

Ours is by no means a tradition limited to respect for the bonds uniting the members of the nuclear family. The tradition of uncles, aunts, cousins, and especially grandparents sharing a household along with parents and children has roots equally venerable and equally deserving of consitutional recognition. Over the years millions of our citizens have grown up in just such an environment, and most, surely, have profited from it. Even if conditions of modern society have brought about a decline in extended family households, they have not erased the accumulated wisdom of civilization, gained over centuries and honored throughout our history, that supports a larger conception of the family.[32]

Thus while it is clear that "the Constitution prevents East Cleveland from standardizing its children—and its adults—by forcing all to live in certain narrowly defined family patterns,"[33] it is unlikely to protect their right to live in arrangements that have not been sanctioned over the years.

Despite the limited reach of this federal constitutional protection for nontraditional living arrangements, greater protection may be accorded unconventional households on the state level. As the concurring opinion in *Moore* noted: "In well reasoned opinions, the courts of Illinois, New York, New Jersey, California, Connecticut, Wisconsin, and other jurisdictions, have permitted unrelated persons to occupy single family residences notwithstanding an ordinance prohibiting, either expressly or implicitly, such occupancy."[34] Some of these decisions simply distinguish the *Belle Terre* decision as involving an ordinance seeking community stability by preventing student transiency.[35] But in determining what regulations they view as reasonable, other courts make plain their state's greater tolerance for new lifestyles and their unwillingness to permit localities to become private clubs where " 'the wrong kind of people,' unable to find decent housing, need not apply no matter how many suitable homes lie vacant and available."[36] In short, modern-living trends influence at least certain state's perception of permissible regulation, although the present Supreme Court appears more concerned with the inculcation of traditional values through traditional family structures.

Illegitimacy Decisions and Women's Role in the Family

Rules concerning illegitimacy appear in a wide variety of state statutes and common-law decisions as well as in provisions governing federal-benefit programs. For example, out-of-wedlock children may not have the same rights to inherit property or receive social security as other children. Similarly one or both parents may be limited in their right to custody or to sue on behalf of their out-of-wedlock children. Such rules, however, can endure only if they can survive constitutional scrutiny. Recent developments—at times seemingly contradictory developments—in the principles governing this constitutional scrutiny reflect ambivalence about changing social mores and equality of the sexes.

The Supreme Court's initial review of classifications involving illegitimacy in the late 1960s suggested that such classifications were as suspect as those involving racial classifications and as unlikely to pass constitutional muster.[37] But it is now apparent that those decisions did not imply approval of adult conduct that deviates from state and socially imposed social norms. In the words of the Supreme Court,

> The basic rationale of these decisions is that it is unjust and ineffective for society to express its condemnation of procreation outside the marital relationship by punishing the illegitimate child who is in no way responsible for his situation and is unable to change it.[38]

But where the Court sees the burden as one imposed on the parent who is "responsible for fostering an illegitimate child and ha[s] the opportunity to legitimate the child but fail[s] to do so," it is "neither illogical nor unjust for society to express its 'condemnation or irresponsible liaisons beyond the bounds of marriage' " by denying benefits available to parents of legitimate children.[39]

In cases explicitly combining questions of sex discrimination and illegitimacy, the Supreme Court direction is particularly unclear. In other contexts, the Supreme Court is able to recognize that distinctions based on sex[40] must "serve important governmental objectives and must be substantially related to the achievement of those objectives."[41] It has, moreover, declined to recognize any interest except the need to compensate for past discrimination as adequate to meet this test.[42] But in the context of illegitimacy, the Court shows some unwillingness to adhere to this test and some confusion about what governmental interests suffice to justify sex-based differences in treatment. Thus when faced with a state statute that permits mothers of illegitimate children to sue for the wrongful death of their children, a plurality of the Supreme Court indicated that where men and women are not similarly situated and a statutory classification is realistically based on the differences in their situations—apparently whether those differences are the product of physical, social, or legal differences embodied elsewhere in the states—the classifications is valid.[43] Under such a formulation the Court could uphold numerous discriminatory provisions that reflect distinctions between men and women that are true in general although not in the individual case.[44] Likewise the type of administrative interest in avoiding fraud-

ulent claims, which the concurring judge finds sufficient to justify the differential, could justify numerous other sex-based classification.[45]

One basis for this apparent backtracking may be an underlying confusion about the part the law plays in reinforcing social roles. The Court
seems to view legislative provisions requiring fathers but not mothers to
legitimate their children in order to have certain legal rights accorded them
as reasonable because fathers do not experience the process of carrying and
bearing the child, which the Court believes makes the relationship between
the child and the mother clear in all cases.[46] Because the father's actual relationship with his children mày vary and because the father of illegitimate
children may not know of his parenthood or may not, for other reasons,
assume any responsibility for them, the Court appears willing to impose
special conditions on men. These conditions function to replace marriage,
which according to one justice is the primary measure by which the validity
of the father's parental claims may be gauged.[47] However, while it is no
doubt true, particularly in the absence of marriage, that as a matter of
social reality, women are left with the "unshakable responsibility" for their
out-of-wedlock children,[48] changes in that social reality will be deterred by a
legal rule which differentiates between men and women on the basis of their
supposed rather than their actual relationship with their children.

A second basis for the seemingly less progressive approach utilized in
illegitimacy cases presenting sex-discrimination questions may be the
Court's aversion to nontraditional, female-headed families. From this perspective, special incentives for fathers to legitimate their out-of-wedlock
children may be seen as sufficiently important to justify certain inconsistencies with prior case law. Certain expressions in dissenting opinions support
this hypothesis. For example, in dissenting from a decision which struck
down a New York law permitting an illegitimate child to be adopted with
the mother's but without the father's consent, one justice wrote, underscor-
ing the importance of the state's interest in promoting the welfare of illegitimate children:

> Unlike the children of married parents, illegitimate children begin life with
> formidable handicaps. They typically depend upon the care and economic
> support of only one parent—usually the mother. And even in this era of
> changing mores they still may face substantial obstacles simply because
> they are illegitimate. Adoption provides perhaps the most generally avail-
> able way of removing these handicaps.[49]

Here too the law's effect in reinforcing existing social mores is ignored.
For if the law justifies differential treatment of men and women on the need
to avoid the handicaps faced by out-of-wedlock children, it not only diverts
attention from other ways of remedying these handicaps—such as improv-

ing the ability of single women to earn satisfactory incomes—but it also solidifies the idea that disadvantage and stigma attach to the status of illegitimacy.

In sum, the constitutional treatment of rules involving illegitimacy is mixed. On the whole, the Supreme Court differentiates between situations in which out-of-wedlock children become the unfortunate victims of their parents' conduct and situations in which the parents themselves are likely to suffer for violating society's norms. Only in the first situation can we say with any certainty that rule will be invalidated. Moreover, rules that impose burdens or conditions on the basis of sex, though not generally likely to be upheld, are likely to survive scrutiny in the illegitimacy context, where they may be perceived as reflecting general differences between men and women, or as promoting a more traditional family arrangement.

Legislation and Regulations Limiting Housing Bias

Access to Housing

Women's access to housing has traditionally been restricted by landlords and brokers who did not want female tenants or who did not want certain kinds of female tenants; that is, those who were single or divorced or dependent on public assistance, child support, or alimony for part of their income. With the exception of a few state statutes, these practices were sanctioned by the absence of legislation prohibiting such arbitrary refusals to rent and by the fact that the Constitution does not prohibit unequal treatment, on the basis of sex, by private landlords.[50]

Sex Discrimination in Housing. It was only in 1974 after a series of court decisions recognized that state action denying women equal treatment violated the Constitution and after the Congress had banned sex discrimination in employment,[51] that attention focused on sex discrimination in the housing market. As a result the Federal Fair Housing Law,[52] which had been adopted in 1968 prohibiting discrimination on the basis of race, national origin, and religion was amended to include sex as a prohibited basis for decision making in the sale or rental of housing.[53] To date twenty-six states have adopted similar legislation affording women an alternative remedy for housing discrimination based on sex.[54]

Although the terms of the federal statute are clear, there are few reported court decisions interpreting the scope of the act as it pertains to women. A more substantial body of law has developed, however, with respect to housing discrimination based on race. Since the same standards of proof apply to sex discrimination, reference to this body of law may be made in construing the statute.

The federal fair-housing law is a good example of how the law appears to reflect social reality but does not address all of the interlocking factors of that reality. While the law protects women from being discriminated against on the basis of sex per se, it does not extend to a number of related forms of discrimination, such as marital status discrimination or discrimination based on source of income. Therefore, the law encourages and enforces the social ideal that women should be treated as equal with men, but it does not foster acceptance of the social reality of the number of single-parent households headed by women or the bases of income on which these families rely, at least in part. Women faced with marital-status or source-of-income discrimination are dependent on state legislation, where it exists, to address these problems or upon judicial interpretation of the federal statute as to whether these types of discrimination are banned.

The federal law against sex discrimination in housing also reflects the legislative reluctance to intrude on the prerogatives of small landlords. For example, owner occupiers of units containing quarters occupied or intended to be occupied by no more than four families are exempted from the act.[55] Similarly, the owner of a single-family house is free to discriminate on the basis of sex provided the owner does not own more than three such homes and only claims the exemption once every twenty-four months.[56] In some states, however, state legislation does not allow such exemptions, and women living in these states have the right to equal housing in all sectors of the housing market.[57]

Despite these exemptions in the federal fair-housing law, judicial interpretation of other statutes has eliminated the right of small landlords to discriminate on the basis of race.[58] Unfortunately, courts have refused to include sex discrimination within the purview of the statutes.[59] Therefore, small landlords are free to discriminate on the basis of sex even if the woman is black so long as the basis of the decision was the applicant's sex rather than race.

The Fair Housing Act explicitly addresses one of the major factors that has precluded black families from large sectors of the housing market and is the practice of racial steering. *Racial steering* is the practice by which whites are shown housing in white neighborhoods while blacks and other minorities are only shown housing in integrated or minority neighborhoods. This practice has been soundly renounced by the judiciary,[60] but the force of law has apparently made little headway in eliminating such practices in the real estate community.[61] Black women, therefore, continue to bear the dual burden of race and sex discrimination as factors limiting their access to housing.

Real-estate brokers, owners, and landlords, with the limited exceptions noted earlier, are bound by the provisions of the Fair Housing Act.[62] The basic premise of the law is that women are to be treated the same as similarly situated men when seeking housing. It is unlawful to refuse to sell or

rent because of the individual's sex.[63] So long as the individual seeking
housing meets the normal qualifications established by the owner or real-
estate broker, she cannot be denied the housing because of her sex. Nor can
sex play a role in the seller or landlord's decision.[64] Tactics of delay or discouragement in the decision to sell or rent or in the negotiation process leading up to the sale are sufficient to establish a violation of the act.[65]

The federal law also prohibits varying the terms and conditions on
which housing is offered because of the individual's sex.[66] For example, a
landlord cannot require additional security because the proposed tenant is a
woman, nor can the landlord require that women but not men have a
cosigner on a lease. Similarly, real-estate brokers cannot require that the
spouse of a woman accompany her in viewing housing if men are shown
housing without their spouses. This practice appears to be based on the
assumption that men but not women can make important decisions regarding the purchase of housing and that it is men who unilaterally control the
family purse. Equal treatment under the law does not tolerate these sex-
based stereotypes.

The ban on unequal conditions applies regardless of the motivation of
the owner or broker.[67] The victim of discrimination need not show that the
alleged offender intended to discriminate or acted in a hostile manner, but
simply that the effect of the offender's action was discriminatory.[68] Increasingly, courts have rejected policies and practices adopted under the guise of
"protecting women" in favor of equal application of the law. In one of the
few reported sex-discrimination decisions under the federal law, a federal
district court rejected a landlord's policy of not renting certain apartments
to single women without cars while allowing single men without cars access
to the apartments. Although the landlord claimed the policy was a benevo-
lent one, based on the unsafe character of the neighborhood and an alleged
greater risk of assault against women walking to and from the apartments,
the court found that this policy violated the antidiscrimination provisions of
the act.[69]

The same court held that the exclusion of child support and alimony
from a determination of the woman's ability to pay was a violation of the
act as it placed an unequal burden on women applicants.[70] This decision is
consistent with the congressional intent that the fair-housing law be liberally
construed and is distinguishable from those cases in which economic discrimination has been upheld.[71] The economic discrimination cases recognize
the right of landlords to establish income qualifications (for example, net
weekly income equal to 90 percent of the monthly income), regardless of the
disproportionate impact of such qualifications on certain classes, provided
the same criteria are applied to all.[72] The federal court which banned the
exclusion of alimony and child support merely recognized that so long as
the individual had the requisite amount of income, the source of the income
was immaterial.

This issue remains subject to further clarification or modification by the courts. The silence of the federal fair-housing law regarding the rights of the female renter to have all sources of income credited in determining whether she is financially qualified for an apartment is not remedied by the Equal Credit Opportunity Law discussed later. Although lenders are prohibited from automatically discrediting certain sources of income under that act, a landlord is not considered a creditor. Hence the provisions of the credit law do not apply in determining a renter's available income. It is only in Massachusetts and Minnesota that women can rely on express state statutory provision outlawing financial discrimination.[73] In the remainder of the states, women are dependent on judicial interpretation of state and federal laws to eliminate the unreasonable exclusion of reliable sources of income in determining the woman's eligibility.

Marital Status Discrimination. Discrimination based on marital status per se is not barred by the federal law. This does not mean, however, that divorced or single women are totally unprotected. While a landlord under federal law may refuse to rent to all single and divorced individuals, the landlord may not rent to single or divorced men but not single or divorced women. Such practices are not discrimination based on marital status but discrimination based on sex, since the prohibition is only applied to women but not men. Eighteen states, however, have adopted legislation that is more comprehensive than the federal statute. In those states landlords may not refuse to rent to anyone because of his or her marital status.[74] To prevail in these states, women need only show that such a policy exists; they need not show, as they must under federal law, that the policy applies to women but not men.

Housing Discrimination against Families with Children. Increasingly women's access to housing is being restricted because of their position in households with children. Although the federal law protects women with children who are denied housing if the woman can show that men with children have access to housing, challenges to a landlord's blanket refusal to rent to households with children are only beginning to take shape. Such challenges involve the development of housing as affected by zoning laws and access to housing as protected by a limited number of state laws.

Discrimination against families with children often results from the goals of communities to limit tax assessments and create housing designed for and limited to senior citizens. While women, who on the average live longer than men, make up a disproportionate number of the beneficiaries of the latter goal, the overall result is to severely restrict availability of housing for families, including single-parent families headed by women. The goals outlined already are met in several ways. First, building restrictions may be designed to limit the number of children living in new apartment projects.

For example, a certain percentage of all apartments must be one-bedroom apartments, thereby excluding families with children from this share of the market. Such restrictions have been held void in two states and have found support in one.[75] Further, the finding of the U.S. Supreme Court that undue burdens on a school system may be the legitimate subject of zoning regulations makes it unclear as to whether less restrictive regulations limiting the number of children in an apartment complex may be sustained.[76]

Zoning classifications that are designed to create senior-citizen housing have been upheld as being reasonably and rationally related to creating planned housing for the elderly.[77] These decisions have a negative impact on families with children not only because such families are excluded but because they support the existing trend to use federal monies for the constructions of low-income housing for senior citizens but not for low-income families. Although the Department of Housing and Urban Development is attempting to shift the emphasis to family housing, it is unclear as to what success these efforts will have given community opposition to such housing and judicial sanctioning of housing restricted to senior citizens.

The problem of housing discrimination against families with children was recognized as early as 1898 when New Jersey passed a statute making it a disorderly-persons offense to refuse to rent to families that included a child under fourteen years of age or to make provision in a lease agreement that the agreement would terminate upon the birth of a child.[78] Arizona, Illinois, and New York have similar statutes.[79] Enforcement of these statutes, carrying fines of $50 to $500 and in some cases possible jail terms, is placed exclusively in the hands of local and state officials and for the most part has been completely ineffective.[80] In Massachusetts and Delaware, statutes provide that prospective tenants who have encountered this form of discrimination may recover damages from the landlord for expenses occurred in securing substitute housing.[81] In Alaska and the District of Columbia discrimination on the basis of parenthood is prohibited, the logical result of which is that the individual with children is protected.[82]

As the foregoing indicates, the problem of discrimination against families with children is gaining increasing attention in state legislatures. Similarly, in states that do not expressly prohibit such discrimination other equal-protection statutes are being construed as protecting families with children. For example, in California the Unruh Civil Rights Act has been construed as preventing arbitrary discrimination based on age.[83] Landlords in California must establish the reasonableness of any policy that excludes children, taking into account "the housing needs of the young and of adults particularly older citizens,"[84] as well as the size, nature, and location of the complex and the interests of tenants with children and those wishing to avoid children.[85] In Michigan, the state's attorney general has construed the state's fair-housing act prohibiting discrimination on the basis of age as proscribing a landlords' refusal to rent to prospective tenants with children.[86]

While this area remains ripe for further legislative action and judicial interpretation, the law appears to be moving toward banning arbitrary exclusion of children in favor of demanding a reasonable basis for such exclusion. It remains to be seen how difficult such a reasonable showing would be in light of arguments that may be propounded in favor of other tenants' privacy rights, noise control, increased liability resulting from the presence of children, and potential vandalism. The important factor, however, is that landlords may have to make some specific showing of these factors rather than unsupported claims that children can be excluded.

Access to Financing

Traditionally, credit practices have reflected the legal status of women. Until recently, upon marriage a woman was faced with the reality that her existing credit accounts would be cancelled and she would be required to reapply for credit, usually in her husband's name. Before the married woman could open an account, she would have to furnish information concerning her husband's creditworthiness, and her credit rating would commonly be altered based on her husband's rating. Creditors routinely refused to issue accounts to married women who would have been eligible for credit if they were not married, and stricter credit standards were applied when the wife rather than the husband was the primary wage earner. Divorced or widowed women fared no better than their married counterparts, having trouble reestablishing credit and being burdened by credit-scoring systems that applied points based on marital status. Divorced women also faced the problem created by creditors who refused to consider alimony and child support as available income.[87]

The Equal Credit Opportunity Act passed in 1974 was a major breakthrough in establishing the economic independence of women.[88] As such, it reflected the growing social and legal awareness of women's rights and independence. The federal act proscribed discrimination based on sex or marital status with respect to any credit transaction. In deciding whether to extend credit, lending institutions may not inquire as to an applicant's marital status except for the purpose of ascertaining his or her remedies regarding the particular extension of credit. Creditors may not inquire as to the applicant's childbearing plans, use assumptions or aggregate statistics relating to the likelihood that any group of persons will bear children or for that reason will receive diminished or interrupted income in the future, or utilize sex or marital status as variables in a credit-rating system. Income of an applicant or the applicant's spouse may not be discounted nor may the creditor refuse to issue separate accounts on the basis of sex or marital status.[89] Credit information that was formerly reported only in the husband's name, thereby compounding the difficulties of divorced or widowed women in securing credit, must now reflect the participation of both spouses where the account is a joint one.

The problems women face with respect to their sources of income are not completely solved by the Equal Credit Opportunity Act, but substantial protections are afforded. For example, creditors may not discount income from part-time employment but may consider the amount and probable continuance of any income in evaluating the applicant's creditworthiness. With respect to alimony and child-support payments, a creditor shall consider such payments as income to the extent that they are likely to be consistently made. In making this evaluation, the creditor may consider the length of time and regularity with which such payments have been received, whether they are received pursuant to court order, and the creditworthiness of the payor.[90] This last factor highlights the fact that even if a woman receives support payments regularly, she may be penalized by the poor credit rating of her former spouse.

In 1976 the act was amended to make it unlawful for a creditor to discriminate because all or part of an applicant's income derives from public assistance.[91] In reality this provision will have a negligible effect on women's access to financing for the purchase of a home since the level of public assistance is insufficient to meet mortgage payments. Moreover, public-assistance regulations require individuals to exhaust available assets which could be used as down payments in securing housing before assistance will be granted.

While the full impact of the equal-credit-opportunity law on lending practices cannot be evaluated at this time, it does appear that the legislature has attempted to recognize the growing rights and independence of women. In this area, given the complexity of the administrative process, which women filing complaints must follow and the expense of judicial enforcement, the symbolic recognition that the law has given to the rights of women may be a significant factor in securing voluntary compliance with the law.

Conclusion

As this chapter has demonstrated, the legal trend is to recognize the independence of women and their right to equal treatment when their circumstances are identical with men's. To this extent the law encourages women's access to housing and necessary financing. The law has lagged behind, however, in addressing problems that compound the difficulties women face in securing housing. Congressional reluctance to protect families with children and families dependent on certain sources of income has been only partially redressed by more comprehensive state legislation and judicial construction. Similarly, the federal courts have been more hesitant than some of their state counterparts to condone nontraditional living arrangements. At times the reluctance of legislative and judicial bodies to address these issues reflects a deliberate attempt to retard social change. But the limited steps the law has made in certain areas does signal that social realities will increasingly be addressed by the courts, ultimately recognizing if not encouraging the results of social experimentation.

Notes

1. For a discussion of the role played by law in the area of women's rights, see Powers, *Sex Segregation and the Ambivalent Directions of Sex Discrimination Law,* Wisc. L. Rev. 55, 63 (1979).

2. For a discussion of the relationship between legal developments regarding the family and employment, see Glendon, *The New Family and the New Property,* 53 Tulane L. Rev. 697, 705 (1979) (hereinafter Glendon).

3. L.W. Blackstone, Commentaries 442. A discussion of the incidents of coverture can be found in L. Kanowitz, Women and the Law 36 et seq.

4. For a useful summary of these developments, see K. Davidson, R. Ginsburg, and H. Kay, *Texts, Cases and Materials on Sex-Based Discrimination* (1974 and 1975 Supp.), and B. Babcock, A. Freedman, E. Norton, and S. Ross, *Sex Discrimination and the Law: Causes and Remedies* (1975 and 1978 Supp.). For a detailed state-by-state analysis, see B. Brown, A. Freedman, H. Katz, and A. Price, *Women's Rights and the Law—The Impact of the ERA on State Law* (1977).

5. As of 1979, only eighteen states retained the rule: Arizona, Delaware, Florida, Georgia, Hawaii, Illinois, Iowa, Kansas, Louisiana, Maine, Massachusetts, Mississippi, Ohio, Pennsylvania, Rhode Island, Tennessee, Virginia, and Wyoming. Massachusetts and Virginia have allowed limited exceptions to the rule.

6. See W. Prosser, *Handbook of the Law of Torts* §125, 4th ed., 1971.

7. Id., at §124.

8. Glendon, supra note 2. See BNA Family Law Reporter Reference File, §§401–453 for a state-by-state compilation of current divorce laws.

9. See Reed v. Reed, 404 U.S. 71 (1971) (invalidating an Idaho statute preferring males to females as estate administrators).

10. Califano v. Westcott, 443 U.S. 76 (1979) (invalidating Aid to Families with Dependent Children provision allowing assistance to families with

unemployed fathers but not unemployed mothers); Califano v. Goldfarb, 430 U.S. 199 (1977) (invalidating Social Security Survivorship Insurance provision granting benefits to all widows of covered workers but only to those widowers who were receiving over half their support from their wives when they died); Weinberger v. Wiesenfeld, 420 U.S. 636 (1975) (invalidating Social Security provisions granting childcare benefits to certain widowed mothers, but denying them to widowed fathers).

11. Frontiero v. Richardson, 411 U.S. 677 (1973).

12. Orr v. Orr, 440 U.S. 268 (1979) (statute permitting award of alimony to females and not to males denied equal protection; allocation of dependent role in family to wife is unacceptable state purpose); Stanton v. Stanton, 421 U.S. 7 (1975) (different ages of majority for males and females denies equal protection).

13. Frontiero v. Richardson, 411 U.S. 677, 684 (1973).

14. Eisenstadt v. Baird, 405 U.S. 438, 453 (1972) (emphasis in the original).

15. Planned Parenthood of Central Missouri v. Danforth, 428 U.S. 52, 71 (1976), citing rejecting and the interest identified by the lower court.

16. 381 U.S. 479, 486 (1965).

17. L. Tribe, American Constitutional Law 987 (1978). Professor Tribe was referring both to husband-wife and parent-child relations.

18. Loving v. Virginia, 388 U.S. 1 (1967).

19. Boddie v. Connecticut, 401 U.S. 371 (1971) (financial assistance to indigents). Cf. Ferrer v. Commonwealth Sup. Ct., 4 F.L.R. 2744, 2746 (26 September 1978) (privacy provisions of Puerto Rican Constitution requires right to instant divorce by mutual consent).

20. H. Maine, Ancient Law 165 (1970 ed.) (1st ed. 1861) quoted in Glendon, supra note 2, at 706.

21. See generally, Kay and Amyx, *Marvin v. Marvin: Preserving the Options,* 65 Calif. L. Rev. 937, 975 (1977) (hereinafter Kay and Amyx); Follberg and Buren, *Domestic Partnership: A Proposal for Dividing the Property of Unmarried Families,* 12 Willamette L.J. 453, 456 (1976) (hereinafter Follberg and Buren); Casad, *Unmarried Couples and Unjust Enrichment: From Status to Contract and Back Again?* 77 Mich. L. Rev. 47 (1978) (hereinafter Casad); Bruch, *Property Rights of De Facto Spouses Thoughts on the Value of Homemakers Services,* 10 Fam. L. Q. 101 (1976).

22. See, for example, Trutalli v. Meraviglia, 215 Cal. 698, 12 P.2d 430 (1932).

23. See, for example, Marvin v. Marvin, 18 Cal. 2d 660, 557 P.2d 106, 134 Cal. Rptr. 815 (1976); Carlson v. Olson, 256 N.W.2d 249 (1977) Minn. (1977); and Beal v. Beal, 282 Or. 115, 577 P.2d 507 (1978).

24. 18 Cal. 2d 660, 557 P.2d 106, 134 Cal. Rptr. 815 (1976).

25. These traditional forms of recovery are described in Follberg and Buren, supra note 21. Questions concerning their application to unmarried couples are discussed in Casad, supra note 21.

26. See, Kay and Amyx, supra note 21 at 966.

27. See, Casad, supra note 21.

28. For example, following the California Supreme Court decision in the *Marvin* case, the trial judge required the defendent to pay $104,000 for "rehabilitation purposes" although it found no express or implied contract and no actual, constructive, or resulting trust. *Los Angeles Daily Journal,* 19 April 1979, at 10.

29. 416 U.S. 1 (1974).

30. Id. at 9.

31. 431 U.S. 494 (1977).

32. Id. at 504–505.

33. Id. at 506.

34. Id. at 516–517 (Stevens, J. concurring).

35. See, for example, City of White Plains v. Ferraioli, 34 N.Y.2d 300, 303–304, 313 N.E.2d 756, 758 (1974) (distinguishing the case of a group home).

36. Holy Name Hospital v. Montroy, 153 N.J. Super. 181, 187, 379 A.2d 299, 302–03 (Law Div. 1977) (local ordinance void to the extent that it limits residential occupancy to single, nonprohibit housekeeping units).

37. See Levy v. Louisiana, 391 U.S. 68 (1967) (state statute prohibiting illegitimate children from recovering for parents' wrongful death unconstitutional); Weber v. Aetna Casualty and Surety Co., 406 U.S. 164 (1972) (state worker's compensation statute barring illegitimate children from recovery for father's death unconstitutional); and Trimble v. Gordon, 430 U.S. 762 (1977) (state statute permitting illegitimate children to inherit intestate only from mother while legitimate children could inherit from either parent struck down). See also New Jersey Welfare Rights Org. v. Cahill, 411 U.S. 619 (1973) (per curiam) (state welfare program denying benefits to households with only illegitimate children unconstitutional); and Gomez v. Perez, 409 U.S. 535 (1973) (per curiam) (state law granting legitimate children only judicially enforceable right to support from their natural fathers unconstitutional). But see Labine v. Vincent, 401 U.S. 532 (1971) (state statute denying acknowledged illegitimate children equal share in father's intestate estate not unconstitutional); and Mathews v. Lucas, 427 U.S. 495 (1976) (federal Social Security benefit eligibility provision requiring illegitimates to prove dependency where legitimates presumed dependent not unconstitutional).

38. Parham v. Hughes, 441 U.S. 347, 352 (1979).

39. Id. at 353.

40. The Supreme Court is at times obtuse about what constitutes a sex-based classification, holding, for example, that pregnancy discrimination and veterans' preferences are not sex based. See Geduldig v. Aiello, 417 U.S. 484 (1974) and Personnel Administrator of Massachusetts v. Feeney, 442 U.S. 256 (1979) respectively.

41. Orr v. Orr, 440 U.S. 268, 279 (1979).

42. See, for example, Kahn v. Shevin, 416 U.S. 351 (1974); Schlesinger v. Ballard, 419 U.S. 498 (1975); and Califano v. Webster, 430 U.S. 313 (1977) (per curiam).

43. Parham v. Hughes, 441 U.S. 347, 354–55 (1979).

44. For example, since it is probably true that men have more business experience than women, a classification which preferred men over women in estate administration would probably be upheld under such a test. Yet the court struck down just such a classification in Reed v. Reed, 404 U.S. 71 (1971).

45. Parham v. Hughes, 441 U.S. 347, 360–361 (1979) (concurring opinion of Powell, J.).

46. See Caban v. Mohammed, 441 U.S. 380, 395, 405 (1979) (dissenting opinions of Stewart, J. and Stevens, J. respectively).

47. Id. at 397 (Stewart, J. dissenting).

48. Id. at 408 (Stevens, J. dissenting).

49. Id. at 395 (Stewart, J. dissenting). See also id. at 402 (Stewart, J. dissenting).

50. The guarantee of equal rights under the law provided by the Fourteenth Amendment to the U.S. Constitution has been restricted to deprivation of rights by the state or its agencies. See generally, J. Nowak, R. Rotunda, and J. Young, Constitutional Law, 1978 pp. 453–475.

51. 42 U.S.C. 2000e et seq.

52. 42 U.S.C. 3601 3601 et seq.

53. 42 U.S.C. §3604.

54. For a table of state statutes prohibiting discrimination in housing based on sex, marital status, and related grounds, see Women's Law Project, Women and Housing; A Guide to Combatting Unfair Practices, 23–1 through 23–3.

55. 42 U.S.C. §3603(b) (2).

56. 42 U.S.C. §3603(b) (1).

57. See, for example, Iowa Code Ann., §601A.8 (1975); Minn Stat Ann., §363.03 (1, 2) (1966).

58. Jones v. Alfred H. Mayer, 392 U.S. 409 (1968), construing 42 U.S.C. §1982.

59. Foreman v. General Motors Corp. 473 F. Supp. 166 (D. Mich. 1979); League of Academic Women v. Regents of University, 343 F. Supp. 636 (D. Cal. 1972); Fitzgerald v. United Methodist Community Center, 335 F. Supp. 965 (D. Neb. 1972).

60. U.S. v. Mitchell, 580 F.2d 789 (5th Cir. 1978); Bradley v. John Brabhan Agency, 463 F. Supp. 27 (D.S.C. 1978); Zuch v. Hussey, 366 F. Supp. 553 (D. Mich. 1973).

61. Policy Research and Development Section, U.S. Department of Housing and Urban Development, *Measuring Racial Discrimination in American Housing Market* (1979).

62. 42 U.S.C. §3604(b).

63. 42 U.S.C. §3604(a).

64. Zuch v. Hussey, 366 F. Supp. 553 (D. Mich.) (1973).

65. U.S. v. Mitchell, 580 F.2d 789 (5th Cir. 1978); Williams v. Matthews Co., 499 F.2d 819 (5th Cir. 1974), cert. denied, 419 U.S. 1021 (1975).

66. 42 U.S.C. §3604(b).

67. U.S. v. Reece, 457 F. Supp. 43 (D. Mont. 1978).

68. Resident Advisory Board v. Rizzo, 425 F. Supp. 987 (E.D. Pa. 1976), aff'd, 564 F.2d 126 (3d Cir. 1977).

69. U.S. v. Reece, 457 F. Supp. 43 (D. Mont. 1978).

70. Id. at 48.

71. Metropolitan Housing Development Corp. v. Village of Arlington Heights, 469 F. Supp. 836 (1978).

72. Boyd v. Lefrak Organization, 509 F.2d 1110 (2d Cir. 1975); Lee v. Minnoch, 417 F. Supp. 436, aff'd. 556 F.2d 567 (3d Cir. 1977).

73. Mass. Ann. Laws, Ch. 151B, §4 (14) (1971); Minn Stat Ann., §363.03.2(3) (1966).

74. See chart cited in note 4.

75. Molino v. Mayor of Glassboro, 116 N.J. Super 195 (Law Div. 1971), (ordinance requiring 70 percent of units to be one bedroom struck down); Duggan v. County of Cook, 60 Ill. 2d 107 (1975) (developer's agreement, as a condition of rezoning, to limit children to 25 percent of the units and to pay school board a fixed sum of money was beyond zoning powers); Riley v. Stones, 526 P.2d 747 (Ariz. Ct. App. 1975) (restricting occupancy of a portion of a mobile home to persons twenty-one years of age and older upheld).

76. Moore v. East Cleveland, 431 U.S. 494, 499–450 (1977).

77. Taxpayers Assn. of Weymouth County, Inc. v. Weymouth Township, 71 N.J. 249 (1976); Maldino v. Ambrio, 36 N.Y.2d 481, 330 N.E.2d 403, 369 N.Y.S.2d 385, appeal dismissed, 42 30.S 993 (1975).

78. N.J.L. 1898, ch. 235, at 794 (1898) now codified at N.J. Stat. Ann. 2A:170–92 (1971).

79. Ariz. Rev. Stat. Ann. §33–303A, §33–1317A (Supp. 1977); Ill. Rev. Stat, ch. 80 and 37 (1973), ch. 80 §38 (Supp. 1977); N.Y. Real Pro. Law §§236–37 (Consol 1968).

80. See O'Brien and Fitzgerald *Apartment for Rent-Children Not Allowed,* 25 De Paul L. Rev. 64, 85–86 (1975).

81. Del. Code Ann, tit. 25, §6503 (1975); Mass. Gen Laws Ann, ch.

151 13 §5 (West 1976).

82. Alaska Stat. §18.80 240 (1962); D.C. Rules and Reg., §34–13.1 (1973).

83. *Marina Point, Ltd. v. Wolfson, et al.* PHEOH ¶16, 548 (Super. Ct. of Calif, L.A. Cnty. App. Dept. 1978).

84. Id. at 16, 780.

85. Id. at 16, 776.

86. Mich. A. G. Op. No. 4973, April 21, 1976, PHEOH ¶17, 013.

87. This summary of discriminatory credit practices is drawn from Gates, *Credit Discrimination Against Women: Causes and Solutions,* 27 Vand. L. Rev. 409 (1974).

88. 15 U.S.C. §1691 (Supp. V. 1975).

89. For a complete outline of prohibited credit practices, see Fed. Res. Bd. Reg. B, 12 CFR §202 et seq. (1976).

90. 42 Fed. Reg. 1254 §202.6(b) (5).

91. 15 U.S.C. §1691(b).

11 Housing and Community Design for Changing Family Needs

Mildred F. Schmertz

The Legal Defense and Education Fund of the National Organization for Women sponsored a National Assembly on the Future of the Family. *Record* editor Walter F. Wagner chaired a panel on new environments for new family needs. As a source for this event *Record* recently held a Round Table which examined current and proposed housing and planning policies in the context of the changing needs and self perceptions of women and families. Our aim was to try and determine the architectural and planning consequences of these changing concepts of single and family life.

Today in the United States, 44 per cent of the mothers of children under the age of six are working and only 7 per cent of existing families are traditional nuclear families in which the man is the sole wage earner and the woman the full-time mother and homemaker. Nearly half of all two-parent families in America are "two-paycheck" marriages. An increasing number of households consist of dual-career couples without children. More divorced or widowed women are becoming full-time workers. The number of elderly is increasing. Further . . .

At the same time that the fuel shortage should be dictating construction at higher densities, suburban sprawl continues. Without regard to these demographic and economic facts, suburban houses and urban apartments are still being built to designs and located in community patterns and densities which more or less suit the traditional, auto-dependent nuclear family. The *Record* Round Table of architects, planners, social scientists and writers suggested that architects, planners and developers must begin by ridding their minds of the female-home maker stereotype and her stereotypical family.

Patricia Carbine, who in her role as publisher and editor-in-chief of *Ms. Magazine* has long been putting female stereotypes to rest, said: "We are finished with the idea that the house is primarily the responsibility of the woman. As women we have reached the point where we understand and want to share with our families the understanding that the place where we live is the place where we *all* live and where we are all responsible. The

Reprinted from *Architectural Record*, October 1979. © 1979 by McGraw Hill, Inc. with all rights reserved.

duties performed in the house are not the function of helping the women but of helping each other in a shared way—literally taking on the responsibility for the running of that dwelling; and I think to approach the whole question of the future with any other notion is exactly wrong.''

Like Ms. Carbine, focusing upon woman's true needs as shared with her household, was architect and developer Lynda Simmons, executive vice president and director of development for Phipps Houses, a nonprofit, philanthropic corporation which provides model housing at moderate cost for moderate- and low-income families. Said Ms. Simmons: ''I would like to make an ideological point—I think for me as an architect, a feminist, and a developer with some influence over this process, my goal is to create housing that will allow individuals—men, women and children—to fulfill themselves. I don't think in terms of 'What does the woman need?' What I am interested in is, how can we create dwelling units in which the people who live in them share the responsibilities? How can we design physical arrangements which don't interfere with that sharing and don't create second-class-citizen status for the women and girls. For instance, what is wrong with interior kitchens, which are black holes of Calcutta, is that the men won't go there. If women think that men are ever going to take over their share of household chores and everything else, as long as such kitchens exist they are wrong. We have to eliminate things that create inequities in social relations and thereby interfere with social relations. The stereotype kitchen is the separated kitchen; the stereotype person is the one who is supposed to go in there and work.

The problem for designers is, how do you create spaces in which many different kinds of households can function. I believe that we must create units that are usable over time by different sorts of households at different stages of family or nonfamily development.

Ms. Simmons' concept that dwellings must be designed to be usable over time was reinforced by environmental psychologist Dr. Sandra Howell, who is a member of the faculty of the School of Architecture and Planning at M.I.T.: ''I am particularly concerned with some of the stereotypes the lead designers and developers to believe that the family does not change over time; that people do not grow and develop; that what is established as a household for a family that has very young children is not seen as a household that has to be modifiable by the members of the family as they change and grow. To assume that once a person is 'there,' he or she is always there, is to create another stereotype.

''We must not segregate by stage in the life-cycle. I am increasingly distressed, and I am really paraphrasing the late Margaret Mead, with the tendency in this society, perpetuated by developers in the private sector as well as the public sector, to say, 'This is all for the family with five kids; this is all for young couples, or singles; this is all for empty-nesters; this is all for old people.' If you had 600 units full of adolescent boys, would you not call it an institution? And yet we are allowing, in the public sector and in the private sector, that many units all on the same site, all clustered, for people over the age of sixty-five. I think this is part of the stereotyping. We allow a false notion of preferences to be used to form the societal goals for which we design.''

If stereotyped dwelling units are being built to fit stereotyped families, who is paying attention to the real housing needs of real people? ''Almost nobody,'' said several of the panelists. Dr. Howell put it strongly: ''It seems to me that housing is often designed as though preferences were needs. When a family goes into the marketplace to look for a home, they really typically do not have free choice. Yet the way they choose is then taken by a marketing expert and read as a matter of preferences when it is a matter of constraints.

''We don't know the answers as to what families need as they change, what women need as they change; and I use the word 'need,' rather the 'preference,' because we have to look at human behavior. I am a psychologist, and I don't think we are looking at behavior in a way which evaluates the match between house and people.''

And women must learn how and when to articulate their needs. Said Ms. Carbine: ''One of the things that has been wrong and has created the problems, is that important users—that is to say, half the population which happens to be female, have not been included in early policy planning, in early development planning, in the whole question of how dwellings get designed and used. I think that if we do nothing else here, we ought to agree that women have to be included in policy planning in the future, in order to overcome some of the inherent problems in having policy set by people who have vested interests in not staying in the dwelling.''

Architects who are women can make more difference than they think. Said Ms. Simmons: ''I think that many things in many apartments would never have been built or designed as they are if they had been designed by women. Male architects, because they aren't at home, have not had the experience of taking care of the kids, taking care of the house. Men talk to each other when they are designing houses and they don't make a point of getting women to go over the plans. One of the things that HUD could do would be to require in the design review process that every job be assessed from the standpoint of the homemaker.

''You have all these regulations about the handicapped, who are five per cent of the population. What about women, who are fifty per cent of the population? We now have ramps in buildings because there are a few handicapped people—when women with shopping carts and baby carriages have been pulling those damned things up steps for generations.''

Much of the research on needs is done from too limited a perspective, according to Dr. Howell, who used current literature on energy conservation in the home as an example: "You discover a very peculiar definition of the American lifestyle, which concludes that the American family will never be willing to give up its picture window; never be willing to have the north side of the house without windows, and never a common wall. That isn't the American way, the reports tell us—as though the American housing consumer actually made the original decisions as to how tract houses were going to be built. Again I think that until we really begin to approach the decision-makers and confront them with who the American family is and what their major interests behaviorally are, we are going to get this peculiar mythology as to what the American lifestyle is all about."

If the needs and preferences of real households were met, what could houses and apartment units be like? Architect and author Susana Torre has done extensive research and documentation in the field of domestic design. She has recently received a grant from the National Endowment for the Arts to develop architectural and infrastructural criteria for housing which reflects the changes in family structure of present day society. "The kitchen I have in mind," said Ms. Torre, "would, in its most radical version, probably look more like a restaurant kitchen with everything hanging out. Everybody in the house could just take things and use them and put them back where they found them.

"When everthing is tucked neatly away behind closed doors, the appliances and the objects somehow have to be organized by one person, usually a woman, who knows where everything is—and often this lack of accessibility and visibility is not the best way to promote ready cooperation on the part of other members of the household.

"There should be a central storage room, or stockroom, in the house, even where there is a limited amount of space. There are commercially available storage units on casters. Everything can be made very compact, as long as you have a two-foot-six-inch aisle in the middle where these things roll. Everything that has to do with maintenance and cleaning would be readily available and visible for all to see, thereby freeing some of the closet space in the individual rooms."

Several panelists suggested that guestrooms, not included in the dwelling units, could be located elsewhere in large developments. Ms. Simmons reported that Phipps Houses has included such rooms in hospital housing it manages to handle the flow in and out of doctors and patients' relatives. Larger developments can also have community rooms and kitchens to be rented out by the tenants for larger gatherings.

Individual apartment and dwelling units, however, will probably continue to become smaller, but as Ms. Simmons pointed out: "We need to use all the design tricks we can to increase the illusion of space—large windows, low windowsills, light colors. There are corners and alcoves that can be successfully furnished separately. In other words, the more you get away from or can vary the rectangular room by putting corners and odd little spaces to use, the more you are providing the ability to carry on different sorts of functions. Such an alcove can hold either a giant stereo set or it can have a daybed or it can have a screen around it and, if it has a window, it can become another room. These corners add little to the total amount of square footage. We don't get these spaces because, unfortunately, architects tend to like to draw straight lines. Corners and alcoves are a relatively inexpensive way of meeting all these needs, and I think that builders who have incorporated them would testify that it increases marketability.

"I think, furthermore, that large developments should be planned in such a way as to increase feelings of neighborliness. In a huge development of ours, I put only six apartments on each floor, so that there is a sense of intimacy on a small scale, despite the fact that the building itself has 900 apartments. People appear to like their neighbors if they don't have too many of them."

Although the housing developments architect Simmons plans and manages encourage neighborliness by their spatial arrangements, she doesn't believe that social relationships can be enhanced by physical design alone. Better social organization, she believes, must provide the human benefits once found within the now-vanishing traditional family. "Something I have been after for years," she told the panel, "and have finally succeeded in doing, has been to hire a full-time person to be what we call a community development specialist—someone who helps create the social organization within the building, especially when people are working, especially when people are under the pressures of being poor. HUD has approved such a post for subsidized housing throughout the country. Now everybody wants to move into our buildings. They are organized by floors. We have committees that work on the youth center; committees that work on joint suppers, where we have 200 families in the back yard bringing down covered-dish suppers and cooking chafers. These committees tell us what is wrong with the management, and the work with teen-agers. They have a tenant patrol.

"We made physical as well as social changes. We put a fence around all the grounds to keep out the junkies and all the other people who cause trouble. The grounds now belong to the tenants. We built a youth center, which was not part of the original HUD program, and we did all this with HUD's cooperation. It is a pilot project. We now have people working on all these things. We have people relating to each other. We have older people coming down two or three times a week and spending an evening with their punchbowl and bridge, having a great time. The teenagers who tried to destroy the building when the blackout occurred two years ago are now helping the old people get in the groceries."

Ms. Simmons' demonstrations of the way a well conceived and implemented social service system within large developments leads to greater community participation by the tenants led to a discussion of another kind of participation—self help.

How much planning should architects, planners, and builders do, and how much should they leave to the users? Should the users have more options than choosing color schemes and pushing furniture around? How much does the developer have to build? Shouldn't we allow people more room to act on their own and develop their own environment within a framework? Should we build loft buildings?

Said Ms. Simmons: "There is a market for that, but I think it would be a mistake to say that should be everything, because if you have a couple of small kids, that last thing you want is one big open space. You have to have rooms with doors.

"The whole New York City loft phenomenon, however, really indicates that there is a tremendous unmet need here of people wanting more spacious surroundings. In the old days many people could afford them, but now you have to be rich."

Self-help is a particular interest of Louis Sauer, architect and chairman of the Department of Architecture, Carnegie Mellon University: "I am an advocate of people being able to choose and intervene for themselves with a minimum of professional help. I want to get architects out of housing. Maybe it will take a hundred years—because it is obvious that there are many people who choose not to intervene for themselves in housing.

"We have the most sophisticated housing self-help industry in the world in this country; but we cannot build a house and leave most of it unfinished. This is because the valuation given in the mortgage is going to penalize the developer for doing this and certainly in HUD it wouldn't even qualify—so forget it!

"The problem is rooted in the institutionalization of codes. Everybody can get in their two cents worth on what is business for them by lobbying to get a code change, so there is not regulatory system over the codes."

Architect Danforth W. Toan continued: "Self-help programs, unfortunately, require two things: one is initiative, and the other one is money. You have to have your own financing to do it, and that limits it to the upper-middle-class to a much larger extent than it should. We must find a way in which banks would risk brownstone adaptations by lower-middle-income people as in the Park Slope part of Brooklyn. But the financial institutions obstruct this process terribly."

Architect and feminist Joan Sprague asked: "Can housing be used as economic development for the residents who are going to live in that housing? Can housing be used as a way of learning skills, especially for women who may be interested in construction skills and don't really have access to learning them?"

Ms. Carbine was realistic: "Let me speak from the point of view of a lending institution. I am going to give you $20,000, and if you don't pay me back, my only recourse is to repossess the house and sell it to somebody else. Then I have got to have a house that I can sell to somebody else for the amount of money that I loaned you.

"So until we have an increase in the level of skill and sophistication of the people who are supposed to be doing the self-helping and self-modification, it is not going to work. And it has to be recognized that this is one of the longer-range things that requires starting small, and a lot of education, not just for the banks but for the people who are going to do it, because right now very few can do it."

Moving up to the scale of the community: What kinds of urban and suburban environments do we want today and what are our chances of getting them in the next decade? Dr. Robert Gutman, professor of sociology at Rutgers University and professor of architecture and urban planning at Princeton, suggested that much that we are asking for many indeed come about: "I don't want to seem like a Pollyanna, but it seems to met that there are a lot of things happening on the American scene at the moment which suggest that some of these things we are asking for are much more likely in the near term than they have been in the past.

"Not only is the gas shortage compelling people to thing about higher-density land-use, but the whole environmental movement which we have been experiencing for the last decade is also encouraging people tho think of a more economical use of land. This implies more compact development. I think the fact that housing costs have been, for some time now, rising faster than personal income—the reverse of the situation that occurred in the decade following the war—means that people are thinking of new ways of saving in the design and construction of housing.

"Then there's the general concern about improving the quality of life, both for men and for women. This is getting people interested in the idea of better community facilities, child-care facilities, and so on. I don't want to minimize the difficulties that we all struggle with on a day-to-day basis. But I think there are certain long-run cultural changes, at least in the area of the suburban housing I deal with, that suggest things are looking up in many respects. We need more push and more resourcefulness, however, in trying to find specific ways of translating some of these cultural dispositions into practical policies. But the public support may be forthcoming.

"There was a recent curfew in Levittown, New Jersey. The reason for the curfew was that the previous night a certain number of the residents of Levittown rioted and burned down some of the local gas stations, and also blocked the main traffic artery.

"Is it conceivable that these people who are embittered—and with good reason, because they really depend upon two cars in the garage and the

availability of gasoline—will now see the wisdom of some kind of new housing policy that will argue in favor of higher density?

"I think the way that question is answered over the next decade has a
lot of implications for whether the things we are talking about are viable or
not."

Although the forces outlined by Dr. Gutman may indeed point the way
to higher density land use in new housing construction with all the community services and amenities concentration makes possible, what can be done
to adapt our existing housing stock to today's needs, such as the requirement to save energy? Socio-economist and energy specialist Eunice Grier
reminded the panel that "one of the things we have to face up to is that we
really did a marvelous job during the 1960's in building housing in this
country, and whatever problems there are with that housing—we do have
comparatively new housing stock. How can this housing be adapted to meet
the needs of the kinds of households we have today?

"During the first part of the 1970's we built more housing units with
seven rooms or more than any other individual-size housing. So our newer
housing is also larger housing.

"We have to take into account what is happening to energy costs. Much
of the housing we have now is built to extremely inefficient energy standards. Houses are poorly insulated; layouts are bad; the locations are bad.
They are low density. Where the big item for low-income people might once
have been the rent or the mortgage payment, today, the energy bill is getting
to be at least as large as the mortgage payment or the rent. One wonders
what a lot of these families are doing for food, because, once the rent and
the utility bills have been paid, there just cannot be a great deal left over.

"Furthermore we are not getting to be a more densely-populated country. We are getting to be a much more spread-out country, particularly in
metropolitan areas. Between 1950 and 1974 the metropolitan population of
this country grew by 79 per cent; but during the same years the growth in
metropolitan land area in square miles grew by 97 per cent. This has caused
a tremendous increase in average daily vehicle miles.

"Our most numerous housing type is the most energy-using—the
single-family detached house. These are in place, and it is going to be a
while before we can turn over to some other type—if we ever can—that
might conserve more energy.

"Even the rehabilitation that is going on now in a lot of inner-city
neighborhoods—so-called gentrification, which can be very attractive—uses more energy. A young professional who buys an old house previously occupied by several low-income families, tears it all out and recon-
structs it, putting in some big skylights and enlarging some windows, may
thereby consume more energy than the previous occupants.

"Income is another important factor in energy and conservation. The higher the income group, the more energy it consumes. Poor households are already pretty close to the limit of what they can do to reduce their energy consumption. They are already using fuel only for the essential elements of life.''

How bad is the fit between what our real housing needs are and what is being produced today? According to Dr. Gutman: "The situation today has declined from the standard set just after the war. Then we saw development of new housing types, new kinds of settlements to respond to the new family formations of the veterans who were coming home. The American housing market at the time, with a good deal of support from the Federal government through Federal mortgage policy and fairly liberal land-use policies, was able to respond to that need and to convert that need into effective demand.

"But for the last decade or so housing production in the United States has been stalled. That does not mean we haven't been producing new housing. But developers have not been in a position to produce the kind of housing which the public would want to buy if it were available.

"You can see that very clearly, I think, in the development of housing forms. The suburban housing form has been locked into the same basic builder's colonial in all parts of the country now for the past decade. The only hopeful sign has been the generation of townhouse developments.

"As we know, multi-family housing is the part of the housing market that manages to support the volume of housing stock that we have now. It is not a problem of the developers. The developers would love to build the kind of housing that would respond to the things that we have been talking about, simply because there is a potential market for them. As we have been saying, there are millions of people who perhaps would like to move, even though they don't move, at the ages of fifty and fifty-five. But there really is nothing for them to move into that has the advantages, both economically and physically, of what they presently live in. The same is true of young people and all these new households that have emerged. For the most part, the housing just is not available for them.

"So in New Jersey we find ordinary fifty- and sixty-thousand dollar suburban houses being occupied by single middle-income males because these are the only places they can find in the area where they want to be. And, of course, there are similar mismatches in the case of single-parent households and households of people living together. There is enough money around so that housing can be bought, but it really is a case of bad fit.

"At some point I hope the question we will tackle is, how can we loosen up the situation? What is standing in the way of giving developers and architects and the other people in the building industry the kind of support that would make it possible for them to respond to this potential demand?

It is not the developer; it is not the architect; it is not the purchaser. There are other policies that are operating in our society that are preserving this mismatch, and it is these that we have to address ourselves to."

Those who suffer the most from the mismatch between their needs and the available housing are the old, the poor, the single and one-parent families, most of whom are women, and those who must rent, many of whom are young and just starting out. George Grier, demographer and policy analyst, is deeply concerned about our accelerating loss of rental housing and apartment units. "We are not building rental housing at nearly the rate we have to use it. We are converting much of what we have to condominiums and we are rehabilitating much of the older rental stock of our cities into either single-family-occupancy townhouses or into condominium status.

"But what is concerning me also is that we are simply doing away with the whole rental class of housing in this country, which is going to do almost unlimited damage to some of the things we hold most dear, including mobility. Once we have done with our rental housing stock—and we are doing away with it at a very rapid rate in this country—young people will no longer be able to move freely from one place to another.

"One of the main reasons we are doing away with rental houses is the tax incentive for house purchases. Unfortunately the people who can give mortgages believe that only certain people are worth giving mortgages to. So that is really not an open option for many people."

Architect Toan pointed out that: "Our big problem today is that houses typically have been designed for the two-parent family, which is no longer in the majority. We must pay attention to the problem of the one-parent family, because that is where the dysfunctional aspects of the house become most critical."

Mr. Grier agreed and supported Mr. Toan's assertion with demographic facts. "We still think in terms of the family-centered household, but a very rapidly-growing number of households do not contain any families. As a matter of fact, between 1970 and 1978, which is the last date for which we have census statistics, 56 per cent of all household growth consisted of non-family households—whose members are unrelated, and who don't have children.

"That, I think, poses a whole different set of questions for designers. How do they take account of the needs and lifestyles of such households? There may be several women living together, several men living together, men and women living together, and there is a lot of popular stuff about that, which overshadows the fact that much of this is a matter of economic necessity. Much of this is adaptation to changing needs and changing housing availability in society. But our units are not designed for non-family households at all."

Nor are they designed for people living alone. Author and feminist

Betty Friedan presented even more startling figures. "Only seven per cent of Americans are now living in the kind of traditional family for which almost all housing, both public and private housing, has been built: mom, pop, and the children—and then mom, pop, and the grandchildren.

"The significant increase that is changing the population mix is people living alone—divorced, widowed, single. In addition to people living alone—i.e., one unit, one-person families, if you want to call them that—one person in need of family, there is an increasing number of couples. While fifty per cent of marriages end in divorce, most of the divorced people do remarry, so the couple is still quite a large demographic unit. Except for the couples, the common denominator for all these people is isolation. The way to break through this isolation is to change the housing built for the individual unit alone. We have to open out the walls, but not just inside the apartment or the house for sharing the housework. We have to do something that is much more difficult for Americans—broaden the concept of family to encompass the needs of all of the great majority now who need space to get out of isolation by the sharing of certain functions. We will be breaking new ground, because there is no model anywhere. The only model you can get usually has something to do with college campuses. Consider the Marlboro Music Festival or look a little bit at the experience of Leisure World which, no matter how it has been criticized, has met needs of older people."

Representing HUD at the Round Table was Allene Joyce Skinner, who is director of the Women's Policy and Programs Staff, Office of Neighborhoods, Voluntary Associations and Consumer Protection for the agency. She augmented Ms. Friedan's argument with significant data on the number of women living alone. "In 1976 there were 18 million women who were heads of households. We don't have data specifically on how many single fathers or other individuals were living alone, but we know that the tendency is greatly increasing. Yet we are continuing to build the kinds of housing units that interfere with their ability to have the kind of shared living that several of you have talked about. That is a great concern of some of the people in HUD.

"As economics of housing price more and more families out of aspiring to home ownership, or even being able to afford to rent unsubsidized housing, it is women who are most affected. Out of the eighteen million women who head families in this country, for example, one-third live below the poverty level. How much housing can you buy if your income is $3,000 a year?

"There is a popular myth that women control the wealth of the country. However, Margaret Griffin reported in recent testimony on the Hill that only 69 per cent of American women, compared with 92 per cent of American men, had income from any source. Among those with income, the average income for men was $9,289. But for women it was only $3,799.

"As we look for solutions to their housing needs, we have to keep in mind that there will have to be solutions that take into consideration the economic status of the 24 per cent to one-third of American families that are headed by single parents who are women, and who are at or below the poverty level."

Women with jobs who have children, even those who are neither single nor at the poverty level, can expect their ability to pay for available housing reduced by the energy crunch. Architect Toan pointed out that "such women are usually relegated to jobs that are close to the home, usually in a service industry at relatively low pay. These jobs are unstable. I think many two-income families are going to find that their second incomes are going to dry up as the mobility of the population decreases, particularly in the suburban area."

Muriel Fox, executive vice president of Carl Byoir & Associates, Inc. and president of the NOW Legal Defense and Education Fund reminded the panel that, today, the prices of homes are based upon two incomes per household. What is to become of the single person, man or woman who can find no place to rent, yet cannot buy?

George Grier argued: "If we believe that certain kinds of people must be accommodated in rental housing because it is the only kind of housing they can afford, since they cannot make down payments, then we ought to be doing something about increasing the tax breaks for the development of rental housing.

"We must also provide increased funds for the construction of housing for the elderly, not just for their sake but because there are a very great many older people who are occupying housing that is too big for them and they are suffering as a result.

"They really don't have an alternative. We ought to be providing alternative housing subsidized by the government. I propose differential subsidies, depending on the degree to which the community facilities, either already in the community or provided with the housing, are adequate.

"If the housing were sited in a place where its elderly occupants could get to the needed community facilities, then the subsidy would go up. It would have to, because the development would certainly be more expensive. This would be one way of promoting the construction of housing for the elderly within communities where the facilities are available. Alternatively, if the developer wanted to build the facilities and the government would subsidize him for that, either way the elderly would get facilities they need in conjunction with the housing.

"Another possibility is simply that the government starts subsidizing the provision of basic community facilities like shopping, laundromats, et cetera, in locations where it would be convenient to the housing as an energy-conservation incentive. I think if we don't do some of these things—and fast—we will inevitably come to the point where we are going to be subsidizing all housing, even for the middle class. It will not take us very many years before that is the only way we can provide any more housing in America.

"Furthermore, in recognition of decreased resources, vastly increased housing costs, land costs, and finance costs we ought to provide a differential taxation for different-sized housing in relation to the size of the household in the housing. In other words, if you have too many rooms for your household, then you get taxed more—relatively more—than the household that has fewer rooms per member. I know this is a very unpopular idea and there are some of us, myself included, who would suffer from it; but it would change the incentive pattern and would encourage development of smaller housing units."

Record editor Walter Wagner expressed reservations: "I am worried about taxing too-large houses. Think of the older people who stay in their homes. It seems to me that they do this partly because of their feelings of belonging to their community, but also because of the fact that the house is paid for, so they are down now to paying taxes. Would it not be possible—or would it not be more palatable—to create incentives of that sort without laying the big tax on the existing homeowner?"

Mr. Grier agreed that this made sense and was probably the only way such a concept would become politically feasible. Dr. Howell, however, found the idea of taxing older people out of their too-large houses unrealistic and totally unacceptable: "Your parents and my parents may have houses that are much too large for them, but the majority of people over the age of sixty-five in this country own houses which are over forty years old. Most are not bigger than three bedrooms; more likely two bedrooms. There was a time in this country when the two-bedroom house was considered the family house. Most of the older home owners are low- and moderate-income home-owners. Of the population over the age of sixty-five, approximately 70 per cent live in their own homes. They are working-class homes bought by working-class people in the thirties.

"More than economics forms older peoples' attachment to their houses. We spent the entire 200 years out of our past history making it a status symbol to be a homeowner—and then, all of a sudden, you are saying, 'Let's disenfranchise these retired people. They can no longer have the same status.' "

Mr. Grier insisted on his point: "I would agree with you that many older people do live in house which, by the standards of housing that we have built recently, are relatively small. But they are still larger—three bedrooms, sometimes two bedrooms—than they need."

Dr. Howell: "Who says so?"

Mr. Grier: "Many of those older people are saying so—and they will be saying so increasingly as the energy bills continue to go up. But they have no alternative. What I am saying is that we really need an alternative, and the middle-income housing that has gone up has been well planned, well constructed, and has consisted of smaller units usually with adequate community facilities for older people."

June R. Vollman, associate editor of *Housing* magazine pointed out that "People do not buy housing the way they used to—to live in all their lives; houses that the children grow up in and the grandchildren, and maybe the great-grandchildren come back to visit. They buy them because they figure that within five and a half years, they are either going to move into a better house, or another kind of house, as their needs change. As the children grow up the couple moves into another house—that is what tract housing is for."

Dr. Howell disagreed: "That is not true statistically. Statistics show it is just at the age of fifty to fifty-five that the mobility curve in the United States drops precipitately."

Ms. Skinner suggested that policies be developed to allow elderly homeowners to remain where they are. "While the statistics of elderly living in small houses versus very large houses may not even be available, there are numbers of elderly who don't need as much housing as they have in terms of their ability to pay the taxes on it and their ability to maintain it. This has been established by studies of housing occupied by elderly women which we have done at HUD. A policy which gives a combination of subsidies, incentives, and grants so that a person or couple still has a portion of the home to occupy but then has a small rental unit as part of it, would provide a flexibility that we need."

Dr. Howell agreed: "It is an excellent idea; and, as a matter of fact, there are about eight such tiny pilot programs on that, and they have received inadequate publicity." Mr. Toan told the panel that his local zoning ordinance has an unusual provision—that a house which is over twenty years old can be divided into a two-family house. "The estimates that have been made by housing study groups within our community estimate that, of the houses both over twenty years old and less than twenty years old, over fifty per cent of them have essentially two households living in them already.

"If we could break into this local institution of zoning and permit this kind of thing to happen on a much larger scale, we would have a chance to revive and to save, perhaps, the suburban community, because we would intensify the use and diversify the use."

Dr. Gutman urged that more women get on zoning boards and gave an encouraging example: "I was adviser to a township in New Jersey that was considering a proposal from a developer for a 1,500-unit suburban townhouse development, and I originally suggested to the planning board that they demand in return for their approval that the developer put in a series of community facilities, including a child-care center, as well as a library.

"Of course the planning board was already prepared to demand schools, but I had a very difficult time convincing them that they ought to ask for the other facilities. This development took a long time to get started and in the course of a two-year period a woman was added to the board. What I was struck by, the second time we went around on this, was that as a result of the views of the female member of the planning board, the township finally asked for the additional community facilities I recommended—and got them. The composition of these planning boards is a very critical matter. If women or men whose consciousness is raised with respect to these issues can be encouraged to serve on these boards, we might be able, at least on the suburban scale, to improve the quality of our residential environments."

Ms. Simmons made the important point that what is needed for political impact is a "larger coalition, not just women, to get our ideas across, because the changes in government policy which we propose involve the great majority of the population. If we limit our attention to the needs of just women, we are not going to have the votes to offset the tendency for government subsidies to be cut out at every level and in every area. I think further that we must develop strategies which require very small subsidies, because we are not going to get large ones."

Betty Friedan had the last word: "This was a good conference because women and the situation of women was not our only subject. We talked about families of single people, and single people living alone, about men, about couples whose children are grown. I think that within the set of basic assumptions that America is built on, including respect for the individual and the need for roots and the need for family, with the woman now defined as a person, we could begin in a pragmatic way to make it possible and profitable for this system to design and build a new kind of housing to meet the new needs we have defined. There is even money from the new kinds of families over the age of forty where there are not any more little kids—and that money is just as useful to pay for housing as the money for that so-called family-forming that all the architects and the designers were geared toward in the past.

"My husband and I took advantage of the GI mortgage in my young married and homemaking years with the children; we all did. Otherwise we wouldn't have had mortgages. We wouldn't have been able to afford them. Should there not be such mortgages available today for instance, for people after the age of forty, or even after the age of fifty, who may still have 35 years ahead of them? Can they get financing to have the different kind of housing that they now need?

"What we need to do here is something that a lot of us in the Womens' Movement have had some experience in doing effectively. We have to change everyone's consciousness so that there will be a wide public awareness of the housing need and the demand. We will bring about new government policies and incentives and mortgage arrangements which will recognize the kinds of populations we now have. Once we have the government initiatives our entrepreneurs will make the most of them—some will even make exorbitant profits, but that is absolutely fine with me if they build what is needed."

Index

Index

List of Contributors

Susan Anderson-Khleif
Department of Sociology,
Wellesley College

Sarane Spence Boocock
Department of Sociology and
Anthropology,
Rutgers University

Galen Cranz
Department of Architecture,
University of California,
Berkeley

Sheila Levrant de Bretteville
The Woman's Building,
Los Angeles

Dolores Hayden
School of Architecture and
Urban Planning,
University of California,
Los Angeles

Ilene M. Kaplan
Department of Sociology,
Union College

Jo Ann McGeorge
Department of Housing and
Urban Development,
Washington, D.C.

Iris Miller
Architect

Geraldine E. O'Kane
Attorney-at-Law

Mildred F. Schmertz
Architectural Record

Donna E. Shalala
President, Hunter College

Nadine Taub
Associate Professor of Law,
School of Law,
Rutgers University,
Newark, N.J.

About the Editor

Suzanne Keller holds a joint appointment in the School of Architecture and the Department of Sociology at Princeton University. Professor Keller has served as vice-president of the American Sociological Association, is a Fellow of the American Institute of Architecture, and was the first woman to be appointed to a tenured professorship at Princeton University. She is the author of *The American Neighborhood* and a standard textbook on sociology, among other works.